The Time of Our Lives

A humorous, detailed and affectionate memoir, dispelling the myth that post-war Britain was lacklustre and drearily austere.
It wasn't.

For most Baby Boomers it was simply TERRIFIC

GUINNESS

My Goodness!
My Guinness!!

GUINNESS

John Burden

Charities supported:
Save the Children
National Churches Trust
Bodmin and Wenford Railway Trust

The Time of Our Lives

Growing up with the well–hard babies
1945 – 1960

Copyright © John Burden 2021

ISBN number 9798711525585

Cover design by Cornerstone Vision

Contents

****

Foreword

There's a popular misconception about the fifteen post-war years which preceded the Swinging Sixties. In particular, the 1950's have attracted a reputation for being a dull and dreary time, full of gloomy deprivation and crushing austerity amidst which a careworn population struggled with seemingly endless rationing and an unusual obsession with over-boiled cabbage.

Do me a favour - the post-war years were anything but!
For the vast majority, it wasn't gloomy at all. It was just terrific!

OK, we didn't have microwave dinners, sex education, disposable nappies or Jeremy Vine… but, what we did have was a truckload of freedom, skiffle groups, bombsite adventures, gob stoppers and shiny loo paper…. plus big and hopeful expectations for the future.

And speaking of expectations, the immediate post-war years also became the breeding ground for an extraordinarily large number of new babies, who went on to share their birth and infancy with the brand new squeaky-clean NHS. How lucky can you get? Not only did you get free milk and National orange juice, but your dad got his teeth fixed, your mum a free pair of specs and grandad some unmentionable truss thingy to help him overcome that long-standing problem with his unmentionables.

And what else? Well, if you take into account that the fifties saw the invention of teenagers, the birth of Rock n' Roll, plastic teaspoons, day-glow socks, bubble cars and winkle-picker shoes, how can you be any other than impressed that the decade was in fine fettle, and just raring to go? In the days before TV really hit its stride, the fifties was also a time of great good humour received and understood via the dear old steam wireless with shows like *'Hancock's Half Hour'*, *'Beyond Our Ken'* and of course, the utterly barmy but entirely glorious '*Goon Show*'. More than anything else, the fifties was a time when the blue touch-paper for the cultural explosion to come a decade later suddenly burst into flame.

This commentary on those wonderful years revolves around my experiences of growing up in Portsmouth. Having been born there in 1946, my founder membership of the Baby Boomer generation is underwritten by a pin-sharp memory for the details of the period, and what follows covers the ridiculous and the sublime in equal measure. To avoid stumbling into autobiography, any family details are used most frequently to illustrate the national picture. Thus, my account presents as a joyful, accurate and affectionate commentary on the post-war experiences of one very ordinary kid whose natural gormlessness was equally – and thankfully – matched with a perceptive eye.

So, if you want unconventional and quirky, it's all here. Just ask yourself: in which other book of post-war reflections could you find a new interview with Adolf Hitler, the graphic details of a mechanical cow with poisonous legs, and the sexy ballet of a bus conductor?

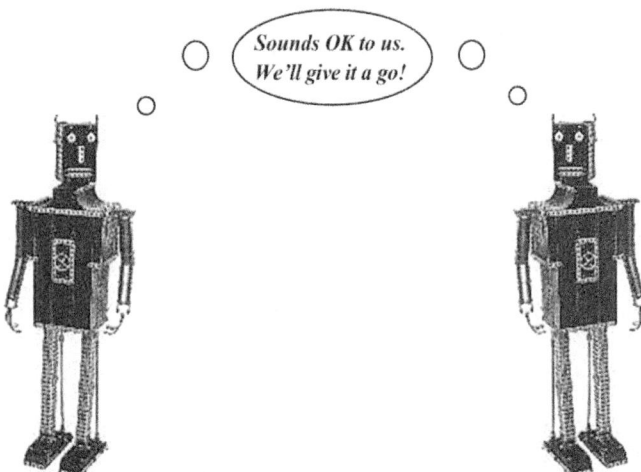

Sounds OK to us.
We'll give it a go!

Introduction

I suppose I shouldn't have been afraid of Ben Parsons and ought not to have gone out of my way to avoid him.

He was, after all, a kindly old gent, who never had anything other than a cheerful word to say to me. The trouble was, it was the way he said it, and well, *the way he was.* If I'm honest, I was squeamishly and quite unfairly rattled by just about everything to do with poor old Ben. His appearance was - let's say, unattractive to an impressionable four year old. For a start he was very, very old and he had a husky voice... a voice that trembled and wobbled around in his throat, and gave the impression of a possible over-supply of spit. Added to that, he had glasses asymmetrically balanced on his nose, and one of the lenses was *greyed out*, giving rise to further four year old speculation as to what lay behind it. But this was not all. He had something wrong with his foot, and this disability provided him with the most sinister thing of all: a self-propelled, black canvas-aproned, creaking and wheezing tricycle wheelchair. This creepy piece of machinery appeared to be set in motion using hand operated cranks – the only saving grace being that its slow and noisome inefficiency meant that everyone could hear its approach and, as far as I was concerned, take necessary avoiding action.

A lot of effort to get somewhere... slowly

Shame really. The old chap must have often wondered why, as he turned the corner into our road, the young JB would suddenly disappear before his very eyes – or to be more accurate, before his one good eye.

In this day and age, it seems cruel that people in need of support should have been so identifiable. Indeed, there was not a trace of embarrassment that such bizarre machines should have been called *invalid* carriages. Not only were they hard work to propel (and I reckon old Ben seldom topped three mph even on a good day going downhill), such contrivances were awkward to get in and out of, completely impractical to park, and almost impossible to store. They were so utterly *obvious*. You might as well have had an illuminated sign on the back saying – '*Hey - look at me! I'm disabled – and if that isn't bad enough, I'm condemned to grind my way very slowly around the town in this weirdo contraption!*'

As time went on, things got a little better. Modernised invalid carriages appeared – but the opportunity to help the less advantaged members of society to merge into the background was almost totally ignored. Not only were the new vehicles (made by a company calling

The Invacar: smoky, noisy and eye-catchingly blue, but it was progress - of a sort.

itself, almost inevitably, *Invacar*) constructed in an eye-catching bright blue plastic, they were all powered by an incredibly noisy and often smoky two stroke engine heard from about quarter of a mile away. Another stroke of corporate genius was to have a large sign on the back of each and every such vehicle boldly proclaiming: **NO HAND SIGNALS**. If such a sign means nothing to you, then let me explain.

Right up until the mid sixties, the drivers of all motorised vehicles were required to communicate their intentions to fellow road users by sticking their right arm out of the window and flapping the hand about in a prescribed manner. Sounds bonkers? You're right – it was. Nevertheless, it was also a vital part of the national driving test and so important that we'll look again at its bizarre applications in a later chapter.

But to return to the motorised Invacar: quite why every single disabled driver should be denied the right to engage in an activity required of all other motorists seems thoughtless at best, if not downright divisive. Wasn't it bad enough to be so identifiable in the first place?

So, the denial of quiet anonymity for those in need of support appears at first glance to almost border on the spectacular... but this was the early 1950s. In recently nationalised Britain, still shrugging off the dust and debris of war, even such meagre provision was PROGRESS, of a kind. And boy - was progress needed!

* * * * * *

As the first day of the new decade dawned, I was busy lining up my toast soldiers ready for their imminent dip into a runny egg yolk – but had I been less preoccupied I might have sensed what might be described as a national sigh of relief. The forties were over: a new decade beckoned and with a bit of luck, no lunatic was going to drop bombs on the population for the foreseeable future... and what's more, you could now get your teeth fixed by the all new National Health Service. Although the country was broke and a vast amount of building was urgently required, the new decade - indeed the new *half century* – was a psychological renaissance and there was confidence in the air. And to prove it, the government had announced that the following year, 1951, London would host the 'Festival of Britain' – an extravaganza of all those things at which we Brits excelled. Deliberately scheduled to coincide with the centenary of the Victorian's Great Exhibition, it was to be a national shot in the arm *sans parriell*… and all of this with the country still in the grip of rationing and rigid austerity. Blimey.

Mind you – that such momentous plans and national aspirations passed us tinies by that January morning was hardly surprising, because we had our very own new-decade achievement to celebrate. And what was that? Why, we'd survived a 1940's babyhood, that's what – and as a little closer inspection will reveal, such an achievement was no mean feat, believe me.

1   The Well-Hard Babies

In recent years, I've been introduced to C Beebies, a whole TV channel dedicated to the very young. I have to say that, yes, it is packed to the gunnels with jollity, fun, slapstick tomfoolery, soft and cuddly animals, fluffy animations of all kinds (even the monsters, one of whom has just one Cyclops-like eye and another which appears to possess two heads are most agreeable) and is eye-achingly colourful.

The scariest episodes seem to involve a cuddly blue dinosaur playing hide-and-seek and unsuccessfully hiding himself behind a very small bush. His multi-coloured playmates are at a loss to see where he might be – even though his enormous bum is sticking out beyond the bush right behind them. Nevertheless, a microsecond of tension is created as the day-glow fluffies are unable to find him for a nano-second. So it's all very safe, and stickily unthreatening.

Not so in my day. Babies brought up in the late1940's were of sterner stuff … no *C Beebies* for us – we just had the wireless for a miniscule 15 minutes per day:

"This is the BBC Home Service. It is a quarter to two. We present 'Listen With Mother' for mothers and children at home"
The signature tune was a very short and frankly unimaginative piece of harp music followed by the query:

"Are you sitting comfortably? Then I'll begin."
Regardless of your domestic disposition, the announcer and a bloke called George then got into their stride with a medley of musical items largely based upon lullabies and nursery rhymes. Sounds innocent enough – but was it? I think there is very strong evidence to support the view that the BBC was toughening up the post-war brood to become *well-hard babies*. Don't believe me? Well,

look at the evidence. Take for example, the favourite and apparently comforting lullaby *'Rock-a-Bye Baby'*:

Rock-a-bye baby
On the tree top
When the wind blows
The cradle will rock
When the bough breaks
The cradle will fall
Down will come baby,
Cradle and all

Now, forgive me if I'm wrong, but the words of this apparently comforting and melodious ditty, designed to get junior into a suitably soporific state prior to a decent sleep, in fact do anything but. On the contrary, they encourage the wee sleepy-head to remain alert to the fact that his parent is preparing to lodge him *cradle and all* in the high branches of a tree, fully aware of the fact that a storm is coming, that the tree is basically unsound, and there appears to be a strong possibility that both he and the cradle will come crashing to the ground. Comforting? *Really?*

Please bear in mind that we Baby Boomers were born into a world where the brand new welfare state proudly proclaimed total governmental support for all people *from cradle to grave* – which according to the sinister implications of the nursery rhyme would therefore last for the extremely short time between being blown out of the tree and ending up head first in the cabbage patch–a period of little more than fifteen milliseconds. Such a scenario puts a different interpretation on a term my mother apparently applied to me when she assured her friends that she had given birth to a *'bouncing baby boy'*. So it suggests, does it not that perhaps her comment was rather more literal than just a description of infantile well-being. So, the apparently innocent *'Rock-Bye Baby'* a recipe for a sound night's peaceful slumber? *I really don't think so!*

Many's the night I can recall that I lay staring out through the bars of my cot, prepared to make a dash for it the moment my mum gathered me up and headed for the nearest unsafe tree, regardless of in-built bounciness.

Probably photographed just after completing a final bounce, yours truly looks quite cheerful (if a little grey) at having survived yet another treetop ejection.

And that's not all. Loads more nursery rhymes of the time were full of violence and merry brutality. For example, another favourite of George and Co on *'Listen With Mother'* was *'Sing a Song of Sixpence'* which kicks off with a couple of lines describing how 'four and twenty blackbirds' were unaccountably able to raise a song despite having been shoved in a very hot oven for an hour or two. Now, as if the baking of two dozen *live* blackbirds for your local regent was not enough, the second verse provides graphic detail surely unsuitable for the young and tender vis:

The King was in his counting house, counting out his money,
The Queen was in her parlour, eating bread and honey,
The maid was in the garden, hanging out the clothes,
*When down came a blackbird and **pecked off her nose!***

Whilst there might be some sympathy with the avian community in seeking revenge for the loss of two dozen of its kind in a pie, the mutilation of a domestic servant does seem a trifle harsh, if not brutal retaliation – and which doubtless will have brought about a needless escalation of hostilities between men and birds. I suspect that this is the reason why there is no third verse.

Further rummaging around in the mental attic brings two more horrors to light:

The Troll Song:

All about violent Scandinavian mutants who live beneath bridges where they rather give the game away by singing the somewhat repetitive ditty:

I'm a troll, foll de roll, I'm a troll, foll de roll,
I'm a troll foll de roll… **And I'll eat you for my supper!**

Oranges and Lemons:

Nothing to do with refreshing citrus fruit, but a tale of church bells. All seems fine and unthreatening until we get to the end:

Here comes the candle – to light you to bed,
And here comes the chopper **to chop off your head!**

So we have on the one hand cannibalism and on the other, random execution – all pretty gruesome stuff, certainly. And that's not the end of it. How about many fairy tales and folk tales which were part of our daily diet?

Take for example the story of *Red Riding Hood, a* little girl who takes a walk in the woods to deliver some groceries to her aged grandmother. Note that this somewhat risky and precarious errand was *sanctioned by her parent* – even though the general public had been warned in '*The Teddy Bears' Picnic'* that ' *if you go down to the woods today, you're sure of a **big** surprise'* … *AND* that her mother had dressed her in the most conspicuous clothing available. Well, almost inevitably, the poor kid mistakes a vicious bed-ridden wolf for her granny, which suggests that either the old soul was unspeakably ugly (perhaps a reason why she lived alone in the woods?) or that Little Red Riding Hood was suffering from severe myopia and had forgotten her recently prescribed National Health specs. Anyway, it all gets very nasty and only concludes when a wood cutter chops off the wolf's head. This violent end also raises a further worrying question…what was a bloke doing alone in the woods with a big chopper in his hand? I could go on. So I will.

Let's have a look at Goldilocks and the Three Bears. Even the most casual acquaintance with this story raises a few moral questions. For example, is squatting in someone else's house, breaking their furniture and eating their food really acceptable? Does the fact that having smashed the place up a good deal and eaten all the food available entitle you to take a nap in your host's property and even then complain about the size of the bedroom suite? I mean, it's a *bears' cottage,* for heaven's sake! What did you expect? King sized mattress with memory foam? Not a good example to set us little kiddies, you will agree.

And if all that wasn't sufficiently unsettling, we can move in to the completely surreal:

> *Hey diddle diddle, the cat and the fiddle*
> *The cow jumped over the moon,*
> *The little dog laughed to see such fun,*
> *And the dish ran away with the spoon.*

Now, if these words had been written in the 1960's, you could have understood it and replied with a languid: '*Yeah man, right on, that must have been some scene… pass me the joint baby!* …but a decade earlier it left us little infants with just the slightest suspicion that perhaps the world of adults was not quite the full shilling, and furthermore provoked a vague sense of uneasy anticipation.

When not toughening up its audience with the horrors of nursery rhymes, *Listen With Mother* had a tendency to stray into the merely puzzling. Often this comprised the broadcasting of songs which left the enquiring two year old with an increasing sense of mystification.

For example, there was the vaguely menacing '*Wee Willy Winkie*':

Wee Willy Winkie
Runs through the town,
Upstairs and downstairs
In his nightgown,
Tapping at the windows,
Crying through the locks
'Are all the children in their beds?
It's past eight o' clock!'

Now, given that such a title might be misinterpreted as a rather unwholesome reference to the dimensions of Mr. Winkie's personal anatomy, all 1950's children were informed that getting a good night's rest was important. Despite the fact that unsound sleeping arrangements in neighbouring woodland was still something of an issue, it could not be denied that a good night's rest was highly desirable and as a result, '*Wee Willy Winkie*' was a popular choice of bedtime tale for adults to read to their kids. Not so sure it was very popular with junior though, as the imagery it created could be a little unsettling. As far as we could make out, if you were still awake at 8pm, some bloke who had been '*running through the town, upstairs and downstairs in his nightgown*' would soon be '*tapping on your window and crying through your locks*' to remonstrate with you for not being asleep.

And as if the thought of some poorly clad weirdo shouting at you through your letter box wasn't enough, there was the thinly veiled threat from your mum that… '*if you don't get to sleep quickly, the Bogey Man will get you… so just shut your eyes and drift off to sleep like a good boy*'.

Drift off to sleep? You must be joking! How can I do that when I'm fully aware of the fact that the moment my back is turned you'll be off to get the ladder so you can shove my cradle up that elm tree that got struck by lightning last winter! It was all most unsavoury.

And Who Killed Cock-Robin? Don't look at me, mate! I was too busy sealing up the letter box and stuffing tissue paper in the locks. To be honest, a nursery story based on an inquest and subsequent funeral arrangements for the unfortunate redbreast lacked a great deal of appeal.

So there you are: BBC's *'Listen With Mother'* ... or perhaps more realistically *'Let's Toughen up the Tinies'*. And with all these crazy rhymes and ideas floating around in our impressionable little heads, it is not surprising that we looked for solace and consolation by withdrawing into the magical world offered by our toys.

Now, you'll remember my reference to the goodly Ben Parsons, the kindly, wheezing and wobbly-voiced old bloke I used to try to avoid like the plague. Did his kindness stop at a distant wave or a rasping and gravelly *'halloo'* from the creaking confines of his pedal powered bath chair? No, it did not. He also provided my mum with a little toy for me...perhaps the earliest toy I can remember owning. A train set? A shiny rubber ball? A cuddly teddy bear? No, it was a model **cow.** Now when I say *cow,* you may well conjure up in your mind a brightly coloured assemblage of fluffy body, swishing tail with heavily lashed appealing eyes plus clippety-clop hooves and even comedy udders. Not so Ben's cow. As a model of bovine accuracy it certainly left a lot to be desired Yes, some of it was brown, but for a start it only had *half* the number of legs normally associated with the beast: the two front legs were fused together, as were the complementary pair at the rear. So really, it was a *biped* cow, and to make matters more bizarre still, both of these appendages were hinged within the cow's less than convincing brown body – so that both front and rear sets swung across an arc of about twenty degrees. Had my parents been more observant in those early days, it might have occurred to them that for its size, (a mere 6cm long by 4cm high … we're not talking BIG cow here) this masterpiece of the toymaker's art was really rather heavy. Looking back, I suspect that the non-matching silvery coloured legs were probably made of unadorned – and therefore highly toxic – lead. *'Anyway'*, I hear you ask, *'why should anyone in their right mind want to make a small brown cow complete with barely authentic brown body and just one pair of fused, swinging and poisonous legs?'* The answer? *Because it walked, that's why!* Hard to believe, but this was a *gravity toy.* Put it on a level surface and, to be honest, it didn't do much – well nothing really … it just stood there on its two fused legs looking fairly un-cow like. BUT, put it on a slope and your little world was

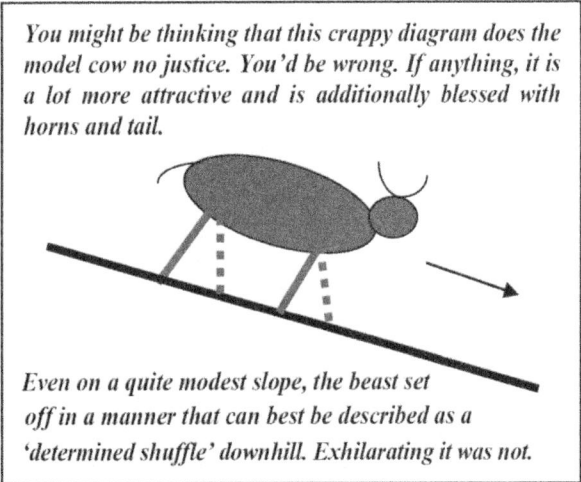

You might be thinking that this crappy diagram does the model cow no justice. You'd be wrong. If anything, it is a lot more attractive and is additionally blessed with horns and tail.

Even on a quite modest slope, the beast set off in a manner that can best be described as a 'determined shuffle' downhill. Exhilarating it was not.

transformed! The body would eventually lurch forward so that it was in danger of toppling over its front co-joined hoof. At the very point you were assuming all was lost and the poor beast would topple on to its bovine nose, the back legs would suddenly spring into life and swing forward to dramatically save the day by altering the centre of gravity of the whole beast. At this point, the back of the cow now had greater leverage than the front, and so the model tipped backwards on to its hind legs this in turn releasing the front legs from their load-bearing responsibility, and allowing them to swing forward once more.

I tell you - excitement? And for the first few hundred times it was. I remember putting that cow through its paces down ever increasing slopes where its poisonously fused legs became little more than a blur of frenzied activity. But like all kids, its attraction started to wane, especially when I found out that it wouldn't go around bends and complained to my mum that it wouldn't go backwards either. *'Never mind darling.'* she'd say *'Real cows don't go backwards much either, do they? Now be a good boy and sit in the corner...mmmmm those cow legs look tasty – why not give them a suck?'*

Bearing in mind that throughout the first post-war decade industrial output was almost entirely focussed on recovering from the exigencies of the war, it was not surprising that so little was available for children. No doubt Mr. Attlee and the boys were more interested in producing stuff to flog to the Yanks in a desperate effort to repay some of the massive war debt than they were of encouraging the production of more life-like cows for us tinies. Thus toys were often a bit bizarre to say the least. The other toy I remember having was of the pull-along type. Unlike the afore-mentioned bovine, at least this playmate had the requisite number of wheels touching the ground – four to be precise. So what was it? A car? A bus A lorry? No. it was a dragon. Furthermore, it was a rather two dimensional wooden assimilation of the mythical beast finished in dull olive green and red. Even the wooden wheels were dull, and for a little boy whose early interest in cars was already flourishing, it was something of a disappointment. *'Why'* I had to ask myself *'would someone go to the trouble of providing two axles and four wheels only to affix them to a* ***bloody dragon?!!!*** Not that I used the expletive in those days – but a

- 15 -

sense of pure indignation and utter frustration made me very aware that *some other word was needed.* I mean, come on! Is a little lorry too much to ask? Is it beyond the toymaker's ability to produce a miniature vehicle that bears even a passing resemblance to stuff you see every day on the road? To be honest, even a simple cart or even a wheelbarrow would have been a marked improvement.

Not that all was doom and gloom for yours truly. Oh no. You see my dad had a shop and therefore there was an inexhaustible supply of cardboard boxes to play in, around and under – and of course, there was clockwork. In these days of fantastically self-propelled, battery powered and remote controlled wonder toys, it is hard to believe that just a few decades ago such things only existed in the realms of fantasy – or in the minds of comic strip writers, and here I'm thinking of *General Jumbo* in my much loved weekly Beano.

Would you agree that General Jumbo's inventive professor friend looks uncannily like Vladimir Ilyich Lenin?

So if power was needed to animate a toy, you had to resort to a small clockwork motor. These mechanical marvels worked on the principle that a wound up spring stored energy which could then be released at a measured rate to provide the necessary motive power for the mechanism concerned. It also worked on the principle that you never lost the key or over-wound the spring…which of course, everyone did. What's more, the amount of energy stored in clockwork motors provided power of very limited duration – usually no more than half a minute or so. Even in that short time span, it would gradually run down so that the animation got slower and slower until it jerked to a convulsive stop. So as a means of powering anything other than, say, A CLOCK, the little spring powered motors had their limitations.

My first clockwork toy was therefore (again) something of a disappointment. Following the by now somewhat predictable theme, you may ask yourself: *'Was the new toy a car? Was it a train / aeroplane / lorry/ bus?* Of course not! It was a MONKEY dressed up as a little drummer boy complete with pill box hat and yellow uniform. The fiddly little key went in between his shoulder blades, and after winding up the spring, the little git would start drumming away as if his life depended on it. That's all … he didn't march about, salute or do a soft shoe shuffle – all he did was beat a thirty second rat-a-tat-tat on his tinny little drum, getting ever slower towards the finale. Mind you, he could catch you out by issuing a final and defiant *tat* just as you picked the little fellow up in order to shove the key back between his shoulder blades. Laugh?

Well, no, not really. Bizarre toys were not just the province of little chaps either. My sister was given a ceramic rabbit. *'So what?'* I hear you say. Well, this rabbit came in an almost inevitable dull green, but weirder than that, *it glowed in the dark!* Unbelievable. Evidently the green paint was of the luminous type, and therefore slightly radioactive. My sister kept it by her bed thereby, no doubt, giving herself a healthy dose of radiation every night. No wonder her hair stood on end every morning, and was it my imagination, or was there a faint crackling sound every time she walked by?

Now I don't want to give the impression that early childhood at this time was one of uninterrupted misery and that the toys lovingly bestowed upon us were any other than kindly meant or, initially at least, joyfully received. It's just that there really weren't that many toys around in the late forties. And don't forget that as far as me and my tiny chums were concerned, there were cardboard boxes aplenty.

With a bit of imagination, these could become just about anything you wanted.

My best toy, though, was undoubtedly my second-hand pedal car. It was kind of basic, little more than a simple metal cylinder with part removed to allow the insertion of a seat, a steering wheel and the obligatory pedals … but I loved it. It had *four* wheels and it could be *steered*. Together with the necessary and highly personalised sound effects, it could be any vehicle your inventive little mind could turn to. Irritating my mum by constantly banging into the furniture, she encouraged me to play on it in the garden, suggesting I should take on the role of *'Mr. Brown the insurance man'*. This involved me in doing a long tour of the garden, collecting insurance money at frequent intervals before returning to collect hers at the end. As this usually took me at least fifteen minutes or so (I was useless at reversing) it could be seen as a pretty cunning ploy huh? Bear in mind also that I had not the faintest idea what insurance was anyhow. So, suitably duped I would troll around the garden making appropriate car sounds suggestive of far greater mechanical performance than my primitive and rusty little conveyance aspired to, as happy as Larry.

Mind you, as the new decade dawned I was abruptly reminded of just how basic and crude my own little pedal car really was when my mum's glossy magazine landed with a dull thump on the doormat and contrived to open itself at the page featuring a pedal car gifted to the young Prince Charles. Not only did it actually look like a real production car (an Austin Devon?) but it had lights, a comfy seat, clean wheels with proper hub caps, realistic tyres and a shiny bumper. I wouldn't have been at all surprised to have been informed that there was also bottle or two of champagne in the boot *to boot* if you see what I mean. Not that I was really that bitter, you understand understand. Even I recognised that Charles was *royal* and probably had a footman or two give his pride and joy a quick polish each and every morning and then spend a little time warming up the upholstery prior to the young chap enjoying a blast right around the corridors of power. Nevertheless, I bet HRH and Her Majesty didn't get to play Mr. Brown the insurance man, did they?

So there you

This particular pedal car is to be found at the wonderful Moretonhampstead Motor Museum in Devon where it takes its place among a huge range of motoring glories from the past. If it is not the one owned by Prince Charles, then it is very similar. See why I was jealous?

have it: the world of us tiny Baby Boomers in the late 1940's. Despite the threatening lullabies, the inane and disturbingly weird nursery rhymes, the gruesome folk tales and the inherent dangers of lead poisoning from some toys and low-level radiation from others - not to mention the puzzling uselessness of two legged cows – we survived.

And talking of survival, it should be borne in mind that this was an age well before the introduction of even the most basic forms of safety equipment. For example, there were no smoke detectors in domestic properties, simply because such an invention didn't exist. And as for carbon monoxide, well, I'm sure most people hadn't even heard of it let alone thought about finding a way of warning against its presence – and this in an age when coal fires and paraffin heaters were the most common sources of domestic warmth.

But perhaps the most noticeable item missing from those things designed to keep us safe was the car seat belt. It is almost mind-boggling to note that even by the end of the 1940's, it would be another ***thirty three years*** before this simple safety device was made compulsory in the UK. And child-specific car safety? There really wasn't any to speak of. Once loaded aboard the car, tiny tots were free to rattle around, squabble, fight, make faces out of the window – just about anything really – without any restraint, whatsoever. Kids could sit in the back, in the front, on the parcel shelf, even in the space right behind the back seat if you wanted to. Child seats, childproof door locks and the other safety paraphernalia required by law these days weren't even on the *distant* horizon in the late forties.

But did we feel hard done by? Neglected? Uncared for? Of course we didn't! Like all kids everywhere, we were bursting with energy, optimism and enthusiasm. I would even go so far as to say that a whole load of us could easily have added a good dollop of *joie de vivre* for good measure, but for the fact that most found stringing together a few words to make comprehensible English difficult enough – let alone going all foreign.

So, were we well-hard tinies? Beyond doubt! And just as well, for the endless possibilities of what was to become the unrestricted mayhem of an independent 1950's childhood were fast approaching - and there was still so much to get our little heads around.

2   The Lino Years

It is quite likely that the earliest and most formative recollections of those of us born immediately after the war were circumscribed by two essential themes. The first was a normal characteristic of early childhood - *everything is really very big* and the second a feature of the time… *we're not as good as the Americans even though we desperately want to be.*

To take first things first. From my knee high perspective, our very ordinary 1918 built end of terrace house was big. So was the dining room which had just been rebuilt by the war damage people, who had replaced the entire back wall of our house after the Germans had very inconsiderately dropped a land mine in the next street, resulting in a blast which had sucked out our entire gable end. In their defence, I suppose I ought to point out that this was *during* the war and not, for example, the result of any post-defeat sulkiness on their part. Anyway, the room was big and smelled of fresh paint and wall paper paste, owing to the fact that my mum had had it completely redecorated in 1947 after I had pee'd all over a cushion.

But no need for complete redecoration after such a small inconvenience, surely?' I hear you ask. Ah, but that doesn't take into account my mother washing the violated cushion and then putting it in front of the dining room fire to dry… which it did very successfully, especially when it burst into flames when ignited by an errant spark. The subsequent blaze set the whole room on fire and filled it full of merry smoke and cinders. Firemen are big too.

So were the stairs, which had an interesting ninety degree turn two thirds of the way up. This necessary quarter turn demanded a whole load of complex calculations for my dad when he fitted the central strip of stair carpet to the treads of various shapes which accommodated the turn. Two or three were almost kite shaped, and meant that at the inner edge, the tread depth was minimal, whereas at the other side it was massive. This provided a great opportunity for the imaginative little git in that the outer edge was great for parking Dinky Toys, marbles and part-used chewing gum, whereas the inner edge was an ideal location for acting out the heroic ascent of Everest, with just toe holds and the base of the newel post for support. The climax of this climb came at the summit, when one heaved oneself up onto the upper landing to lie breathless, exhausted and yet modestly triumphant. Such heroics also had the added bonus that the final recumbent position allowed one to look through the banisters at the *back* of anyone climbing the stairs in a less dramatic way – a most tempting opportunity for dribble or a manic shout designed to startle, for example. At the top of the stairs was a small landing with three doors leading off, one to the front bedroom, another to the bathroom and the third to two more bedrooms. You will draw the obvious conclusion that the first room beyond this third door was therefore both a bedroom *and* a corridor. Guess who got that one?

No ordinary houses at that time had central heating, and coal fires were the order of the day. These were nice to look at but limited in efficiency. They were also a frequent cause of houses burning down, which although the ultimate form of keeping your property warm, was not entirely to be recommended. Usually, your average coal fire heated an area up to about five feet from the hearth, and, as domestic double glazing had not yet been invented, left the rest of the room chilly and draughty. A basic law of physics dictates that hot air rises – thus most of it created by the fire disappeared up the chimney. As this evacuation of warm air created a minor vacuum, replacement and unheated air came rushing into the room – mainly under the door, through gaps in the window frames or from cracks between the floorboards, creating a merry draft to keep your back as cold as your front was hot. After what can only be described as a campaign of incessant moaning, my dad was eventually arm-twisted by his better half into working out a way of eradicating this over-supply of cold air blasting in through every nook and cranny. And I have to say, he came up with a pretty damn good idea. What he did was to cut a small rectangular hole in the floor boards in front of the fire grate. This apparent act vandalism didn't meet with much wifely approval at first, owing to the fact that my dad wanted it *'to be a surprise'* and also because he had a habit of leaving over-long gaps between stage one and stage two of any particular project. So my mum's response of *'Wally! What on earth are you up to? There's a great hole in the front room floor, and I've got the vicar coming round next Thursday week!'* was really not at all surprising. The further development however, stilled all criticism and indeed, became something of a source of pride, something with which to impress visitors - rather than to place a rug over it and hope the good cleric didn't notice. What my dad did was to build a little box-like structure up from the hole in the floorboards and over the top of the fire grate. It really resembled a miniature version of one of those prompter's boxes you used to see at the front of the stage in a theatre, and from which the incumbent would whisper an actor's forgotten lines such as:

'Look out Lady Fortescue – the bounder's right behind you, and he's got a candelabra shoved up his jumper!... and similar. But what did come out of my dad's little invention though, was a steady draught of air drawn up by the open fire - from under the floorboards. What a great idea! Not only did it eradicate the cold draughts from under neighbouring doors and windows, but it provided a good deal of under-floor ventilation too. Oh, and it also provided a lot of puzzled and resentful spiders who suddenly found themselves wafted up into the fireplace.

In most small houses like ours, fires were confined to just one or two rooms downstairs, and that meant that upstairs could be pretty chilly in the winter, and it was not unknown for ice to form on the inside of bedroom windows during particularly cold spells . As a result, bedclothes were voluminous and heavy, with the usual sheet plus two or even three heavy blankets covered by a counterpane. These were tucked in tight - which helped to keep you warm, but made two things more difficult, namely *getting in* and, more essentially – *breathing*. On top of this, and of particular note, was an eiderdown which was often quite garish in colour and had visual similarities in its soft lumpiness to the lava pool in an active volcano – or magnified tapioca pudding if you like. Eiderdowns were certainly warm, but because they were covered in some sort of shiny material, had the habit of slipping off during the night to land with a muffled *flump* on to the lino... and thereby hangs another tale.

The dictionary defines lino – or *linoleum* to give its full name – as '*...a durable, washable material made in sheets by pressing a mixture of heated linseed oil, resin, powdered cork and pigments on to a burlap or canvas backing, and used chiefly as a floor covering...*'

Although no doubt technically correct, for me, lino was the cold, hard shiny flat stuff your dad hacked and cursed at when it came in an unyielding and brittle roll. We should remember that in the fifties, Mr. Stanley's invention of his eponymous knife was still at the drawing board stage, and DIY was not yet common – so any lino cutting operation had to be done using blunt and chipped chisels, (my mum had a habit of using them to get the lids off Golden Syrup tins) old screw drivers with half the wooden handle missing, secateurs from the garden shed and even totally inadequate kitchen scissors. Furthermore, as this was still decades before the days of aerosol glues, this reluctant and almost *spiteful* material had to be beaten into submission and nailed to the floor with tin tacks. These in turn, were particularly vicious little black spiky nails, long enough to give you a serious puncture wound, but too short to hold easily between thumb and forefinger when hammering them home. This enhanced the chance of swollen, hammer beaten digits... with the lino still at liberty. In addition, tin tacks rusted easily, and in our damp houses would see it as their collective duty to congeal themselves into an inaccessible and violently fanged ball of rust and spikes that made sea urchins look positively cuddly. Against this dubious background, you have to bear in mind that when unrolled, lino took on a malignant life of its own and fought every attempt by your enraged parent to get it to lie flat and to render itself willing to be cut into awkward shapes to fit around doorposts etc. And as regards *used chiefly as a floor covering* ...try as I might, I cannot think of a single additional use for the stuff; putting it on walls or even the ceiling seems pretty unlikely doesn't it?

So, 1950's householders spent a great deal of time and energy in hiding their lovely wooden floorboards, by covering them with this vindictive, unforgiving and demanding material which more often than not, was finished in a depressing stripy deep snot-green colour, or bore a striking resemblance to the results of a particularly prolonged and liberally applied bilious attack. From all of this you might be drawn to the conclusion that I was not a fan of the aforementioned floor covering... *but say not so!* For indeed, lino did have one over-arching and supremely important redeeming quality for an aspiring mini athlete: *you could slide on it! Like anything!*

Given the propensity that house designers of the Victorian and Edwardian eras had for building dwellings with long, dark hallways, the temptation to cover them in merry lino was overwhelming – and thus provided us little chaps not only with our very own mega-slide, but with sufficient space to get a really good run up as well. Bear in mind too, that all 1950's children were obliged to wear long woollen socks. Whilst fairly gruesome as a fashion accessory, an unintended outcome was that they were the excellent 'other half' of the lino/woolly sock combo – a match made in sliding heaven, if ever there was one.

And as if that was not enough, some parents, perhaps in an attempt attempt to offset the livid colours of their favourite floor covering, would place a small 'occasional mat' on the said lino, thus inadvertently providing the intrepid child Olympian with a *sledge* for all and sundry to investigate.

Of course, it was not all plain sailing; the occasional tin-tack would somehow manage to raise its battered head to visit last-gasp retribution on the unwary slider by slashing a neat cut through an unprotected sock, and lino was also prone to pick up all sorts of unintended marks in a random but uncomfortably *identifiable* way. Let me leap forward a couple of years to give you a perfect example concerning me and Michael, my infant school pal. I had invited Michael round to my house 'to play boats' during our dinner* break from school. Yes! We had a long enough break to get home, have a play with pals, enjoy a meal and still get back to school in time for the afternoon 'muck about with bits of very old clay / plasticine / powder paint' lesson. Normally, Michael and I would play buses in the street, but it was a wet day, and so floating my clockwork powered plastic cabin cruiser boat in a part filled bath seemed the obvious alternative. And thus fifteen minutes of exuberant play - with a little splashing and a few arguments as to whose turn it was to bomb the boat, and by the way, *whose boat is it anyway?* - went by remarkably quickly. It was only when called for dinner that Michael and I suddenly noticed that, having not removed our school shoes, the bathroom lino was now covered with an interesting and diverting pattern of shiny black lines in what one could only really label as '*random rubbery smear*' pattern. I looked at my shoes at the same time as Michael looked at his, and with one voice we each blamed the other... before desperately trying to remove the new design with water and toilet paper. Those of you who can remember the pre soft tissue days of such a product, will know that *Izal* and *Bronco* weren't really up to this job.

* *We didn't have 'lunch' in those days. Dinner was at... well, dinner time, the time between morning school and then going back to mucking about with clay in the afternoon.*

Come to think of it, they weren't much good for their intended purpose either, being more inclined to simply spread the offending matter around, as I recall - but such unsavoury concerns were not really the focus of our attention at that precise moment. No amount of vigorous rubbing would remove the wretched marks, it simply added to the grimy smear effect. So, we adopted plan two: Michael cleared off home for his dinner as fast as he could, and I spent the rest of dinner time being extraordinarily polite to my mother, complementing her on the excellence of the stewed apples and custard, offering to fetch the dustpan and brush to sweep up wayward lunchtime crumbs, suggesting an earlier than usual return to school in order not to miss a particularly exciting powder paint session – and all the time hoping like hell she'd not want to go to the bathroom. Well, at least it deferred the inevitable. So there you have it, that's 1950's lino for you: great skating surface, supreme tobogganing medium... but give it any leeway, and it would stab you in the back, and leave you deep in the brown stuff – or snot green / random puke, to be more precise.

Dads in those days were big and small. Let me explain. My dad was a lot bigger than me, and quite a lot bigger than my mum, who was small, but still bigger than me. It was hard for me to know whereabouts on the scale of dad sizes exactly where my own parent fitted, but he was certainly bigger than many grown up blokes in the car advert pages of his 'Motor' magazine. I know this because I would often pore over the publication desperately searching for a British car that looked anything like an American one. To any random reader of such advertising material it seemed that people in the 1950's were either a) a lot smaller than they are now, or b) the car you got delivered had somehow shrunk between leaving the factory and arriving at your door. For example, the brochure for our 1950's Standard Companion estate showed a blissfully happy family of four out in their new car. Clearly, owners of this model had a lot to live up to as the publicity material showed the dad in a smart sports jacket and matching hat. Whilst driving, he was also smoking a pipe which stuck out of his mouth at an angle that can only be described as 'rakish'. Even so, the space between the end of his pipe's fragrantly fuming bowl and the brim of his wife's hat, (also worn at a matching coquettish angle), was still a good two or three feet. Seated in the back were two beautiful children of indeterminate age – the boy dressed in school blazer and cap, a collar and tie, smartly groomed with neatly parted hair and holding a cricket ball. Inevitably, the girl was blessed with long blonde locks cascading about a cherubic face only minimally obscured by her dolly whose bonnet ribbons she was adjusting. The overall effect was one of immense space, with ample room remaining for at least one more adult with her accompanying portmanteau and hat box. Even then there would be plenty

The US export version of our Standard Companion. The name was changed to Triumph because the Yanks saw the word 'standard' as meaning 'average' or 'normal' and this didn't go down at all well. No amount of explaining that standard meant flag or pennant could persuade them, so Triumph it was. Note also the US additions: ours certainly didn't have white-wall tyres and chrome over-riders.

space left over for the family's pet St. Bernard and a Pye radiogram the size of small wardrobe.

Well, that's not how I remember it. Sure, it was a nice car, though it was really just a four seater. It left precious little space in the back seat for me and my sister to conduct our acts of sibling rivalry and even less between my parents. Had he actually been a pipe smoker, there would have been a good chance that my dad might have knocked mum out with it should he have turned his head to the left in anything approaching a vigorous manner. Nevertheless, and despite having no heater, no radio, no windscreen washer, no power *this* or electronic *that* the little Standard was much liked and in some respects seemed quite innovative.

Most noticeable was the fact that the seat covers were red and white; gone were the days of boring old brown leather – we now had two tone wipe-clean plastic, and although you tended to stick to it a bit in hot weather, it did make that interesting farting sound when you pealed your sweaty legs away from it prior to disembarkation. Also, it had green and cream bodywork, and new technology introduced brake lights and winking orange indicators operated by a little stalk next to the steering wheel. Gone were the days of the old semaphore signalling (I'll explain later), which only ever worked when it felt like it, and seemed prone to sulkiness. OK, the car had no reversing lights and a radio was still a distant aspiration – and we'd never even heard of servo assisted brakes and power steering. Still, this was the fifties, and if you could now have cars painted in any colour, it showed we were on the way up, didn't it? And even though my dad had less elbow room than the ad man suggested, he could still enjoy the integrated ashtray and wind-down the windows on all four doors. Clearly, he had every prospect of being as highly chuffed as the bloke sitting next to his yacht in California.

And it wasn't only cars where dads played a prominent part in advertising. They seemed to appear a lot in promotions for many products designed for boys, presumably to lend authority to whatever was on offer. Take Meccano, for example. This excellent and versatile construction kit was extremely popular in the fifties, and like most of my pals, I was a great fan. Models you were encouraged to construct from the kits varied from a modest wheelbarrow to a fully functioning model of Tower Bridge. Well, in my experience, most of us in those post-war years were at the bottom end of this scale - and the fascination for wheelbarrow construction had its limitations. My kit was a hand-me-down inherited from my cousin, and seemed always to have some important pieces missing. Thus, after a couple of frustrating hours trying to bend a piece to fit to the - by now - somewhat warped garden implement, I might well be reaching the point where going outside to play marbles, or even staring vacantly out of the window seemed attractive alternatives. Clearly, what was needed was an injection of paternal enthusiasm, and if the highly successful ads were anything to go by, there were vast amounts of it. This one is pretty typical: dad and son have constructed an amazingly large and complex model from what must be a very extensive kit. What's more, it is reassuring to see that they both wear collar and tie, dad, (who must be Errol Flynn's brother?) has on his jacket, his hair is neatly styled and Brylcreemed into place and, of course no domestic scene

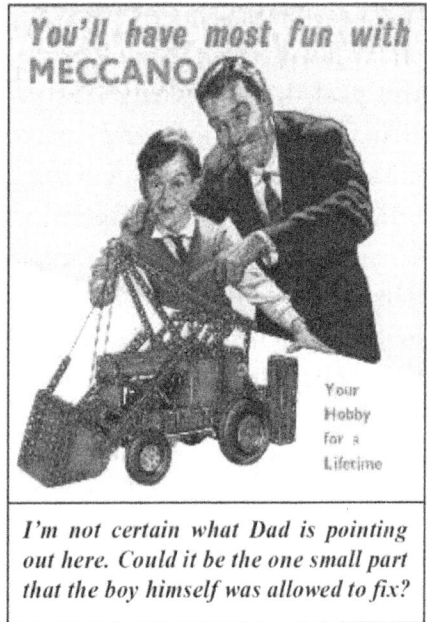

You'll have most fun with MECCANO

Your Hobby for a Lifetime

I'm not certain what Dad is pointing out here. Could it be the one small part that the boy himself was allowed to fix?

would be complete without the trusty pipe clenched manfully between snow-white teeth. Such a setting begged for the insertion of imagined dialogue, and proved irresistible to my friends who were prone to add a make-believe dialogue along the lines of:

'Well done Algy! Our Meccano masterpiece is just tickettyboo! As soon as your mother's finished hoovering the house with the new Goblin Upright I bought her for her birthday, hung out the washing, done the ironing, been to the butcher's, popped into the greengrocer,

the newsagent, the baker and then come trotting home to cook our tea, we'll show her just how clever we've been before she does the washing up. Oh, and by the way, I'm sorry I set fire to your ear with my pipe. Now stop snivelling, put some ointment on the worst bits – and hide that bendy wheelbarrow of yours in the cupboard'.

Clearly, a successful strategy, for here he is again. This time, the model's even more ambitious and with jacket off, sleeves rolled up and his pipe left smouldering on the sideboard, he has taken over. His son is relegated to an advisory role as his pointing finger suggests. And my chum's suggested dialogue ?

'Dad, when can I have a go? – and by the way, I think your pipe you put on the sideboard has just caught the curtains alight.' 'Quiet Algy – this is the trickiest part – I'm just about to slide the jib into place, and my

darned shoe has come off. Go and tell your mother to bring me my slippers and a welcome cup of tea and Digestive biscuit – there's a good fellow!'

So perhaps in our imaginary world, Meccano endeavours were best undertaken when the enthusiastic parent was out, and a boy could take revenge... and have we here a credible attempt by the youngster to make a model of his father, complete with moustache? All that is now needed is the Meccano pipe, and then it will be ready to hurl bricks at down the end of the garden – provided, of course mother is not still there digging up the last of this year's potato harvest prior to making a satisfying gristle-and-mash pie for Dad's tea.

Almost inevitably, the advertising for the product and the reality of ownership was a little different. Like lots of 50's kids, I loved my Meccano, but spent a lot of time scrabbling through the box looking for an errant part, or trying to unbend the screwdriver (also used to open a tin of Golden Syrup) and feeling down the sofa cushions for a missing bolt. Unlike the boys below, I knew of no one who:

a) Had a kit that could build anything remotely as grand as this. The best most of us could do was a wheelbarrow or windmill, or a soap box cart with one wheel not matching the other three, and

b) Who *looked* remotely like the boys on the box. Hair brushed? Socks pulled up? Shiny shoes? *Cheerfully cooperating?!!* You must be joking – but perhaps they're just pleased to be having a go with Dad's latest effort while the domineering bread-winner is out at work... indeed, they might be just about to *remove* some important structural pieces – or at least to loosen a few critical nuts and bolts. Shame though. It's a nice model. Took Dad weeks to complete. Shame mother ran off with the milkman too.

To do them credit, those responsible for producing the Meccano kits throughout our childhood years did a fine job. Based in Liverpool, the company set up by the great Frank Hornby continued to intrigue and challenge thousands upon thousands of children... and quite a few dads too. Quite elaborate plans and well-made parts really did introduce many youngsters to a greater understanding of mechanical engineering. The pulley systems on cranes for example, were really quite complex and as long as you didn't get the green string provided into a cat's cradle of knots, could be both effective and revealing. The gears set, beautifully made from polished brass was another case in point and taught many a youngster a great deal about the science of how you could get rotation to reverse - and change speed as well. Decades before the battery powered motor, the little clockwork item which set your windmill in motion was a revelation, even though such it had its limitations. It often seemed that coiled spring energy only lasted about thirty seconds which, coincidentally, was about the same amount of time that it took to lose the key, rendering you powerless in more than one sense of the word.

A mark of the company's success was that it was able to move with the times, and to update its designs to reflect modern developments. Nevertheless, it came as a surprise to learn that after about sixty years in Liverpool, production of this quintessentially British brand moved brand moved to France in the late seventies. Whilst some famous and well liked developments took place during this period, we can only speculate that a touch of *'oooh la la'* may have influenced an over-imaginative designer...

Strewth! Wouldn't Dad be surprised?!

les sous-vêtements

MECCANO

...or could this be Mum's revenge? Having run off with the milkman to Paris, she finds an original use for the family's favourite kit.

For people of the Baby Boomer generation, it's sort of comforting to know that Meccano still thrives to this very day, and thus provides proof positive of the product's outstanding inter-generational appeal. It is also interesting to note that countrywide Meccano Societies flourish, often populated by folk who would now qualify to be dads and grandads in their own right, producing astounding models of the sort of complexity which outshine even the post-war ads.

Whilst you are still trying to work out what the French advert means, or wondering why the dear soul hasn't bothered to acquaint her under-arm areas with a lady-razor, let me remind you that we jumped into this chapter in the late forties. Whilst we have been re-visiting the lino Olympics, dawdling through the toy cupboard, analysing the role played by over-ambitious and multi-sized dads things have moved on. The change to a new decade meant that for those of us born at the cutting edge of the Baby Boomer years, the grim prospect of having to go to school had arrived.

'*So what about pre-school preparation?*' I hear you ask. Good question. But I have to say that if my own experience was anything to go by – well, there wasn't any at all. The existence of pre-school play groups and lavish nursery school provision was a distant aspiration, and a large proportion of pre-schoolers simply stayed at home with their mums until they were dragged (sometimes screaming) into school. And believe me, for many this is no exaggeration.

Of pre-school visits or preparation of any kind, I have not the faintest recollection: you just got a letter from the Local Education Authority which told you which school you were going to, and that was that. It was expected that mums at home would be just that... at home, looking after the children. Thus your pre-school years were spent in blissful ignorance of what was waiting. The only experience most little kids had of what to expect when they started school was hearsay from older siblings... plus any sights and sounds emanating from local schools as the children hurtled around the playground.

So, apart from the pleasurable distractions offered by our toys what did we do for the five years before compulsory schooling started? How did we fill our time? Well, for a start, domestic life was a lot more labour intensive, and our mums had to expend a great deal of time and energy just keeping the happy home functioning. Food preparation in particular was a lot more arduous, and required daily visits to a range of shops. Inevitably, this entailed dragging the offspring with her, and so like thousands of other pre-school kids, I spent a lot of time staring up at various shop assistants, my vantage point being just about level with shop counters. I also spent a lot of time wishing my mum would get a blooming move on. To be honest, her discussion with the shopkeeper concerning the state of Mrs. Jenkins' arthritis was of limited fascination; I was keen to get back to my pedal car in order to practice the necessary sound accompaniment required for reversing round the corner of the veg patch.

Pre-school life was generally uneventful and highly regulated, circumscribed as it was by domestic necessities and predictable outcomes… and there was also the extended family to take into account. In the days before social mobility was the norm, most families stayed within shouting distance of eachother – some literally so. To move away to a distant location was very uncommon and so the proximity of one's grandparents, aunts, uncles and a shed-load of cousins was all part of the domestic scene. Although the life of the pre-schooler wasn't nearly as varied as it is today and we were ignorant of much of the world around us, I think most of us infant Boomers were very happy with our lot.

And by the time the powers that be said we had to go to school, were we ready? Were we toughened up enough to face the rigours of the playground, to meet the challenge of powder paint, grubby bits of plasticine and the unlikely tales of Dick and Dora?

In comparison with today's littlies, we were as green as grass. Apart from dire warnings gleefully provided by older siblings, most of us had little idea of what was coming… but after spending hours being dragged daily around the local shops, I suppose we were at least looking for something a bit more challenging. And don't forget, we also had four winter's worth of scraping the ice off the inside of our bedroom windows, and by now were quite skilled at digging out splinters and sliding on the lino, so perhaps we were a lot tougher than we looked.

Good job, really.

3 And the Lord said *'Let There Be Sellotape'*

The observant amongst you will note from the previous chapters that the things described were made almost exclusively from natural materials – wood for toys (and splinters), pressed tin for toy cars (and laceration), lead for toy soldiers (and poisoning), lino for slipping (and dislocated joints) - and so on.

What things were *not* made of in those days was **plastic**... because, even by the late forties, *plastic hadn't been invented*. Well, that's not squeakily true, as there was some hard, brittle, heavy brown stuff called Bakelite, which seems to have been produced for the sole purpose of encasing inefficient and static filled radio sets, thus making them only moveable at risk of a hernia. Today, it seems almost incomprehensible that there are still a few of us who can remember a time when plastic did *not exist*, especially when you consider that currently, about ninety percent of our physical world seems to be made of this ubiquitous material. For example, picture yourself sitting in the comfort of a modern airliner... and then remove everything made from plastic and its derivatives. Chances are you'd be left sitting on a small aluminium ledge accompanied by just the engines, a few wires and about three hundred other semi-naked people wearing little else than a small bracelet and a startled look – prior to plummeting earthwards accompanied by that bullet ricocheting sound so beloved by cartoon makers. Now I'm well aware of the current serious environmental issues regarding single use plastic – but we are talking the other end of the spectrum here: *virtually no plastic at all.*

However, come the early fifties, things started moving ahead plastic-wise, and suddenly manufacturers found that they could produce an almost limitless range of products from this new, cheap and easily formed material – and what's more, it could be just about any damn colour you'd like. Which was a bit of a problem really, in that the post-war population, being sick and tired of the austerity-ridden grey drabness of everything, welcomed the new material without restraint: the more garish the colour, the better. Inevitably, this led to many a 'repent at leisure' moment when perhaps those bright orange dinner plates accompanied by mauve cutlery didn't quite cut the mustard... in fact, to be honest, plastic cutlery didn't cut anything much, and was a perfect example of a slowly growing realisation that this new wonder-material wasn't good for *everything*. But what it was spectacularly good for was a) making cheap, colourful and relatively unthreatening toys, and b) sticking stuff together. We've had enough of toys for a moment, so we'll take the latter first.

Compared with modern excesses, the habit of present-giving at this time was a very restrained affair. True, people didn't have a lot of disposable income and there wasn't much to buy to give to others anyhow, but most of all, I think people just couldn't face the prospect of *wrapping up* presents and sending them. You see, everything had to be wrapped in brown paper, and then tied up with string. I'll repeat that for emphasis and dramatic effect. String! Yes -the long thin hairy stuff, little balls of which had virtual permanent residence in the pockets of small boys' trousers... and before any dodgy association of *balls* and *boys' pockets* raises its ugly head, let us return to the problem in hand. To do a satisfactory wrapping job in the early fifties, you also had to be proficient in tying slip knots and flipping over the package without tearing the brown paper and having to start all over again. What a performance – and all this prior to trailing down to the local post office with a pocket full of pre-decimal coinage which weighed about half a hundredweight. One questionable aid to this laborious process was *brown paper tape*. This was a reel of – guess what? - brown paper lavishly coated with some thick brown sticky-when-wet stuff that looked like congealed gravy. When moistened, this was supposed to turn into a useful string-replacement packaging medium. In point of fact, it often turned into an unmanageable ball of wet tacky goo, forever determined only to stick itself to itself. At the same time it also made you feel very sick because you had licked the glue rather than shelling out for the little water trough produced for the purpose.

So, you can imagine the delirious joy with which our generation of Brits greeted the arrival of the new wonder plastic based product **Sellotape!** It was light! It was transparent! It was reasonably sticky! You didn't need to lick it! It came with a groovy little plastic dispenser which had a serrated edge for tearing off just the right amount! It consigned string, slip-knots and the vomit associated with brown paper tape to the annals of history, along with other undesirables such as the plague and the hopeful but useless application of leeches.

My family's bright green plastic dispenser held pride of place on top of the bureau, and it was my responsibility – nay, my *pride and pleasure* – to report to my mother when the roll was getting near to replacement time. And what's more, it could be used for purposes beyond simple parcel packaging – oh yes. It had numerous applications including providing the transparent part of a visor in a cardboard box space helmet, (assuming you didn't mind it occasionally sticking to your nose), and holding a cupboard door closed that was always, *always* springing open of its own accord. It could also be used to cover up the holes in the bodywork of your rusting Ford Anglia, though it has to be said that this application had its limitations – especially when the next rain shower came. But most of all, Sellotape was at its best when sticking bits of cardboard and paper together. Later in the decade, this fact was not lost on the presenters of BBC's '*Blue Peter*', whose endless production of useful pots in which to put things for kids to press upon their unsuspecting parents, were always held together with the stuff. Not that the BBC could be seen to endorse a commercial product, so

Sellotape was always referred to as '*sticky-backed plastic*'. Valerie Singleton and John Noakes, ably assisted by the brilliant artist Tony Hart created a real bond with children throughout the succeeding decade, and there can be few homes which were not blessed with gaudily decorated ex baked bean tins wrapped tightly with wallpaper stuck on with Sellotape. These were duly presented to a parent on Christmas morning as a wonderful, thoughtful, utterly unique and artistic solution to his or her storage needs. They were also dirt cheap to make, and provided you did not lacerate yourself on the sharp edges of the tin, or failed to get rid of *all* the baked beans before applying the Sellotape, you were on to a winner.

Regardless of the ability of humankind to mess up just about everything, Sellotape was proving its indispensible worth – and the very name of the product soon gained the same status as Hoover and Thermos, in being able to drop the capital letter. Thus, just as the vacuum cleaner was always referred to as a 'hoover' and any insulated flask was called a 'thermos', so 'sellotape' *was* sticky-backed transparent tape, regardless of which manufacturer's product you chose. It is my contention that the introduction of such a useful and labour-saving material as sellotape assisted the nation in shaking off its post-war blues, in discarding its gloomy austerity-inspired lethargy and re-energising its entrepreneurial spirit. After all, if you could stick cardboard together with just a few bits of plastic tape, what else could you do?

Along with this wonder of the modern age came an avalanche of other new materials. Perhaps it was because in post-war Britain there was not much of anything, and so it was therefore good commercial sense if you could make something out of virtually nothing. Take for example, the residue left at a sawmill. What unprepossessing and apparently useless bits and pieces are left over? In this case there's sawdust by the cartload, scrap wood, splinters and the twiggy bits remaining after all the good stuff had been used. So what can be done with this unappealing collection of waste? Well, in the late forties someone had the bright idea of shredding it all up, mixing it with some gluey stuff, heating it up a bit and then rolling it out like pastry - and what do you get? Hardboard, that's what.

When my dad brought home the first sheet of this stuff, it was subjected to whole family examination. My mum noted that one side was quite shiny, whilst the obverse was textured and matt. I said that it was not very thick, to which my sister added *'Not like you then!'* Since her only other contribution to the family debate was the pathetic observation that the new material *'was brown'*, I chose to ignore her caustic remark, treat it with the disdain it deserved, and vowed to stick up her bedroom door with sellotape the next time she went to her room. However, to return to the family analysis of the wonder that was hardboard. My dad then made the mistake of mentioning that the dimensions of the purchased sheet made it *'about the same size as the dining room door'*. Now, on its own, this seems a pretty innocuous remark, but of course, you have to remember that this was the early fifties, and that the first faint tremors of the avalanche that was to become the DIY revolution were already being felt. You could buy screws, you could buy nails, Brolac paint was available in more than one colour and if you knew a bloke who knew another bloke you could get some turpentine and *more than one grade* of sandpaper.

Mum looked at dad, dad looked at mum… we all looked at the dining room door and saw in our mind's eye not the plain, old-fashioned solid wood with attractively embossed panels and rather charming ceramic door handles mounted just above a decorative back plate. No, we saw an opportunity for *modernisation*... a chance to move into the new up-beat world of home improvement, to replace such fuddy-duddy symbols of a bygone age - such as well made polished timber doors - with something new, exciting and colourful. It was the opportunity to show off to the neighbours that avant-garde *something* that hardboard represented!

So, like tens of thousands of others, my family demonstrated its artistic liberation by embarking on a sort of *collective madness* of modernisation – effectively acts of near vandalism - which saw quality materials and elegant joinery replaced by cheapo rubbish… and beautiful fireplaces ripped out to make room for an electric radiator.

To be fair, my dad didn't rip things out so much as *cover them up*. Thus, all our wooden panelled doors were covered with a sheet of hardboard almost, but not quite up to the edges, and then had added a frame of wooden beading before painting the whole ensemble in '*a colour of your choosing*'. Fortunately, in our case, this was generally white or cream, but in many other houses it was possible to see quite violent colour variations, and if a striking combo of purple and yellow was to your liking then the dawn of DIY was a time and place for you. And not only that: lovely old china door knobs with charming lock plates and escutcheons were chucked out in their thousands. In our house we replaced the traditional door furniture with a basic ball catch, and the door knobs with plain green plastic handles. We then stood back to admire the very chic and up-market appearance such vandalism had achieved.

By the end of the fifties, DIY was beginning to hit its stride, and garden sheds all over the country were becoming the epicentre of the DIY revolution, and ours was no exception. Being a grocer by trade, my dad had a plentiful supply of quite sturdy and well-made wooden boxes, which in those days were commonly used by suppliers to send consignments of goods such as butter and various soft fruit deliveries. Responding to my mum's complaint that she never had enough storage space in the kitchen, dad retired to the shed accompanied by four empty wooden butter boxes. These became the subject of much banging, sawing, sanding and painting in the dusty confines of his shed - before emerging as a five cubby-hole storage set complete with (slightly bendy) hardboard doors and our, by now, family trademark green plastic handles.

'*So, how do you get a five cubby hole set from just four boxes?*' I hear you ask. ***Well, like this:***

Good, eh? Only thing was, the bendy hardboard doors got increasingly bendy as the unit was mounted close to ye olde gas cooker, thus subjecting the new material to a quite concentrated steam bath each time it was used. As a result the hardboard doors would suddenly and quite randomly burst open having released themselves from the tiny spring catches which were supposed to keep them captive and_compliant. For a little lad, the entertainment value of such erratic cupboard behaviour far outweighed my parents' irritation in having their Heinz Tomato Sauce bottle, Paxo stuffing packet and slightly crushed-so-that-it-would-fit-into-the-space Kellogg's Cornflake box revealed to any passing visitor... and my sister's claim that the cupboard was haunted didn't add to their overall ambience of our oh so modern 1950's kitchen. Hey ho.

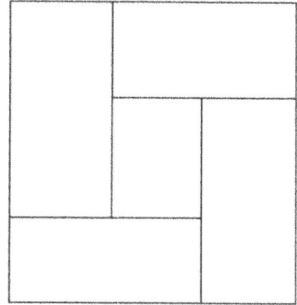

Undaunted by such trivialities, however, new materials continued to be welcomed and tried out regardless of practicality, colour or taste. Formica was one such, and was probably the earliest example of what we now call a laminate. For the first time, you could buy a sheet of non-bendy stuff that had a wipe-clean plastic like surface, and could be just about any colour or artistic style the manufacturers liked. As a result, a whole range of uses were discovered – some of them good and practical, such as flat and hygienic kitchen surfaces, others less well advised. One of the latter that springs to mind was the questionable fashion for hubbies at that time to impress family, friends and neighbours by making their own bar. By this, I don't mean a strong beam, such as the type you might pair up and set parallel with one another in order to then over-exert yourself with flamboyant, ill-advised and lycra-clad gymnastic manoeuvres. I mean the sort you lean up against in the snug of your favourite local, passing the time of day with others dedicated to emptying the contents of landlord's latest barrel of the finest ale.

It seems that many a chap, on seeing the versatility of the new material, was immediately impressed by the thought of mounting a sheet of the more colourful sort in the front room. So far so good – but he then pictured himself standing behind it in a landlordly way, dispensing frothing pints of bitter-and-mild to his mates whilst impressing the ladies with the elaborate cocktails he could conjure up from the beautifully displayed racks of the finest liqueurs mounted on the wall behind. Add a table lamp made from a recycled Mateus Rosé bottle plus an advert for Sandeman's Port, and mine host was in his element.

In truth, it seldom - if ever - worked out like that. For a start, most suburban front rooms were quite small and included the intrusion of a sizeable fireplace, hearth and chimney breast. The latter thus created a useful recess each side - one of which was perfect for the insertion of your new 14 inch black and white telly and the other... well, equally perfect for the in-house bar, surely?

Well, no. Many tried, but their valiant efforts to combine a curved kidney shaped yellow Formica top with a purple painted quilted hardboard front seldom took account of the fact that even if you were quite small and managed to get behind the damned thing by squeezing around the side, there was hardly any room *behind* the bar. You therefore risked either banging your head on the optics display (comprising a bottle each of sweet British Sherry and Cinzano Bianco mounted enticingly behind you), or nudging the bar sufficient to cause the three unmatched wine glasses assembled there to make an immediate and noisy dive for freedom. Added to this, the tiny space available behind the bar top made it near impossible to lower yourself sufficiently to retrieve the large half gallon *'Jackpot'* can of beer stored on a lower shelf. There was simply not enough room to bend from the waist in any direction, and thus an ungainly combination of twisting to one side and slowly bending the knees whilst groping about with one hand was the best you could hope for. To be able to do this with any dignity whilst still maintaining a manly conversation about United's promotion prospects for next season required considerable aplomb – and in consequence was almost universally absent. Nevertheless, there was at least a little compensation in pouring the painfully retrieved ale into the dimpled pint glasses placed next to the little Spanish doll centrally displayed amongst the purloined beer mats, and put there expressly to demonstrate your cosmopolitan, international, barman-about-town appeal.

Another problem was the fact that, being squeezed into a tiny space and totally hemmed in by the adjacent chimney breast and the Formica monstrosity in front, there was no way the incumbent could see the telly in the other recess. So, many an aspirant barman spent his time squashed up against the wall, *listening* to the TV programme that other family members and guests were enjoying watching. I suspect this presented an opportunity for *mine host* to reflect upon the wisdom of the whole enterprise: was a love of beer mats really worth missing Hughie Greene's *'Double Your Money'*? And, of course having to put up with the steady leakage of sweet sherry dripping down the back of your shirt from a faulty optic didn't help. Thus it was that many an attempt to create the lounge bar ambience of the local pub ended up with the yellow Formica bar top being re-cycled as a pair of shelves at the back of the broom cupboard or, more likely, appearing in several broken parts in the dustbin. So let's get back in the shed for a bit of a re-think.

Few homes were blessed with any garden utility building that was purpose-built, and the vast majority of blokes just cobbled together whatever they could to provide some degree of shelter from the rain, with perhaps a modest bench and even a vice. Ours was typical, and like many thousands of others, was made from the remains of the wartime Anderson air raid shelter. These had been distributed to the civilian population just before hostilities started in 1939 and were installed in many back gardens. They comprised four large, curved sheets of corrugated iron which were bolted together to make an arch. When joined to the end pieces, one of which contained the tiny doorway, they formed a surprisingly strong structure made even

Anderson shelters - in theory and practice. Despite the spiders, they were a step up from the Morrison shelter which was a wood and wire cage installed under a hefty dining table.

more bomb-resistant by then burying them up to two thirds of their height in the soil. To add the final touch, turves or sandbags were then applied to the top, and *voila!* Bomb-proof... or more or less. Certainly, the old Anderson shelter was damp and a bit of an attraction for the many local insects, worms and rodents who were also seeking safety from the Nazi hoard - but generally a lot safer than sitting under the kitchen table or in a cupboard under the stairs.

And the proof of the pudding? Well, as you may recall from the previous chapter, my own family home had been subjected to the unwanted attention of the Luftwaffe in 1941. On this occasion a bomb dropped in a street nearby created a blast sufficient to quite literally suck out the back wall and a proportion of the roof of our modest end-terraced house. Up until that point, my folks had little premonition that the destruction of the back of our house was critical to Hitler's ambition of world domination. Unknown to my parents and their neighbours, it had been decided by the German High

Command that there was no chance of final victory for the Fuhrer and his Teutonic chums until our family's back wall had been blown out and unceremoniously re-distributed across the back garden. You can picture the scene, can't you?

Hitler: *Vy hef ve stopped at der channel? Vot are ve vaiting for?* *

Goebbels: *Der English are digging in, mein Fuhrer!*

Hitler: *Who is behind zis brilliant strategy?*

Goring: *Already ve hef been using spy planes from our 'Letstakealookatvotthebastardsareupto' Service, and I can report that der reason vy ve are apparently up shit creek is that der Burden's back wall is still standing!!*

Hitler: *Still standing? Still standing!! I vont der whole Luftwaffe, der Wermacht, der Kreigsmarine, der Hitler Youth, der Berlin Philharmonic Orchestra und der Hamburg Girl Guides if necessary to destroy zis last obstacle to my complete domination of der world!!*

Goring: *Cool it mein Fuhrer! Your vish is my command*

Hitler: *Afterwards, I vill then say: 'For you, Tommy, der vall is over!!!' Ha ha! I make my first joke.*

Goebbels: *Don't give up der day job. Ve hef a var to vin!*

And so it was that one night in 1941 our little old Anderson shelter suddenly found itself covered in bits of brick, splintered floorboards, some rather dodgy looking green lino and three china ducks that barely a moment before had been serenely flying up the dining room wall. But apart from a few dents, it stood up very well to the Nazi onslaught, and continued to defy the enemy's worst intentions until it was dismantled in 1945. The dip in our back lawn which marked its location was still there thirty years later, as was half of the shelter itself – in the form of my Dad's garden shed, relegated to sit, rusty but proud up against the back garden fence. And all around the city,

* *As you can see, this script of this (until now) undiscovered interview is written in German to add to its authenticity*

and decades before the notion of *recycling* became common, you could see where the elements of Anderson shelters had been used for a whole range of purposes. At my grandparents' house for example, the previous owner had obviously acquired two shelters, and bolted the eight corrugated sheets together to form a small but usable garage. That such a double sized structure could just about squeeze in a Morris Ten indicates just how small pre-war motor cars were.

But back to the wonders of early DIY and my dad's garden shed. It was from this location that such magnificent articles as our Anchor Butter box *'five for the price of four'* kitchen cupboards were created and sheets of hardboard were cut, planed, and all too often inadvertently snapped in half in the quest to ruin our plain but quite attractive Edwardian internal doors. It was also the place where I insisted that seven years was quite old enough to begin my career in furniture making, and immediately set about building for my mum a *coffee table*. This was none too artfully constructed from orange box wood nailed together and then lovingly stained with creosote. Was she pleased? I'll leave you to guess. Nevertheless, in a somewhat roundabout way, the Second World War promoted the growth of DIY in providing many a workshop facility for the aspiring craftsman. Also, for a little chap, there was an almost endless supply of DIY materials to be gleaned from the local bombsites. Let me explain:

There were scores of bombsites in our city alone, and some of them were really big. I can only suppose that the Luftwaffe crews sent to destroy our back wall must have been pretty useless, as they seemed to have dropped a lot of their bombs near the huge naval dockyard which takes up most of the western side of Portsea Island. Thus they missed our house by as much as three miles; it was almost as if they were trying *not* to hit it! I have to say however, that in their attempt to get our strategically vital back wall, the Luftwaffe made one hell of a mess everywhere else. This was brought home to me much later, when in 1967, I was working on modifying a telephone exchange in Portsmouth. On that day, one of the GPO engineers found a wartime pamphlet which had slipped down the back of the exchange test desk, collecting dust for over twenty years. This modest publication was dated 1943, and its centrefold comprised a 360 degree panoramic picture of Portsmouth city centre. I remember being quite shocked at the level of devastation thus recorded... it seemed as if the whole of the Portsea area of the city, with its densely packed two up, two down houses and narrow streets had been completely flattened as far as the eye could see. It was said by some that in a way, this was a blessing in disguise, as much of the original housing had been quite severely sub-standard. Nevertheless, they had been people's homes however modest, and to see them completely wiped out was a sobering experience. But however dire the circumstances, the old adage concerning clouds and silver linings rang true even here, for the clearance of such devastation and the urgent need to provide quick and effective solutions to the appalling housing crisis gave birth to another icon of the 1950's, *the prefab*. Designed as a stop-gap measure to meet immediate needs in at least providing displaced people with a roof over their heads, thousands and thousands of these compact and efficient little housing units were installed in areas where the original housing stock had been destroyed. Although many were located on cleared bombsites, they were subsequently used as the initial housing units in green field areas beyond original city limits - and in time would become the large post-war council housing estates which flourished in the 1960's. And very welcome they were too. For many people it was the first time they had proper dry,

Inevitably the term 'prefabricated House' was quickly abbreviated to 'prefab'. Most people loved them.

draught-proof and self-contained accommodation, complete with often quite generous gardens and other most welcome benefits such as your very own bathroom with that great luxury, *an inside loo*. From the perspective of the 21st century, it might seem bizarre that such basic amenities should be regarded as a luxury, but it has to be borne in mind that pre-war inner city housing was often very poor indeed, with several families sharing one outside toilet, and no internal plumbing beyond a cold water tap. So, to be suddenly granted a much greater level of comfortable privacy in your own little detached home was warmly welcomed. Add a couple of pairs of gingham curtains, stick the china ducks back on the wall, go and prod about in the garden for a while, tune in to '*Two Way Family Favourites*' each Sunday...well, what more could anyone ask? I suppose the only downside might have been that 'prodding about in the garden' might reveal the occasional rusty metal cylinder which, once the mud had been scraped off revealed a chalked on message in a vaguely familiar Teutonic hand:

'Zis one is for you, Tommy! Ve know vere you live! Your back vall ist doomed!! All der best for now,
Your enemy,
Adolf (Hitler)'

Unexploded ordnance was indeed something of a problem post-war, and thus made the exploration of the many bombsites yet to receive a visit from the bulldozers an even more hazardous proposition. Getting lacerated by rusty bits of iron, pierced by shards of glass or falling through into a previously undetected cellar were occupational hazards; finding yourself staring at the rusty fins of an unexploded bomb was something else.

Given the apparently random distribution of the aerial attack, some bombsites were quite small, and thus the areas of some produced land only sufficient for three or four prefabs. The weapon which eventually did for our back wall was a particularly nasty thing called a land mine. This was designed to explode about fifty feet above the ground, and thus caused a lot more devastation than the traditional type which often half buried itself before exploding. In our case, the land mine destroyed about a dozen houses, but the immediate post-war rebuilding just filled in the gaps thus created in the four neighbouring streets surrounding the site. And so it was that for us local children, the only approach to this particular bombsite was via a narrow alley that ran between two houses, and which was guarded by a very stern lady who seemed to spend most of her waking hours watching out for mischievous kids for whom the bombsite wilderness just over her back garden wall was an absolute magnet.

It never really occurred to us that the whole environment could be dangerous; that jagged pieces of iron, planks of splintered wood and sheets of rusting metal might be in any way hazardous – not to mention the brambles and stinging nettles which immediately colonised such abandoned land. Unexploded bombs? What bombs? Come on! We were kids! The freedom we had to rush off out was just part and parcel of everyday life, and the local streets, parks and bombsites were our natural playground.

Street games were possible because residential roads were largely free of traffic. Give a kid a stick of chalk, and the cricket stumps appeared on nearby walls as quickly as hopscotch squares transformed the pavements. And bikes and trikes of course. Ring-a-Ring-a-Roses anyone?

'*So*' I hear you say, '*apart from being blown up on the nearby bombsite, wasn't playing in the street dangerous? What about the traffic? Wasn't being run down by a passing Ford Anglia or Morris Eight an ever present risk?*'

Well no, not really. In most residential areas, there wasn't much traffic to speak of. Even in the mid fifties private car ownership was still relatively uncommon, and the likelihood of being knocked down by Ben Parsons' creaking invalid carriage tearing down the centre of the road at 3mph was somewhat unlikely – in fact you were more likely to be bored to death if by some mischance he happened to engage you in lengthy conversation. Kerbsides were relatively free of vehicles of any type and it was quite usual to see only one or two cars parked in any one street. Strange to reflect that in just a decade or two, such a scene would be impossible, and that streets which had been blessed by such scant parking would become the home of twenty or thirty vehicles parked nose to tail. So, for us there was plenty of room for play, and few moving cars to avoid.

It's odd to recall too, that the Highway Code at that time insisted that all vehicles parked on a road must be *lit at night*. Now, considering how poor battery technology was in those days, leaving a car's sidelights on all night was never going to be practical. Thus it was that vehicle owners had to invest in alternative light sources, and this would often be in the form of a little paraffin lamp, (one side of which would be painted with mum's nail varnish so that it appeared red) which was taken out each night at dusk, and tied on to the bumper of your beloved Austin Seven. The reverse operation was, of course, needed each morning, but the overall effect was of an increasing number of little flickering lights dimly illuminating your street from dusk to dawn. Seems laborious? It was. But I suppose it could be said that street lights in the fifties were nowhere near as powerful or as omnipresent as they are today, and so giving some indication as to where your limousine/heap of rust was located was to the unwary cyclist, perhaps necessary. Those with their own garage, of course, were free of this nightly duty, but many older cities were ill provided with such facilities. Added to this, most suburban streets, by today's standards, were quite narrow, and so it was perhaps fortunate that our little family cars were just that – little. Put beside a modern equivalent they seem – well, *spindly,* almost fragile, and bearing in mind that the MOT test was not introduced until 1960, many of them were in a parlous state. To be honest, the little paraffin lamp was sometimes the best part of the whole set up. At least while your 1932 Austin Seven was leaking oil, petrol, water and various other bodily fluids in to the gutter, your little night light was burning cheerfully away.   There was also the benefit of it lighting an area near your vehicle, enabling you to more easily locate various pieces of car which might well have fallen off during the night. Thus, during the daylight hours, when the small number of private cars that parked overnight were away on their daily round, the streets were virtually clear for the ambitious marble player, the confident leap-frogger, the trainee roller skater, the hastily assembled footie team, and most of all, for the dedicated go-cart driver.

That's not to say you didn't need your wits about you; there was still a certain amount of traffic, much of it in the form of delivery vans. The first of these, very early each morning, was the milk float.

Smaller electric milk floats had no room for a milkman... so rain or shine, he had to walk the round. When you recall that his working day started at around 4am, you get the idea that milkmen were well-hard too.

Many horse drawn milk floats worked well into the sixties. My grand-parents' house was on the main A27 but that did not stop a horse-drawn delivery right into the decade, main road or not.

A typical early morning scene replicated in its thousands countrywide. It was just so ordinary, it was never noticed. Note also the lack of parked cars.

These little battery-powered vehicles were a constant presence throughout the fifties and sixties. They were so omnipresent as to represent just the ordinary backdrop of life. The whining of their electric motors, the clinking of the milk bottles in their crates and the slamming of your front gate as the bottles were delivered were as much a part of the morning scene as toast and marmalade. In fact, they were only ever noticed if they failed to turn up ... which they never did. Getting the milk in from the doorstep was just part of normal daily routine.

Other street-borne hazards which occasionally would interrupt our play included the weekly visit of the dustman whose refuse collection lorry was no more than an ordinary truck with a semi-circular metal cover designed to keep the rubbish in - and the smell out. That it failed spectacularly to do the latter, and sometimes the former as well, was frequently all too evident. All dustbins were of the galvanised iron type (remember, we're still before plastic?) So their collection, emptying and return to your front door made a hell of a noise. It seemed some of the crews took a delight in making as much noise and mayhem as possible, and may even have indulged in pursuing their hobby of mixing up the dustbin lids with something that approached joyful abandon. Still, I suppose when all you've got to do is go up and down streets emptying heavy, dirty and often very smelly dustbins, you deserve a little entertainment, don't you?

It's odd to reflect that, although the bins themselves were as described, they were never kept in the front of the house. Whether you were lucky enough to have a front garden or not – and most didn't - the vast majority of dustbins were kept 'out the back'. Thus, dustbin day got off to a merry start with having to carry the damned thing to the front door, and for people in terraced houses, this meant tripping the light fantastic right through the house. It's quite hard carrying a heavy bin through a long lino-slippy passage whilst at the same time holding your breath and trying to avoid sweeping the carefully mounted flying ducks off the wall, believe me... and especially so when you find the front door has slammed itself shut in the sudden breeze created by the opening of the back door. *Well-*

hard? You betcha! Delivery vans were another hazard for the aspirant street athlete, and were more frequent than you might expect. At a time when domestic fridges were still a rarity, housewives (and yes, it was nearly always the ladies' task) had to shop for food on a daily basis: essentially, any perishables you bought in the morning, you ate that day. As a result, the slightly more affluent got local trades-people to deliver, and thus the arrival of the bread van was nearly as common as the milkman, and there were also delivery boys aplenty on their weird bikes. To us kids, these were the very opposite of what we wanted our bikes to be: our heart's desire would involve white-wall tyres, drop handlebars, sparkly reflectors and battery powered lights. Delivery bikes looked like a mutation of the penny-farthing with odd sized wheels - and quite often pretty odd riders as well. The disposition of their wheels made them more like *farthing – penny* bikes I suppose, and they were certainly bereft of any glamour. Nevertheless, such delivery bikes were just a part of the street scene, and no doubt for many housewives, quite indispensible.

Talking of bikes, the fifties was a time when nearly everyone owned one and used them for work more than for pleasure. Seeing many neighbours cycling off to work each morning was very common, and they were also used for the transport of goods. '*How so?*' I hear your incredulous cry. Well, for a start, this was the age of the *saddlebag.* Most bikes were equipped with a comfy saddle which sported two little eyelets along the back edge. Through these you attached the short leather straps of your large saddlebag so that it hung somewhat precariously over the back wheel, and hey presto!

You were a van! Not only were the bags quite large, many also sported additional pockets which when filled made your saddle bag balloon out in all directions, rather like an over-ambitious hamster. For the serious cyclist, claiming pride of luggage space would be your wet weather gear comprising bright yellow rain cape and sou-wester, making you entirely water proof, albeit at the expense of looking like a small yellow volcano. And as if one rain sodden saddle bag was not enough, some cyclists would go even further by adding panniers to hang dangerously either side of the back wheel.

The truly delusional took the final step of mounting an additional bag on the handlebars, thus converting their bike into more of a heavy goods vehicle. Getting on and off such encumbered vehicles – especially when wearing a rain cape and leggings - was often a source of much entertainment for the casual onlooker, and frequently involved an extravagant amount of one legged hopping along prior to limb elevation. This final stage of the mounting process was the most precarious, and involved strenuously trying to disentangle your foot, cycle clips and flapping leggings from the numerous luggage carriers distributed about the back wheel, whilst still maintaining some kind of forward motion.

Another abuse visited upon the bicycles was to use them as carriers for items far beyond their dimensions. Some people insisted on strapping long lengths of wood, or stepladders or Christmas trees *across* their bikes, and held them in place using the tightly buckled flap of the saddle bag. Thus the bike, in addition to teetering along under its overladen weight, had now expanded to about two metres *in width* and was quite capable of scratching parked cars or knocking the hats off people on the nearside whilst forming a major obstacle to traffic wishing to overtake. Lest you should think this is becoming something of a rant, let me just draw such considerations to a close by saying that I loved bikes and the eccentricities and inventiveness they encouraged. In an age before most people could afford a car, using two wheels to do the job of four was a challenge happily met. Using a bike as a trolley was just another example of solving a practical problem with the limited means at your disposal. Besides, how else could you get a large sheet of Formica home if not on your bike?

So, the street scene was enlivened by visitors and trades people. I'm not sure the rag and bone collection qualified as a trade; I suppose the nearest match these days would be a *'recycling operative'*. Their job was to collect unwanted items from the neighbourhood, and such men would roam the streets with their handcarts crying *'Any old rags and bones?!!'* From a modern perspective, to employ such street cries seems like a throwback to Victorian times – and perhaps it was. Rag and bone carts were generally piled high with, well, odds and ends, as just about *anything* seemed to qualify. Certainly there were clothes and other fabrics aplenty, and to see items such as a previously wall-mounted moose's head would not have raised so much as an eyebrow, and neither would the occasional chamber pot, (don't ask), aspidistra or recently scrapped bright yellow Formica front room drinks bar. One thing I never did see, however, was any *bones;* plenty of rags, plenty of scrap, plenty of chipped and broken crockery, but never so much as a glimpse of any skeletal remains, so why the call for rags *and bones* persisted, I know not. It may have been that the cry was just a habit or, eternally hopeful of being graced by the donation of the odd femur or two, rag and bone men just included the plea in a spirit of optimism. Seems unlikely. Rag and bone men understandably seemed keener on making a quick buck by re-selling better quality stuff, as my mum found out one day when my sister, feeling sorry for our local man's apparent lack of business, offered him her new gabardine raincoat. Evidently, he saw it as an opportunity not to be missed and gave her twopence for the coat before disappearing at a rate of knots round the corner. Unluckily for him, his handcart was heavy and slow and my mum caught him two streets away. Suffice it to say that in the unequal battle that ensued, the only addition to the tradesman's stock that day was a rather large flea in his ear. My sister wasn't that popular for a day or two either, so all in all... result!

As well as trades peoples' handcarts – and builders at the time used these a lot - other weird vehicles would suddenly hove into view to get in the way of a particularly intense game of marbles or the critical phase of a football match. One such was the Reliant three wheeler van. This curious vehicle was clearly a hybrid of motor bike and small van body, and I can only assume that it was designed by a heavy goods cyclist (see above) who got fed up having to push his overloaded bike around in the pouring rain. In reality, it always looked like someone had ridden a motor bike far too fast, only to come into sudden and unexpected collision with a van body- and then nearly penetrating right through the front. I also suspected that at the end of the day, the driver would rev up the engine of the bike, and burst out from the van body to go careering off up the road with a yell of *'Yahoooo! – free at last!!'* Perhaps not. Whatever the speculation as to their design and use, these strange little vehicles were quite popular and presumably quite economical, which was just as well, as 1956 saw the Suez Crisis. Even for a carefree and gormless nine year old, I could sense that something was not quite right. Grown-ups were muttering stuff about someone called Nasser and things like *'well, it's our canal, innit?'* and so on. Also, even I became aware of the term *'petrol rationing'*. Now, if the Second World War had taught us one thing, it was that necessity is the mother of invention. Thus, when petrol was severely rationed in 1956, did we reach for the

smelling salts? Cave in, put the Morris Ten up on blocks, drain off the oil and with a heavy sigh start rummaging through the kitchen drawer in order to find the old cycle clips again? Well no we absolutely didn't!

Instead, the nation turned its attention to obtaining a whole range of little vehicles which were designed to go a lot further... for a lot less petrol. And believe it or not, we had one already. If you think that the Reliant motor bike van was weird, then let me introduce you to the ultra light-weight, extremely economical and slightly more than bonkers Bond Mini Car.

Picture in your mind a plastic bath tub, mount it on three wheels, pop in a noisy little two stroke motorbike engine – and you get the idea. They were immediately appealing because, well, they were so tiny and so colourful. OK, there was no luggage space to speak of, they didn't go much above about 30

Just add in a cloud of blue smoke, hear the angry buzzing of a little two stroke engine, and there you have it: the Bond Minicar. Lovely!

mph, – oh, and the earlier models had no reverse gear, not that this mattered much, as the front wheel could be turned ninety degrees in either direction, and thus the little car could be spun around *within its own length!* No wonder we loved them. Even more of a hoot was that early ones did not possess a reliable self-starter. Now remember, the power unit was a motor bike engine, and all such engines were fired up using a kick-start. And so it was with the earlier and more primitive versions of the Bond Minicar, – they were kick-started. Ok, so what? Well, the kick-start was located *under the bonnet*. So, to start the little car, you had to open the bonnet, step inside the engine compartment, and kick away until the engine burst into noisy life. To be honest, such a procedure could not be described as sophisticated. Extracting yourself from the eager embrace of the new girlfriend in order to step inside the engine compartment with a view to kick-starting your little pash-wagon into reluctant life, didn't really do much to demonstrate your suave man-about-town credentials, I'm sure. On the up-side, however, if the engine simply refused to start, she could give you a hand to lift up the front end and *wheel-barrow* the little car home, as the early versions only weighed 129 kg - quite possibly a lot less than the passengers.

No, not an illegal immigrant - just a Minicar owner going through the engine start-up routine. Maybe the dog will be required to blip the throttle when the engine fires, otherwise the driver could be there all day.

Not that the lovely Bond was the only kid on the block when it came to making your gallon go further: the Suez crisis spawned that other peculiarity of the late fifties, the *bubblecar*.

Most of these curious little vehicles originated in Germany, where they were manufactured by the Heinkel, Messerschmitt and BMW companies ... organisations which, not a few years before, had been busy building aeroplanes whose express purpose was to blow out our back wall. So, their introduction as an apparently harmless little runabout caused

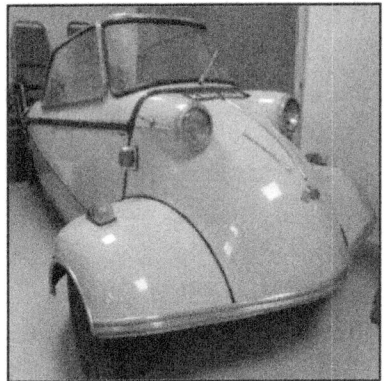

something of a sensation, and became the butt of many a tasteless joke. The Messerschmitt in particular came in for a lot of stick, as its design, with one passenger behind the other and a fold up cockpit canopy, looked just like it had been sliced off the top of an aeroplane. Added to this, in place of the more conventional steering wheel, it had a handlebar, which if inverted, would have been a dead ringer for a joy-stick; it even had the same wheel arrangement as an aeroplane, for heaven's sake! As you can imagine, the jokes about being the *rear gunner,* or the *bomb aimer* were legion. Nevertheless, the little car was very popular, and although the only luggage it could carry had to be balanced on your lap, or strapped to the engine cover behind, it

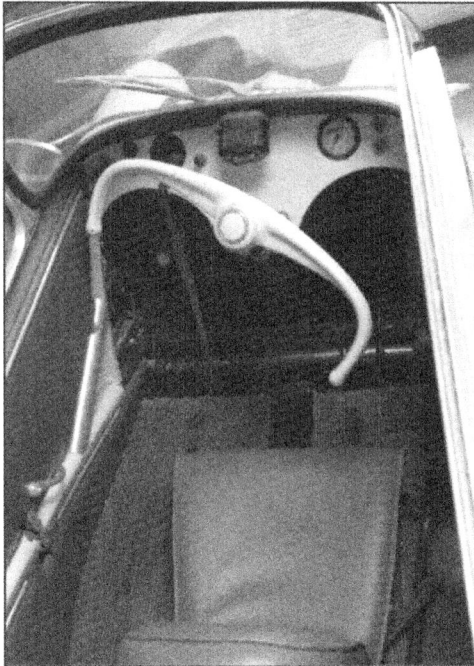

The top of the Messerschmitt hinged along its nearside length. When lifted, it revealed sparse instrument panel and fairly basic seating. Note also the handlebar-like steering wheel, and lack of stowage space.

quickly became quite an icon of the age. Another unusual feature of the Messerschmitt was that to reverse the little car, you had to re-set the ignition by double pressing the switch. This operation meant that the engine would then rotate in the opposite direction, and thus the car would reverse. An unforeseen consequence however, was that it could therefore *go as fast backwards as it did forwards.* A car salesman friend of mine was determined to show off this unique characteristic to gathered customers at a demonstration held in a local park. As with many young men of the time, the ability to reach forty miles an hour *in reverse* rather went to his head. The result was that he over-turned the little car. Whether it was due to the strength of its construction or to pure good luck, I am happy to report that he walked away uninjured, although the perspex hood was smashed beyond repair. Also rather ruffled was my friend's customer - a naval officer who had been sitting in the back seat for the demonstration drive. He too was uninjured, but as my friend ruefully reported... he subsequently refused to buy the car! True story, honest.

Oddly, the tricycle wheel arrangement of the Messerschmitt was not one preferred by the Germans, but was introduced because of a need in Britain to meet the requirements of the Road Tax: if you had a three-wheeler, then the duty you paid was the same as for a motor cycle, and therefore much cheaper. It was fortunate, therefore, that the companies that really put the *bubble* into *bubblecar* - Heinkel and BMW - already had a three wheeler design which came to epitomise the genre. Unlike the little Bond, the single wheel was at the back,

The BMW built Isetta was popular, but getting three adults on the bench seat would be something of a miracle, despite what the advert overleaf suggests. If you parked too close to a garage wall, all three of you might be destined for a 'cosy night in'. Note how the steering wheel and other controls swivel out with the little car's only door.

thus making steering and stability a bit more precise. What really amused us, though, was how you got in and out of the bubble car. Unlike the Messerschmitt, the whole front of these vehicles opened outwards, taking with it the steering wheel and other very essential

One wonders if many of today's proud owners of their very own 'Beamer' would be pleased to be reminded of the prestige make's quirkier and humble post-war model?

odds and ends. It also meant that you had to be careful not to park too closely to anything in front, as you could not open the door. This was particularly important when driving into a garage, as the little cars *had no reversing gear.* Thus, if you were not paying attention, and parked up against the back wall of your garage, only your screams and shouts were likely to lead to a timely release.

Isetta was the name that BMW traded under in the UK, and Trojan was another company which produced these little runabouts. They were very popular, and perhaps because of their bright colours and cheerful demeanour, became almost chic - certainly so, when compared with that other example of 1950's economy motoring style which decorated our streets – the motor bike and sidecar.

Now, if you think squeezing into a tiny bubblecar was tricky, then the motorbike and sidecar combo might help you to realise that you were really quite fortunate. Many sidecars were single seaters, but larger versions seating two adults -as here- were also available. No doubt they were great for economy, but I'll leave it to you to assess how they rated for comfort and luggage space. Although like many budget conscious necessities, this form of transport had lots of

devotees, sitting almost on the ground beside a very noisy and often smelly motor bike engine is not an endeavour that appealed to the faint-hearted, however economical. Given also that visibility through a small plastic window was often extremely limited, and that the only means the passengers had to communicate with the driver was yell or tap his left knee, meant that the whole experience could be deemed somewhat less than romantic. Negotiating corners was also a challenge: turning left was OK because the driver could lean on the sidecar, whereas an over-enthusiastic right turn might lift a small single seater sidecar off the road. Not likely with the two in the illustrations however: a mighty Brough Superior and a BSA Golden Flash, no less. Despite this, such combinations were quite common and many motor-cyclists swore by them. I suspect a good many sidecar passengers did too, though perhaps in not quite the same spirit.

Many years later, such devotion to this form of transport was brought home to me when I was living in digs with several other students. One of our housemates was from a farming background, and he told us that he was going to bring his motorbike up from home the following weekend, so that he could take his new college girlfriend 'out for a 'spin in the country'. When we suggested that sitting on pillion seat for hours on end may not be an ideal way for the young lady to enjoy a first date, he said – '*It'll be fine. I've got a sidecar: she'll love it*'. So when the sidecar arrived we were all a trifle gob-smacked to find that it was little more than a big wooden box with a couple of cushions in the bottom. Its similarity to a lidless coffin was commented upon, with the proviso that a coffin might have been a lot better padded. Undaunted, our farmer friend continued with his courtship – and do you know what? It actually flourished! Not that the lady in question put up with such rudimentary transport for that long, you understand, but the fact that she put up with it at all and actually enjoyed their days out says something doesn't it?.

So as you can see, local domestic traffic in the 1950's was varied and quite interesting, being populated by far fewer – but perhaps more interesting -forms of transport than today. From a child's perspective of course, even its relative scarcity was an inconvenience that had to be tolerated: it only took the approach of just one bubble-car to mess up a grudge football match which had just reached a critical stage, or for some thoughtless motorist to park his Bond Minicar right in front of the garden wall where your cricket stumps had been painstakingly chalked, and you were up the creek.... talk about inconsiderate!

And as regards the wisdom of playing in the street at all, it is odd to reflect that in the fifties, apart from the unpleasantness of dog fouling, the streets were actually a lot cleaner than many are now. There was relatively little litter about for two reasons: first, packaging was minimal - for example, most sweets were sold loose in paper bags, as were many grocery items. Second, plastic was not commonly used for wrapping and storage at this time and thus accumulations of the freely available, cheaply produced and near indestructible litter which nowadays adorn every street, park, and beach of the country had not yet become a grim fact of life. That's not to say that folks of the fifties were more environmentally aware: we weren't, and the term had not even been introduced. It was just that the litter which did accrue was smaller in quantity and nearly always totally bio-degradable. Fish and chips, for example, were ladled into a small, overflowing grease-proof paper bag, and then wrapped in a couple of sheets of newspaper. Even if these wrappings were discarded on the completion of the meal, it did not seem to take that long before a couple of rain showers reduced them to a pulp which then miraculously disappeared down the drain. Polystyrene trays, multilayered wrappings of colourful cellophane and plastic moulded containers were yet to be produced in the massive and readily available quantities the modern consumer requires, and as a result, streets, parks, hedgerows and beaches were relatively litter-free. That disposable '*one use*' plastic wrapping should become such a menacing pollutant never entered our heads... and nor would it for another half century.

Although the decade after the end of the war was one of pretty acute austerity, there is a tendency these days to paint the era as one of general gloom and greyness. Archive footage showing queues of shoppers waiting to get their meagre ration of meat from the butcher tend to make the viewer feel that *all* life was equally dour. But it wasn't. Sure, waiting in a long line of shoppers is hardly a fun-provoking occupation, so looking a bit cheesed off is hardly surprising. But what such footage may obscure is the fact that the majority of folk felt that something better was coming... the world was at peace, rationing wouldn't last for ever, and manufacturers of the better things in life were gearing up for what would soon be called the consumer age.

For children growing up in such an environment the period was one of excitement and innovation. Although not recognised by us littlies, the very fact that the country was at peace had a massive effect upon the population... indeed, the chance that when you ventured forth each morning, there was every likelihood that when you returned in the evening, the back wall of your house would more than likely be exactly where you had left it, and this was a situation not ignored by many.

Even national emergencies such as the Suez crisis provided an opportunity for people of imagination to come up with radical and inventive solutions that were a joy to behold. If you couldn't get excited about the prospect of whizzing your own Bond Minicar round and round in ever decreasing circles, then that was a real shame. Added to that, the opportunity to do some improvements to your own house with the dawning of the DIY age was a revelation for many, and despite the many disasters in terms of over-ambitious *booze at home* projects, it was an age of great experimentation with new materials. Above all, the availability of plastic *everything,* set us in a flat spin of expectant curiosity as to what on earth would our inventive nation come up with next. I mean… come on! The prospect of finding a plastic deep-sea diver in your box of Corn Flakes… need I say more? And wrapping up stuff and sticking all sorts of unsuspecting bits and pieces together with consummate ease proved to be of limitless fascination.

The sellotape revolution was with us, and it was here to stay.

4   A Dog's Dinner

I think everyone would acknowledge that the advent of the global internet, and the accompanying advances in communications technology have had a seismic effect upon the pace and *immediacy* of our modern world. Who would have thought, even ten years ago, that you could have instant visual communication with anyone the other side of the world, using a device about a quarter of the size of a Ladybird book, as well as having with you all the music you could ever want, a library full of books and several top feature films as well? You have only to go into any public place and take a look around you and count the number of people using their mobiles, tablets or i-pads: it is most likely that there will be more who are thus occupied than those who are not. There was a time when we would fight shy of people walking down the road apparently mumbling to themselves; nowadays non–participants almost feel the odd ones out.

There is good reason to conclude that there is not one thing of any import that goes on in today's world that is not instantly made available to the global audience. Our connectivity and the associated information overload is as vast as it is extraordinary, and leaves pre-internet days in the dust. However, I would contend that it is the *second* major life-changing social revolution of recent times.

The first was the introduction of mass television in the 1950's. Prior to that, news coverage was mainly down to the newspapers. As well as the vast number of folk having a national daily delivered each morning, quite a substantial proportion also had an evening paper for more local news. The other source of information was, of course, via the radio. However, broadcasting was far from the 24/7 coverage we have today, and beyond the formal news bulletins – which seldom longer than about ten minutes - the range of programmes was very limited. And don't forget, radio reception was a much more unreliable and tricky business in those days, and for many the 'wireless' could only be listened to with some difficulty since:

a) Sets could be almost the size of a small cupboard and were therefore anything but portable;

b) You often found yourself hanging half way out of the nearest window waving the aerial wire about to get a signal and

c) Broadcasts were accompanied by much static interference whose whistling and farting excesses could be described as *imaginative.*

On a weekly visit to the pictures, there might be a short Pathé Newsreel presentation, but their content was somewhat random, hardly ever topical and frequently of the *'It's good to know that bee-keeping in the outer Hebrides is in the safe hands of good old Jock McKay and his family'* type.

As regards product advertising and information, I can't for the life of me recall much in the way of such material in those early 1950's cinema visits – but a decade later they became a feature in their own right. The memorable (if almost totally alien) adverts for the classy in-crowd knocking back their poolside Martinis and Babycham to the accompanying and memorable signature tune provided by the famous Pearl and Deane agency were particularly popular. Nevertheless, in the fifties, exposure to advertising was limited to magazines or via the huge billboard adverts which adorned many vacant plots, house gable ends, on the side panels of buses. Also of great interest - often because of their quirky nature - were the classified ads in the local and national newspapers. The latter were usually buried in the middle of the publication, and bearing in mind that the majority of newspapers were still in broadsheet format, taming the paper to see the tiny adverts took some doing. That the classified ads themselves lacked the imaginative energy and vivacity of their modern counterparts I'll leave to your judgement (next page). The compilation is of interest too: nice to see that the hernia ad is placed so close to the memorial headstone.

A genuine 'Classified Ads' page from the Daily Express, Saturday 16th March 1957. OK, it's a bit grey and faded, but then so were some of the things for sale.

So, the introduction of TV, spurred on by the Queen's coronation of 1953, had the electrifying effect of bringing an inaccessible and largely unimagined world right into our own homes. OK, there was only one channel to start with (BBC) but the effect it had was enormous. It seems inconceivable these days that people would look forward to being invited to go round to a TV owner's house to watch *Dixon of Dock Green* on a Saturday evening. I can easily remember the spine-tingling anticipation of going to my grandparents' house, thrilled right down to my socks at the prospect of seeing another episode of *The Lone Ranger* complete with his faithful redskin chum Tonto - of *'Kimo-sabby'* fame.

It's really little wonder that were all so taken by the new medium; to be able to view someone walking and talking in some far off land was as incredible as it was mesmerising. To see up to the minute pictures - *in the privacy of your own front room* - of news events which had only just been reported was equally gob-smacking, and the introduction of outside broadcasting brought yet another mind-blowing element to this wonderful new invention. Bear in mind also, that TV was all monochrome, that screens were small (usually 14") and that broadcasts were over only 405 lines. As a result, the picture presented was like looking through a finely slatted venetian blind.

And then came ITV. Have I mentioned advertising before? Oh yes... the Meccano bit and family cars etc. The thing is, the fifties in particular saw an amazing transformation in the way we saw ourselves, and TV advertising played a pivotal – almost *explosive* - part in this revolution. Not only could we see the lives of other people at home and abroad, we were introduced to their lifestyle, and the choices they made. The art of advertising is to make you drool after the product in question, and to have it so warmly presented by those cheerful, glamorous, successful and damn near perfect people on the telly, that it makes the product virtually irresistible. Never mind that you didn't actually *need* a plastic bird bath in a tasteful shade of yellow, the fact that the lovely TV family with the whiter than white smiles, their dear little dog, shiny car and weed-free lawn had one was enough!

I would say that the dawn of television, and commercial television in particular, opened the floodgates for a social change of hitherto undreamt proportions. With the final abolition of wartime rationing in 1954, the spectre of austerity Britain had finally been sealed up again in its gloomy vault. It is hardly surprising therefore, that the reaction to this - fuelled by a heady mixture of post-war optimism, almost full employment creating disposable income and the explosion of attractively portrayed goods advertised at least every fifteen minutes right into our living rooms - was that we were ready and very willing victims of the ad man's persuasive tongue. I suppose you could say that the late fifties saw the birth of the consumerism that would blossom and flourish over the next decade. In the early days we fell for just about any of the ad man's smooth talk with an almost joyful abandon. And it didn't really matter what was for sale... whatever it was, if it was on the telly, and a smiley lady and her cheerful pipe-smoking hubby said their happiness knew no bounds since they had bought their over-the-bath clothes airer, who were we to argue?

Anything and everything was now advertisable, and product promotion was particularly persuasive when it impacted directly on our day to day personal choices. Thus anything you could eat, drink, smoke, give to your adoring, well-mannered and unrealistically clean doggy was of immediate interest... and if the ad backed up its often preposterous claims with *scientific validation*, then it was job done: order a gross now!

I suppose that, having just survived a war, folks of the fifties had an almost reverential regard for the scientific community... after all, hadn't these bespectacled and kindly boffins invented radar, built the jet engine and discovered antibiotics? If they were good enough for that, then their endorsement of *new and enriched Can O'Meat* for your doggy must take the...well, biscuit, mustn't it? Picture the ad:

In a busy crisp white and clinically sparkling laboratory, a serious but kindly scientist wearing a modestly confident smile and a freshly laundered white coat is walking purposefully about clutching a clipboard, upon which he enters data. Every so often he pauses to examine a test tube or two full of coloured stuff, and then nods sagely. His modest but quietly triumphant smile indicates to his many purposefully engaged colleagues that he, the genius, has added yet another successful recipe which will bring untold happiness, everlasting health not to mention a very shiny coat and permanently wet nose to the country's canine population. His obvious joy at such an outcome he shares with other similarly clad scientists who gather round in an oddly hierarchical manner - colleagues of equal white coated starchiness to the fore, more humble but essential juniors behind. The entire staff is united in triumphant acknowledgement that all that work - the endless hours of looking at test tubes, stirring bubbling pots of stuff, measuring anything that could be measured - has been totally worthwhile.

In a decade that was in many ways as stiff and starchy as the scientist's lab coat, one can be forgiven for taking the absurdity of the advert one step further. Picture if you will, the home of the above-mentioned genius. It is nearly 4.30pm, and anticipating the arrival home of her dedicated and hard-working husband, his pretty wife puts on her pearls, touches up her lipstick, checks her stocking seams are straight and fluffs up her perm a little. She pauses only to gather up hubby's pipe and slippers before going to the window to wait expectantly for the hero's return... and sure enough, just at that moment, his green and beige dual-tone Humber Sceptre (complete with walnut fascia and chrome plated ashtray) glides into the drive, narrowly missing the abundantly flowered rose bushes which the gardener has pruned that very morning. She flings open the front door:

She: *Hello Darling! Has it been another trying day for you, my pet lamb?*

He: *Yes, but in all due modesty, not without some success, I might hasten to say.*

She: *I thought I noted a triumphant glimmer in your eye, and a rakish up-turn of your manly moustache... tell me, don't keep me in suspense any longer... will Can 'O Meat's **Bison and Broccoli Yummy Chunks** be yet another success?*

He: *Hold on, old thing.... I've had a hard day of striding purposefully about with a clip board noting down absolutely irrelevant facts and figures. And, don't forget, Daphne, at the same time I had to maintain a thoughtfully engaged yet confident appearance which had to develop into a modest yet becoming smile of triumphant satisfaction. By the way, where's my pipe?*

She: *I've got your favourite shag ready... Oh Darling, I'm so proud of you! I'm sure you set a fine example to all the others – those with smaller clip boards, whose only duty was to provide supportive smiles and a general sense of aching ambition to aspire to your dizzy heights!*

He: *Yes, there's many a junior who would like to swap their place in the bike shed for a Humber Sceptre-sized parking place, but I hope my example has shown them that they have to work their way up, from background 'looks of admiration' routine, through earnest but confident discussion with colleagues, all the way up to attractive, sophisticated but unassuming triumphalism. Are we having fish fingers for tea?*

Get the picture? And the hyperbole wasn't just limited to TV. Suddenly, it was everywhere – and what's more, the term 'jingle' had just been invented. Therefore, you were as likely to meet a friend bursting forth with a rendition of the recent Omo washing powder ad: *'Omo washes, not only clean, not only white but BR I I I I GHT! Omo adds bright, bright brightness!!'* ... as you were a somewhat less enthusiastic rendition of *'Oh Sole Mio'*.

Hindsight, as they say, is a wonderful thing – but if granted its undoubted benefits in relation to career choice in those post-war days, I think I might have opted for *package printing*. To be more specific, food packaging in general - and sweet packaging in particular. To explain:

You have only to take a cursory look at any modern food packaging (and I'm sure that's all we ever do) to note that it is eye-catchingly colourful, artistically creative, frequently humorous, often endorsed by the famous, and full of clearly printed written information including ingredients, calorific values, chemical composition, point of origin, sell-by dates, consume-by dates, allergy information to prevent you killing yourself, and even where to complain if the contents are not perfect. Not only that, the even smaller print has the same information in a variety of European languages, as well as some unrecognisable stuff important to the people of Russia and Japan.* No doubt, as we rip off the several layers of hygienic wrappings, pausing only to look for a knitting needle or *anything sharp* - after giving up trying to tear open the last layer with your teeth - we give little thought to the poor sod who has spent months and months of research into market trends, current fashions in presentation, commercial demographics and all the myriad complexities of local and European legislation to produce the finished article. And the person who's laughing? Why - the packaging producer, of course.

* *I am convinced that by comparing such translations with the original English, it is quite possible to learn both Russian and Japanese by studying food wrappers alone. Mind you, you might be limited to just buying 'Whizzo Chocolate Knobs' in Vladivostok or Tokyo, but it's a start isn't it?*

A comparison with sweet packaging in the 1950's could hardly be more stark. Most sweets were available in large glass bottles with big screw-top metal lids, and were dished out by the sweet shop lady onto some scales, and then put in a paper bag which she deftly twirled to give the pretence of sealing in the contents. When I say 'dished out', it is more probable that they were *hacked* out, as most were sticky, and having been jar-bound for some time, had often managed to congeal into an amorphous lump. So, when you went to your local sweetshop with a threepenny bit clasped firmly in your sweaty palm and asked for 'a quarter of Pineapple Chunks', there might follow a few moments of fairly aggressive hacking with a long metal spoony-shovel thing before several lumps of the requested item was popped into your bag. If you were lucky, you might just be able to prize apart some recognisable pieces, and still be left with a few shattered remains to grudgingly share with your sister.

And that's not all. Some sweets were really quite... well, *feisty*. Take, for example the mystifyingly popular *Pear Drops*. These too were boiled sweets whose characteristics were as follows:

1. They were shaped like a pear;
2. They came in two different colours;
3. As you sucked them, you became more than vaguely aware of a heady smell rather like the dope sprayed on model aeroplane wings;
4. The skin on the roof of your mouth had all but disappeared owing to the fact that the sugar coating with which the pear drop was liberally dusted had more in common with the abrasive qualities of a particularly aggressive rasp file than with white granulated stuff to which we had become accustomed.

Some sweets were wrapped, of course, but they tended to be dearer. Smarties came in a cardboard tube from which you could winkle out the first few with your finger – before tiring of the whole process and simply up-ending the tube into your mouth. Girls seemed to like the red ones in particular, as they could lick the coating and then smear the result on their lips to mimic lipstick. We boys had better things to do with our time.

Take, for example the popular Bounty Bar, which came in its own brightly coloured wrapper. Tearing this away revealed two smallish chocolate covered 'sausages' of the confection, sitting in their own little cardboard tray. Now, bearing in mind my childhood was spent in a naval town where naval traditions, folklore and slang were part and parcel of everyday life, the comparison and similarities of the unwrapped Bounty bar with the Devilled Kidneys provided by the navy – and called *"Shit on a Raft"* by sailors - was unnerving to say the least. However, putting that unwholesome thought aside, the coconut bars were delicious, and provided the intrepid consumer with a fair bit of post-nosh fun in the shape of trying to extract errant pieces of coconut from between his teeth. Better still, you could crease the cardboard tray down its centre line, pinch the ends together and with the merest application of sellotape, make yourself a very serviceable model canoe.

Perhaps the most bizarre sweets of all, however, were really anti-social. I well remember a 1956/7 episode from the hugely popular radio programme the *'Goon Show'*, where Eccles (the idiot) was talking to Bluebottle (the... er... bluebottle) about what they were getting for Christmas:

Eccles: *Hey Bluebottle – guess what I'm getting for Christmas!*

Bluebottle: *I don't know – what are you getting for Christmas?*

Eccles: *I'm getting a bow-wow.*

Bluebottle: *Cor. I'm not getting a bow-wow, I'm getting a Junior Smokers' Kit complete with toffee ashtray and liquorice dog-ends!*

(Laughter)

And he was right! Though I never came across liquorice dog-ends, Junior Smokers' Kits were very popular and comprised:

Sweet cigarettes in their own cardboard packet – complete with red tip to represent burning;

Liquorice pipes with red hundreds and thousands, again to represent a successful conflagration;

Sweet matches with which to simulate the initiation of smoking pleasure;

Sweet tobacco made from brown shredded coconut;

Chocolate cigars wrapped in silver paper with distinctive cigar band, and finally…

Chocolate or toffee ashtray included in the more up-market kits.

Not only that, the more sophisticated child was also able to buy loose lemonade crystals which were eaten by wetting your finger, sticking it in the paper bag and licking off the resulting bright yellow harvest. In this way you could stain your fingers yellow to perfectly mimic the nicotine stains of heavy smokers!

One is led to speculate that if the encouragement of such dangerous habits through the medium of children's sweets were allowed today, we might well have *'Junior Druggies Kits'* with edible syringes, liquorice tourniquets and sherbet powder aplenty to snort to your heart's content. Strewth.

The first rumble of the packaging avalanche probably came from those popular dimpled square boiled sweets called *Spangles*, which in the late fifties claimed to be the first confection:

"Double wrapped to keep all the flavour in, and all the dirt out!"

I can't really see modern advertisers implying that your home is full of dirt, but then these were early days of mass marketing, and clever sophistication was as yet untried. In fact, even a brief foray in the world of consumerism in the fifties shows that one of the main advertising techniques was to simply stick an O on the end of any product you wanted to shift - so we got *Toffo, Rinso, Draino, Brasso Brillo, Minto, Omo, Bisto, Paxo…* and so on.

Added to that, actually *seeing* people on your very own telly thoroughly enjoying the product in question was a new experience in the fifties. That the nice lady with the low-cut blouse and sparkly necklace could clean her whole kitchen floor with just one gentle application of her combined *'Sponge-o-Tex Supermop and Carpet Cleaning Applicator'* without breaking into a sweat or treading on the cat was enough to convince us that it was our absolute duty to go out and buy one right now.

There is little doubt that we were putty in the hands of the advertising folk – but to be honest, we enjoyed it. The ads themselves were a new form of entertainment, and gave you a moment's respite from having to worry about what was happening in some far flung corner of the still pretty much existent British Empire. Also, of course, there was the need to take a breather between the exhaustingly exciting progress of the latest contestant on *'Double Your Money'*.

So, yes – the advent of TV was a social revolution of immense influence. It brought the seemingly unattainable and distant right into your living room. The technology was primitive by today's standards, but the impact was virtually immeasurable. Our little black and white window on the world not only gave us all sorts of insights previously unachievable, but they were instant, they were accessible, they were presented by nice looking people in nice looking clothes. What's more, it enabled people to feel *involved.* Whatever your personal circumstances, you were a *participant* in the modern world as never before. Blimey. Fetch me a pear drop, someone!

So if the growing expectation and fevered anticipation of the fifties was like a bottle of pop which was being shaken violently, what – apart from lack of money - was holding the pressure in? Whilst the wartime habit of self denial was still surprisingly strong, in the light of the new advertising to which we were all exposed, its grip was clearly slackening. But behind that, there was still a very strong measure of self-restraint which might loosely be termed *'the establishment'*.

We are told, are we not, that one of the most attributable characteristics of the British is that we are as a nation very *reserved*. Whilst more exuberant nationals might be delighting in such excesses as Mardi-Gras, or shaking their stuff with consummate vigour at the Copacabana, we Brits are inclined to settle for a nice cup of tea and a chocolate digestive aren't we? There is little doubt that our tendency towards being reserved hails from the Victorian era, when at the same time as massive economic, political, military and global expansion, rigid rules regarding people and their place in the social, political and work-based hierarchy were wrought to be as hard and inflexible as the ironwork which quite literally underpinned such development. What is more, the country had failed to be torn asunder by the sort of political shenanigans seen in France, and our social strata remained firmly in support of the status-quo. *'Twas ever thus: we are British... we don't get over-excited, and be wary of the use of too many exclamation marks my dear fellow!'* Even the birth of the BBC which opened up a new world to its original listeners in 1921 was firmly controlled by the formidable Lord Reith, whose strict moral code permeated the organisation right through until the days of television. From the very beginning, BBC announcers were required to wear formal evening dress when they went on air ... and bearing in mind this was the *radio* for heaven's sake, you begin to get the picture.

It's something of a juxtaposition therefore, that the surge in TV sales caused by the coronation in 1953 – itself a re-affirmation of the nations desire to celebrate all that tradition demands – was an element in liberating folk from what some might see as the repressive grip of traditional values. But did we give much thought to this contradiction on June 2nd that year? Did we hell! All we wanted to see was the royals and the aristos dressed up to the nines. The coronation had a massive effect on our collective consciousness, and drew us even closer together – crikey! We had a new Queen, TV and sellotape ... what more could any nation want?

Well, perhaps a little easing of the *big brother knows best* mentality would have been helpful. People in positions of power and influence were still very much held in high regard, whether they deserved it or not. There was still also a lot of deference to the status determined by class, and this was rubbed in just about every time you did something as ordinary as getting on a train. Right up until 1956 tickets were sold First or Third class, and woe-betide anyone who tried to sneak into a compartment of higher class than that which had been purchased. Even on the BBC, if there was a *Lady this*, or a *Lord that* involved, there was an immediate obsequiousness in the tone adopted by the announcer - and this in addition to the viewers' anticipation that the words offered by our elders and betters would be of significantly more value. There was even aristocracy in children's comics for heaven's sake – remember *Lord Snooty* of the *Beano*? This popular character first appeared in 1938, and lasted for decades after that. More formally known as *Lord Marmaduke of Bunkerton,* his antics and that of his many pals from more humble backgrounds amused and entertained youngsters throughout the fifties and beyond.

Perhaps to give some social balance, Lord Snooty and his pals were all members of the 'Ash Can Alley Gang'.

Although that was about as close as any ordinary kids got to the aristocracy, I think it would be true to say that society in the fifties was certainly more class conscious. For example, there was a lot made of the type of work you did – whether your dad was manual or professional, blue collar or white collar. In society at large, the term 'officers and gentlemen' was used surprisingly frequently, and not always with tongue in cheek. The sporting world was also a place where class showed, and we were schooled in the philosophy of:

'*It is the taking part that matters – not the winning of the game!*'

Oh yeah? All very stiff upper lip and proper I'm sure, but as the decade progressed there was a growing feeling that *'play up, play up and play the game'* might be all right for you mate, but for us kids beating the school down the road into a whimpering defeat in the cup semi-finals was starting to be just a little more alluring.

Nevertheless, the social hierarchy was there, and if you want proof, you have only to look up the curious upper class custom of 'coming out'. This was specifically reserved for debutantes, the young society ladies of considerable wealth and position who right up until 1958, were presented at court. This was seen as their formal entry into society, and a proclamation that they were now eligible for the attentions of any available young earl, lord or viscount who happened to be ambling by, perhaps on the way to his gentleman's club.

Believe it or not, the coming out ceremony was still quite eagerly followed in the popular press where the society pages still held many enthralled. It must be noted however, that the 1950's term 'coming out' should in no way to be confused with its contemporary counterpart, and perhaps just as well.

Regardless of the fact that the bizarre behaviour of the upper classes was remote for the majority, such emphasis did have a way of percolating right down through the strata of society – even, it might be said, as far as the basement. Whereas the days of large houses with live-in servants had almost completely disappeared after the war, many home owners would employ home helps or char-ladies to do some of the manual work about the property, whether or not the lady of the house was working. The fact that such a home help was often known as '*a lady what does*' probably hails from the wartime radio show favourite *ITMA* (It's That Man Again) when the lady in question always announced her eagerly anticipated entry accompanied by the crashing of a metal bucket and the phrase *'Can I do you now sir?'* And so it was that even the humblest occupation took its place of the bottom rung of the social ladder.

During the early fifties in particular, the lingering and pervasive influence of the Victorian era meant that there was hardly any reference at all to sex in the majority of newspapers. The only place where you were likely to encounter smuttiness of any sort was on the raunchy postcards sent from the seaside. Believe me – we little BB's did a lot of research and spent as much time as possible sniggering at the big bums and boobs on such products, even if we didn't understand the captions. But of page three type models in the press, there was not even the glimmer of a glimmer of hope, so the urges which afflicted us had to remain constrained and under control. Cold shower anyone?

And the other way in which society kept its young in check was by the imposition of the need to be mannerly. We were frequently told that *'manners maketh man'* as if the introduction of pseudo-biblical speech would make your adherence all the more likely. Gentlemanly conduct – *playing the straight bat* – went hand in hand with impeccable manners. Yeah, right. And yet it did. My mum, like thousands of others, was very keen to stress the importance of good manners in her feckless offspring. *'Good for her!'* I hear you say. Well, yes, in as far as not gobbing on the carpet or picking your nose in church were concerned, I agree. But really… raising your cap? Being required to always walk on the gutter side of the pavement when out walking with a lady? Let me explain the near inexplicable.

You may have noted in scenes from a variety of period dramas, the custom of your toff about town to smartly lift his top hat when approaching a lady of his acquaintance. Quite why this was deemed the height of courtesy I know not, but nevertheless, my mum and her cohort considered that what was right for Beau Brummell was also just the ticket for her scruffy git of a son. In those days, little boys frequently wore caps, either as an essential part of school uniform, or just as ordinary day to day wear for keeping warm. I was no different. The downside of such sartorial elegance however, was that my mum demanded that on meeting another adult in the street, I was to raise the said cap and bid the on-coming lady a formal greeting of the *'Good afternoon'* variety. Quite apart from the exquisite embarrassment any ordinary street kid would suffer in such circumstances, one has to ask oneself the question WHY? Why does showing a perfect stranger the top of your head make you a better person? Is it, for example, so that the approaching female can ascertain that your parting is straight? That the Brilliantine you so carefully applied still retains its lustrous luminosity? That at very least, you are relatively dandruff free? Beats me. It also beat my mum when for the nth time I would ask why I had to do such a bizarre thing, and received a less than satisfactory response along the lines of *'because that's what polite people do … and stop scratching that rash!'*

At least the other bit of street etiquette which was pummelled into us had a reason. This involved always walking on the outside of a lady when taking a stroll along the pavement. This meant that all blokes had to ensure that they were closest to the carriageway in general, and the gutter in particular. Now I didn't mind this too much, for if there was anything likely to be of interest – like the odd forgotten marble or discarded fag card, the gutter was the most likely place for it to end up. And the reason for this gutter-hugging etiquette? Evidently such a custom dates back to the time of horse-drawn transport, days when road surfaces were unmetalled and full of potholes into which large amounts of dirty rainwater (and presumably, horse dung) would collect. In such circumstances, passing carriages would frequently throw up great showers of watery sewage, and it was the gentleman's task to prevent his lady companion from arriving at her destination covered from head to toe in watery effluent. So, we chaps were required to act as a *human shield*. Oh good. Well, I suppose there was just a teeny-weeny bit of logic to all this, in that it might seem rather more gallant for the bloke to protect his missus from such inundation… but as I pointed out to my mum on many occasions, there weren't that many slurry filled potholes in the local streets, and her raincoat was a lot more weatherproof than mine. Also, had she taken on board the very real prospect that, at the very moment of protecting her from a veritable *street tsunami,* I might also be raising my cap to an approaching lady – with the inevitable disastrous consequences? Didn't make any difference: *rules was rules.*

It could well be that you consider all this street-side etiquette a bit bonkers, but of course, the imposition of manners didn't end there: indoors offered a whole lot more of life's essential rules and regulations.

Whilst I am all for mealtimes being pleasant and socially as well as physically restorative occasions, I think that the imperative of good table manners hit an all-time peak in the 1950's. This was because it was arguably the last decade during which the family nearly always sat down to all their meals together. There were no TV dinners, almost no instant meals, and apart from the chippy, no take-aways. Pizza delivery? What's a pizza? Never heard of it! Bunging an instant meal into the microwave for a half minute blast of the finest radiation, or drooling over the prospect of an instant Cuppa Soup were still things of science fiction. TV programmes such as the BBC's excellent *'Back in Time for Tea'* series remind us that although diets were restricted and their preparation laborious, meals of the fifties were very much more of a social occasion. All well and good. The only thing is that eating all together makes your typical git-at-the-table the subject of fairly intense adult scrutiny, offering seemingly endless opportunity for the consequent correction.

Picture the scene: you have just come in from a longish walk spent leaping about from side to side of the pavement in order to keep the mater free from puddle splashes. Furthermore, you have heroically sustained what in more enlightened times would be called *'repetitive strain injury'* through continually having to raise your cap on meeting the entire company of the local Towns Women's Guild. Thus it is that you flop down exhausted onto your very own utility* chair and draw it up to the utility table in eager anticipation of minced beef and mashed potatoes followed by bananas and custard. Lovely... except that the meal is bound to be punctuated by adult disapproval of your slovenly and unmannerly behaviour, of the order:

1. Take your shoes off, put your slippers on!
2. Wash your hands!
3. Call that a wash? Do it again!
4. Don't drag the chair across the lino, you know it leaves a black mark!
5. Sit up straight!
6. Get your elbows off the table!
7. Don't talk with your mouth full!
8. Don't drink with your mouth full!
9. Elbows!!
10. Don't play with your food!
11. No, you can't get down – wait till the rest of us have finished!
12. ELBOWS!!!

* *Utility furniture was produced after the war as an economy measure to enable people to replace the thousands upon thousands of items destroyed by enemy action. With designs strongly influenced by the Arts and Crafts movement and made of solid wood, the items produced were surprisingly stylish, and very durable. Our dining table and chairs were still going strong when I inherited them in 1975.*

13. Don't stick your tongue out at your sister!

14. Stop grizzling!

Well of course, at least some of these table manners are still required today – but in my opinion, are not as stringently applied as in the past.

So we were regimented, and if you consider my mum's reaction as being a bit OTT, let me assure you it was not. There's many a kid who would have to have spent the rest of the evening banished to his or her bedroom after receiving a thick ear from either parent. We knew our place, and more often than not kept it.

But don't interpret such apparent controlling severity as the description of an unloving or unaffectionate home. The family jollity captured by the *'Back in Time'* TV show mentioned above was pretty accurate. There was a great deal more social interaction, especially around the meal table, and families in the fifties played together a lot more as well. To be honest, unless you made your own entertainment, there was not much else until the growing number of TV sets began to have an effect on social interaction in the closing years of the decade.

What was very different, however, was the way we expressed our affection for each other – especially in terms of physical contact. I can honestly say that the only time I ever saw my dad shake hands with anyone was on meeting another adult *for the first time.* Thereafter, such physical contact was never repeated: it was as if it was a matter of:

'Well, we've been introduced, done the touching bit and the 'How Do You Do?' so that's that. Thank God the physical bit's all over'.

Prolonging this form of greeting to subsequent occasions might have been seen by more than a few as distinctly *foreign* – and most blokes at the time were caustic in their comments about the French habit of kissing one another on both cheeks. I think most of the men I knew would rather have cut their own heads off rather than plant a smacker on Uncle Stan's cheeks. I suppose very close friends might just have been the recipient of an encouraging slap on the back, but as regards MAN HUGS…just forget it! Similarly, men were not under any circumstances allowed to cry, and were expected instead to compose themselves so as to present as the very epitome of manly determination and undoubted pluck. And for dads and their sons? Well, it was much the same really. Whilst you might have received a smacker or two from your proud father when you were still a babe in arms, it certainly didn't carry on into the boyhood years. Holding hands with your dad was OK when out for a walk when you were four or five – but after that?

For women, it was a little different. The planting of a light kiss on the cheek of a close friend was acceptable, and the shedding of a tear or two to be delicately wiped away with a scented hanky was seen as a mark of how the sophisticated lady could manage her emotions.

But don't misinterpret this apparent reserve as indicative of a lack of family love and mutual affection. It really wasn't… it's just that most of our parents were in their turn born and brought up by a generation whose roots were firmly planted in the Victorian era. Enough said.

Kids, of course, were a lot less inhibited, and like all juveniles were apt to let their emotions show regardless of who might be nearby. Nevertheless, letting the family down was a pretty big issue: if you could restrain the scream of rage you wanted to expel when cousin Steve spilt his tapioca pudding all over your new copy of the Beano until you got within the privacy of your own four walls then so much the better. Also, with little boys especially, being able to silently take physical punishment meted out by the likes of teachers, coppers and park keepers was a mark of growing manliness – even if you did spend a lot of subsequent time when you got home hopping about your bedroom going *'Ooch! Ouch! Bugger!!'* .

So were the Baby Boomers of the fifties restrained and repressed?

Well, viewed against current thinking and behaviour, I think the answer is pretty much an unequivocal 'Yes'. The only thing was, we were too naïve to recognise it at the time – and as everyone else was much the same, we really didn't notice, or care... and by and large, we were very happy with our lot.

But one thing I think even the most gormless of the young in the fifties did recognise, was that *something big was brewing*. The world was opening up. Nearing the end of the decade, there appeared to be more money around; teenagers had been invented, and they spent more and more of their hard-earned on bright new clothes specifically designed for them. Optimism was at an all time high and with the coming of Rock 'n' Roll, the fuse to the powder keg of the sixties had been lit.

All we had to do now was to stand back and wait for the show to begin.

5   "Ode Tetnyaah!"

Like many an old bloke with too much time on his hands, I'm an interested observer of films and TV programmes depicting the post-war years, and all too frequently find myself turning to my wife and saying – *"they've got that wrong! Flashing direction indicators on cars didn't come in until 1955, you know… and just look at that Spitfire! The four bladed propellers were only introduced on the Mark IX's in 1942, not during the Battle of Britain! Huh!"* Her response may well be compared with that of Grommet, when Wallace has made a particularly inane comment, and he just rolls his eyes, ruffles and raises the pages of his newspaper with a barely audible *"harrumph"*, and settles more deeply into his armchair.

Nevertheless, there is one mistake that is frequently made, and this concerns the relative age of products featured. A perfect example is the motor car. Often, you can almost sense the satisfaction of the props department in securing authentic vehicles from the 1950's to deploy around their carefully composed sets, frequently appearing a good deal more than once in long shot in different settings – depending presumably, on the film's budget. The trouble is, the vast majority of cars on the road in the 1950's were not from that decade at all – they were nearly all pre-war, with many dating back to the twenties, and were nearly always a homogenous black, liberally interspersed with patches of rust. I can still picture my own childhood street... what few cars there were comprised one very rusty baby Standard 8 which frequently back-fired, scaring the life out of me, our own 1939 Morris Eight and next door's pre-war 1.5 Riley, which had a curiously husky sounding engine... always sounding as if it wanted to clear its throat. Of modern cars, there was not a whiff – except when the doctor came to call as he had a new Ford Consul, complete with front bench seat and column gear change. What's more, it was painted uninterrupted *green,* with chrome bits that actually shone, and didn't look like they had a nasty dose of measles as was so often the case with the decrepit pre-war rust buckets that constituted most car ownership. So when you see a film depicting shiny new Austin A30's, Morris Minor Travellers in pristine condition, let alone the odd - and rust free Vauxhall Victor (pretty rare even then) - you are not looking at a typical 1950's street scene. There were no MOT tests, and so the number of cars with bits hanging off the bottom and scraping along the road, bumpers tied on with string, exhausts that emitted billowing clouds of blue smoke, misaligned wing-mounted headlights that made the vehicle look a bit like silent movie star Ben Turpin– outrageously cross-eyed - were quite common. Nearly all cars had starting handles dangling from the front bumper, no brake lights, and semaphore turning signals which, in the case of my Dad's car, needed a thump on the inside of the door pillar to get them to work. It is perhaps in recognition of the fact that these seldom worked properly (even with the applied thump, ours came up in a manner one might describe as 'languid' – somewhat akin to a sleepy teenager being aroused from bed – and more often than not, refused to illuminate itself) that all drivers had still to use **hand signals!!**

Unlike most, this semaphore arm is clean and illuminated. Note that if the signal arm itself missed a passing cyclist, the unbelievably non flush-fitting door hinge might well do the job.

These days, it is quite amazing to think that in the fifties and sixties, sticking your arm out of the driver's window and generally waving it about a bit was considered quite adequate to indicate your intentions to other road users. In fact, doing it properly was very much part of the Driving Test. Now, if taking one hand off the wheel, winding down the window and flapping your hand about in the breeze seems a trifle bizarre – let alone unsafe - picture the situation should you at the same time need to: change gear/ switch on the windscreen wipers/ search desperately for the burning cigarette your pursed lips have failed to retain and which has just bounced gracefully down the front of your paisley pattern jumper, and is likely to have ended up, still burning, uncomfortably close to your goolies. And perhaps all three at the same time. But all of this mayhem is as nothing compared to the weirdness of the hand signals themselves:

I intend to turn right: pretty obvious really. Arm straight out, palm at ninety degrees, fingers extended. Great also for punching an unwary cyclist in the face, or getting your arm ripped off by a lorry coming in the opposite direction that's got too close to the crown of the road.

I intend to turn left: now the problem with this is **a)** your left arm is not long enough to stretch out of the passenger door window, let alone wind it down **b)** if you tried it you might at best wipe the nose of your front seat passenger, or quite possibly be charged with assault and **c)** pointing over the top of the car with your right hand was probably a non-starter. The prescribed signal was therefore to imitate the direction of rotation your off-side front wheel would shortly be taking: thus your extended right arm would rotate in a comely anti-clockwise fashion, such that its forward most extremity was closer to the side of the car than its rearmost. Get the idea? No? Neither did most motorists.... and bearing in mind that you only had your left hand available with which to steer the car, change gear, light up a fresh cigarette to replace the one which has now burned a small but impressive hole in the front seat between your legs, it is hardly surprising that this rather complex manoeuvre deteriorated into a somewhat hurried and frantic flapping.... all too easily confused with...

I intend to slow down: On the face of it, this seems much easier. This time, you stuck your hand out of the window, palm downwards, and raised and lowered your forearm in the manner of a swan's wing on takeoff. Now that's OK, but it does depend a bit in how quickly you need to slow down. Bearing in mind cars at that time were not fitted with power brakes, the rather unhurried oscillation of your arm as required by the Highway Code did nothing to impart the sense of urgency required when slamming on the brakes in order to miss a marble playing urchin seeking to retrieve his acclaimed 'Super Sixer' which after a particularly vigorous exchange with an opponent's ball bearing, has leapt into the middle of the road. Suffice it to say that the slowing down signal often deteriorated into giving the appearance of a genuine desire to take off, or was frequently a case of 'too little, too late'.

Lesser known hand signals included those to be shown to a police officer on point duty, who would be standing at a cross roads right in front of you. To prevent him having to approach your car and ask you personally about your turning intentions - *("Good evening sir. May I ask you where you intend to go next? May I recommend a sharp left to take you to the seafront promenade, or perhaps you might like to go straight on to the High Street where Woolworths have an excellent End-of Summer Sale of plastic spoons?")* - you indicated your intentions through the windscreen using the position of your hands - the palm of your left for going straight on or turning right, with your right completing the range by offering a left turn. If you couldn't make up your mind, you could end up with no hands on the steering wheel at all, and providing the puzzled policeman with a display not unlike that of a tick-tack man at the 4.30 at Cheltenham race course. Needless to say, if drivers gave any sign at all, it was to point – and the vast majority just went where the rozzer told you to go, regardless of your need to get home in time to listen to *'Educating Archie'* on the Light Programme.

Bearing in mind the vagaries of the hand signalling system, and the fact that they couldn't be seen at all after dark, it is not surprising that so many cars were in such a deplorable state. On the other hand, there were far fewer cars on the road; even subtracting the number that at any one time must have been in garages having their rear ends bent back into shape, car ownership even in the mid fifties, was still far from common. My grandad had a relatively dent-free pre-war Morris Ten, which to a little boy was quite luxurious, with its shiny brown leather seats and comforting aroma of polish and Erinmore pipe tobacco which he habitually smoked, whether on the move or not. Mind you, he did have other difficulties to put up with – the most notable being his wife.

My nan was a real product of her Victorian up-bringing, and had no interest in, or understanding of, things technical. On one particularly spectacular occasion, we were bowling along at a fair clip in the trusty Morris Ten. Nan was, as always, sitting beside grandad dressed fully for the great outdoors, with coat, scarf and hat, and her handbag clutched tightly to her bosom. The road was a little bumpy, and unknown to the rest of us, she had been getting increasingly irritated by the jangling of a set of keys dangling from the dashboard. As with all cars of that period, one of these keys was required to be inserted into the central ignition switch which was located on the dashboard between driver and passenger. Well, it was all too much for nan. With an abrupt *"Daddy, that's enough of that!"* she grabbed the offending bunch, pulled out the ignition key and promptly deposited the set in her handbag which she then closed with a satisfying snap. The effect on the car, and on grandad was interesting: the former let out a sort of surprised *whoop* before spluttering and juddering to a complete and jerk-ridden stop whilst the latter was stamping on the brake and grappling with the wheel in an attempt to control the induced skid with which the car, in what can only be described as a fit of sulking, had awarded itself. When we finally came to a breathless halt, nan turned to grandad and said *"What on earth do you think you are doing?!"* Perhaps she was referring to the fact that grandad, in all the excitement, had failed to wind down his window, and give traffic behind a clear hand signal to indicate:

"I am slowing down, as my barmy wife has just removed the source of any further perambulation by kidnapping the ignition keys, and is currently holding them under confinement in the depths of her handbag."

So, even from the unlikeliest of sources, travelling by car in the fifties was not without its hazards.

However, getting around was becoming increasingly important, in particular as work places were tending to move out to the newly created industrial estates often located at or beyond the edge of town. A public bus service was therefore absolutely essential, and consequently very highly utilised. Most cities had their own Corporation Transport Department with its own distinctive bus livery. Portsmouth Corporation buses even had the city's coat of arms emblazoned on the side of their double deckers, and kept well away from the adverts for *Horlicks* and *Craven A* fags which adorned the upper portions between the top and bottom decks. One gets a sense that Corporation buses were to some extent a reflection of civic pride – an extension perhaps to the Lord Mayor's opulent regalia, the grandeur of the Guildhall and the number of public loos. Also, the size and modernity of the fleet was a factor, and the good citizens of Pompey (about twelve of us) took some pride from the fact that we, like London, were blessed with trolley buses.

For those unfamiliar with this rather trendy form of transport, our trolley buses were of the double-decked variety, and were almost completely silent as they were powered by electric motors. *'But how'*, I hear you ask, *'did they get their electricity?'* Well, on the roof of each bus were mounted two long poles which stretched up to power lines suspended above the road. This gave each bus the appearance of sporting two enormous antennae, which when clipped on to the aforementioned wires, often gave off brave and entertaining showers of sparks, much to the delight of we tiny chaps. But wires do not suspend themselves, so along every trolley bus route, large street-light sized poles were erected, each having its own gantry

Bound for the Dockyard, a very smart No. 6 trolley bus. Note the network of overhead cables which provided the power. The connecting poles are very foreshortened in this view.

extending out over the carriageway to support the cabling. Complicated? Well, yes – especially where routes divided, thus necessitating the installation of overhead points. Believe it or not, when a trolleybus neared such an intersection, the conductor would have to jump off, run to the post nearest the junction, reach up on tippy-toes and pull down a handle – not unlike an old-fashioned loo – and await a satisfying *kerchunk* as the points overhead changed. He would then dash back to the bus and with an athletic leap, throw himself on board, to the general admiration of the passengers – and even a light smattering of applause if the bus had continued to move throughout this entertaining interlude. Occasionally, of course, things did not always go as planned, and the result of **a)** the conductor not pulling hard enough on the handle or **b)** forgetting entirely to perform his duty, the bus would go one way, and its poles would go the other. The result was the detachment of the poles from the wires, leaving them asymmetrically arranged about the roof of the bus giving it a rather bedraggled 'insect in the rain' look. Such an event would then require the hapless conductor to pull out a very long pole, stored beneath the bus for just such an eventuality, and attempt to catch the end of each antenna prior to pushing them back up to clip on to the wires above. Now, if you bear in mind that the bus itself was a double-decker and the connecting antenna were at least twelve feet long, (another picture later this chapter gives a much better impression of their true length) then you can imagine the difficulty of this task. Suffice it to say that the perambulations of a bus conductor undertaking this strenuous activity were not unlike those of a demented pole-vaulter/ caber tosser whose pole has gone completely out of control. Needless to say, we all enjoyed it enormously. Despite these occasional dramas and the heavy street architecture required to provide their power source, the trolley buses were very popular: they were quiet, surprisingly quick, and very environmentally clean.

The same, I regret to say, cannot very often be said of the interiors of the buses – trolley or petrol - which were *never* quiet, and all too frequently very far from clean, a state that was due entirely to the heavy use and less than hygienic habits of passengers. Take for example, the top deck. In those days, smoking was tantamount to a national pastime, and non-smokers were a relative rarity. Thus, bus companies made provision for their travelling smokers, but confined them to the top deck. As a consequence, this level was frequently littered with dog ends, empty fag packets and discarded matches, which mixed merrily with sweet papers, and bits of chewing gum which recent users had thoughtfully squeezed into any available nook or cranny. It seems, too, that the bus company had fairly low expectations of passenger behaviour, as, printed in bold lettering above the front windows was the quite extraordinary warning:

'NO SPITTING'.

I kid you not. I suppose the origins of such an instruction might just possibly have dated back to the time when chewing tobacco was common, and part of this ghastly habit was to spit out the residue into a spittoon. Well, I doubt even the most thoughtful bus company would probably have stopped short at providing such receptacles on the upper decks of their fleet – hence the sign. Of course, the only real effect such a sign had was to *introduce* idea of spitting to the hoards of little boys who daily clambered up to the upper deck, and took a good deal of perverse delight in perfecting their 'chewing gum projectile' routine. I can well remember the many times I travelled on an early evening trolley bus service. It usually seemed to be raining, and so the fug of cigarette smoke and warm but damp gabardine was almost a physical presence that pervaded every inch of the dimly lit upper deck, where condensation covered the yellowing ceiling. I would wait wide eyed in anticipation of some grown-up having a good spit. Never happened.

So, travel by bus was both entertaining and informative – and that's even without the added value of the included floor show. I

A topless half- cab Leyland Titan on the popular Seafront Service. Note the large starting handle.

speak, of course, of that uniformed and badge-covered delight, *the bus conductor.* Buses at that time always had a crew of two. The driver sat in splendid isolation in his cab. On a motor bus, this was a half cab alongside a very noisy engine, but in a trolley bus, the driver had the luxury of a full width cab all to himself. One assumes that such apparent largesse was provided so that in the near silence of the vehicle he could **a)** drive in peace, and **b)** listen out for people spitting upstairs.

The conductor, on the other hand, did everything else and had to be surprisingly athletic. His main activity, of course, was to collect fares and call out the location of various stops, but there was a lot more, and the amount of physical fitness required, and the degree of athleticism displayed was a source of public admiration that added to the glamour. We have already noted the relatively rare but entertaining *pole reconnection routine*, but there were others. For example, the necessarily frequent use of the twisty metal staircase which went from the boarding platform to the upper deck, was a location where a descending conductor really on his mettle could launch himself down the last few steps by swinging through a complete half turn using the vertical pole positioned there to assist passengers. Expertly performed, he could land perfectly - with a dramatic jingle of loose coinage from his money pouch - right into the little cubbyhole under the stairs which was his sole preserve, and the location of a locker storing such exotic items as new ticket rolls and last year's timetables. Done to perfection, I am sure I wasn't the only passenger to think of bursting into applause, with the words *"...and...dismount!"* running through my mind as well as perhaps, as little timely helpful advice such as *" ... excellent, but perhaps bend the legs a little more on landing?"*.

Another regular and frequent requirement of the conductor's job was to wind a handle which would change the destination boards at the back and front of the bus. Seems simple? Not so. For changing the back board a little handle was provided in a barely reachable position (presumably to deter mischievous passengers from giving it an odd twist to confuse would-be customers and following motorists) and a tiny internal window allowed the conductor to read what the board was displaying. Not all that exciting – but the front board was something else entirely. The changing handle for this was placed outside the bus, and mounted upside down right beside the driver's cab. The conductor had therefore to run to the front of the bus and heave himself up on one leg on to a footplate installed for that purpose next to the radiator. He then had to lean backwards in order to see the destination board, cling on for dear life with one hand whilst turning the handle with the other, and at the very same time, ignore the merciless and self-satisfied grin of the driver sat in his warm cab barely two feet away – perhaps occupying himself with idly thumbing his way through yesterday's Daily Mirror, whilst using his little Rizla machine to make a new roll-up. If in a particularly vindictive mood, the driver might also drum any remaining fingers on the dashboard in an impatient manner.

The sang-froid exhibited by the really great conductors of the time was a source of immense admiration, and complemented the rich dialogue which supported the show. A true master of the craft would bring his own personality into the act by entertaining passengers not only with jingling the money in his leather collecting pouch by swivelling his hips in a curiously suggestive thrusting manner, or by ringing the bell whilst winding out and simultaneously tearing off and presenting a fresh ticket, but would deliver his own dramatic and stylised banter. For the accomplished performer, this was metamorphosed into a patois which only regular passengers could understand, and bore only a fleeting similarity to the place names and safety instructions themselves. I well remember one particularly famous conductor whose lively and fulsome commentary was delivered in a highly singular nasal but throaty voice, with each instruction or place name having an added, entirely meaningless and stupendously breathy suffix, included, one assumes, for verbal effect. I can hear it now. Thus the simple request "*Fares please*" became **"Fez plizz-aah".** The well known bus stop at "*Copnor Bridge*" was transformed into **"Conner eeej-aah"** and "*South Parade Pier, all change please"* became an impressive **"Solpray pee-aah, orl chinj plizz-aah".** My all time favourite however, was the safety instruction given repeatedly to all passengers throughout the journey – whether seated or not – to: **"Ode tetnyaah!"**… which, of course translate as: *"Hold Tight Now!"*

It is quite conceivable that you might want to practice the phrase yourself and I am confident that you will find it a surprisingly rewarding experience, especially if accompanied by the entirely authentic stance described above... but may I suggest selecting a quiet corner in which to perfect your routine? The bottom of the stairs is a really good choice for such historic dramatisation: here you can lean against the newel post, place one foot on the bottom step in a casual but confident way, thrust your hips forward in a manner which might be described as 'provocative', reach up to an imaginary bell push, and then let forth with a full blooded '*Ode Tetnyaah!*' sufficient to frighten the neighbour's cat. Get the 1950's feeling? No? Well, keep trying – and possibly make sure next time that your nearest and dearest is *out* before letting rip.

Oddly enough, the one person who never did 'ode tetnyaah' was the conductor himself; it was apparent that a mark of his prowess was to remain balanced and poised throughout whatever the bumpy roads and deviant aspirations of the driver could throw at him. This was most evident when taking fares. Bearing in mind the bus could be rattling along at a fare old lick, the experienced conductor displayed his total mastery of the craft by bracing himself against the nearest seat, and with the additional support provided by putting legs akimbo, could work with both hands free to twiddle the dial on the ticket machine, rotate the handle and deliver the ticket all in one fluent and most impressive motion. A superb refinement to this routine was when change was required from the large leather bag suspended from a cross-chest strap and worn quite deliberately at the hip. It seems that coins taken were just thrown into this bag, and were therefore in an entirely mixed and unregulated heap at the bottom of the pouch. In order, therefore, to extract the correct amount for change, some agitation of the assembled coinage was required. This most refined and impressive action was achieved by only the most practised and skilled conductors *without the use of their hands* by using only thigh and groin gyrations very similar to the newly popular and provocative Mr. Presley when he was *All Shook Up*.

So, bus riding in the fifties was a lot of fun, and the show provided by the conductor a stimulus to the passengers getting in on the act as well. Bearing in mind that folding your paper ticket into a small dart and hurling it across the deck had its limitations, a more entertaining way of displaying panache and bravado had to be found, and there was no better place than that dusty, open-air boarding platform at the back of the vehicle.

In these days of one man operated buses with their electronic destination boards, air conditioning and powered doors operated by the driver, it is hard to imagine that passengers of the fifties and sixties were free to hurl themselves on and off the bus at any point. Young men wishing to demonstrate what later became known as 'street cred' were particularly attracted to this activity especially if a group of young ladies happened to be waiting at the bus stop, and in such circumstances running and leaping on to a bus just as it moved off was quite

Passengers at the back of the lower deck sat sideways-on which afforded an excellent vantage point from which to observe the boarding platform performances.

common. However, it was not without risk; for example, missing a firm grip on the safety boarding pole was inadvisable, as such a misfortune would inevitably leave the aspirant street athlete in an undignified heap in the road while the busload of amused and well entertained passengers drove off into the distance.

A much greater opportunity for street cred however, was *the dismount*. Provided you were on the landing platform first, and thereby took possession of the safety pole, the stage was yours. The most accomplished disembarker would, with a good ten yards still to go, hang off the back of the bus whilst it was still travelling quite quickly towards the stop, and step off on to the pavement. In order to do this well, you had to judge the relative speeds of yourself, the bus and the pavement, and ensure that your legs were ready to run at the appropriate pace to prevent **a)** falling flat on your face or **b)** colliding with passengers waiting to board the bus at the stop - neither of which were helpful in attaining the desired devil-may-care outcome. Quite often, this judgement was mistimed, and it only took a micro-second of inattention, or slipping on a hitherto unnoticed dog turd deposited on the kerbside for the whole thing to end up in disaster. Recovering from such a situation was very difficult indeed as scrambling up from the pavement nursing a grazed knee, or desperately trying to scrape off dog shit on the kerb stone lacked a certain dignity. Nevertheless, for many a testosterone-filled young man, the perfectly executed bus dismount was a rite of passage, especially if it was completed with your Woodbine stilled apparently carelessly hanging from your lips, and your Brylcreemed hair blowing lazily in the breeze.

So you can see that what with the antics of the crew and the behaviour of the passengers, a trip by bus passed in no time at all, and often left the observant child thoroughly entertained, exhausted and impressed. And such enthusiasm wasn't overlooked by the world of commerce either. As these days, post-war children loved to dress up, and common outfits available, especially at Christmas time included cowboy sets for boys and nurses' outfits for girls. However, another highly popular acquisition was a *bus-conductor's set*. Although the packaging with its jolly picture of a child conductor grinning inanely as a mighty double decker sweeps by in the background, the actual contents only comprised a peaked hat, a money pouch on a cross chest adjustable strap, some cardboard coins, some paper tickets and another cross chest ticket holding pouch ..... *not*, you will notice, a ticket machine with an interesting rotary handle, ready and willing to regurgitate smartly produced and multi-coloured tickets. To be honest, after the initial excitement of getting your sister to sit on the suitably arranged dining chairs and demanding *"Fares plizz-aah"* a few times, ringing an imaginary bell and making bus noises, it quickly lost its attraction. Nevertheless, the fact that these sets were produced in quantity throughout almost two decades says something about the social status and nation-wide admiration of the public omnibus. For example, the popular musical entertainers Michael Flanders and Donald Swann, whose repertoire included such memorable titles as '*Mud, Mud, Glorious Mud*' and '*The Gasman Cometh,*' went on to record a witty and perceptive song about buses. Entitled *"Transport of Delight"*, and dedicated to the ubiquitous London Bus, it contains these memorable lines:

> **If tickets cost a pound apiece,**
> **Why would you make a fuss?**
> **It's worth it just to ride inside,**
> **That thirty foot-long by ten foot wide,**
> **Inside that monarch of the road,**
> **Observer of the Highway Code,**
> **That big six-wheeler, scarlet-painted,**
> **London Transport,   Diesel-engined,**
> **Ninety-seven horse power... Omnibus!**

It is interesting to note that after this closing verse of the song,

Flanders and Swann would call out *"Hold Very Tight Now!"* prior to a *'ding ding'* on the piano... *not,* you will notice, the correct:

"Ode Tetnyaah!"

I'm not sure the same level of interest and almost affectionate public pride accorded to buses can be said of the railways. Despite doing sterling service week in week out, regular services from local stations failed to live up to the vividly coloured pictures in my *'Boys' Wonder Book of Railways'*, where a gleaming top link express train, driven by a smiling engine driver with his arm resting nonchalantly on the cab side, hurled his mighty charge across dramatic viaducts set in a green and verdant countryside.

We are, of course, talking about the age of steam, when all little boys wanted to grow up to be engine drivers. Well, to be honest, I'm not so sure this was correct. True, there was an adult perception that this is what we little chaps wanted, but in reality most of us wanted to be *modern* – to be spacemen, or racing drivers or frogmen ... the allure of driving the filthy, clanking, wheezing smoke enshrouded and, without exception, *slow* trains, lacked that certain pzazz, and to many was about as exciting as becoming an accountant. Nevertheless, I did quite like trains and as a little lad, would sometimes persuade my dad to take me on a Sunday afternoon stroll to the local station. The overall impression of Fratton station was one of warm sootiness; the enclosed footbridge over which we passed was windowed throughout its length on both sides, yet let in virtually no light at all. The exterior of the panes was covered with a layer of sooty grime, and the insides had obviously become a home from home for the local spider population. Should a steam train pass underneath the footbridge as you were crossing, you experienced a further dimming of light on the approach side as the steam and smoke enveloped it, and then had a matching performance on the other side to complete the experience. Together with the huge noise and vibration such an event generated, it was all highly satisfactory, and perhaps pre-dated the sort of experience one pays a fortune for in dimly lit tunnels at major theme parks these days.

In pre-nationalisation days, this local stretch of line had once been part of the Southern Railway, and as such sported its yellow and green paintwork ... which could *just* be discerned beneath the ever present layer of sooty residue deposited there by passing locomotives. And that is what most of them did – pass, that is; Fratton was not a major stop at the best of times, but it did have a large goods yard and engine shed next door. As a result, express trains just roared through, and clanking goods trains wheezed and complained as they dragged their heavy loads of goodness knows what into the neighbouring yard. Even so, getting within six feet of train travelling at even a modest thirty mph was, for a little boy, still quite exhilarating, and on the odd occasion when in an unaccustomed and rare fit of *joie de vivre* the driver blew the whistle, could lead to an unexpected and unwanted leakage in the trouser area (me that is... my dad and the driver remained their imperturbable selves... or at least if they suffered similarly it wasn't as visible as it was for me on my snake-belted khaki shorts).

Still, even through the rose tinted spectacles of youth, it was hardly the sort of image depicted by extravagant and colourful railway advertisements of the time, let alone the heroic and glamorous image generated by the W.H. Auden's famous poem "Night Mail", the subject being the Travelling Post Office express:

> *This is the night mail crossing the Border,*
> *Bringing the cheque and the postal order,*
> *Letters for the rich, letters for the poor,*
> *The shop at the corner, the girl next door.*

This rhythmic poem immediately brought to mind the image of a speeding steam train hurtling through the night with its heavy load of personalised mail, each category quoted having an immediate appeal and familiarity to the reader. Not only that, the meter of the poem was cleverly designed to replicate the internal 'diddly-dum' rhythm which all railway trains provided. Another excerpt illustrates this perfectly – depending, of course, if you are old enough to remember the days before welded rails robbed us off such pleasures...

Letters of thanks, letters from banks,
Letters of joy from girl and boy,
Receipted bills and invitations
To inspect new stock or to visit relations....
.... diddly-dum... diddly- dum...diddly-dum...

I have given a lot of thought to the *diddly dum* question, as it was an essential part of railway travel in the post-war years. Such academic introspection has resulted in two things: first, the scientific analysis printed below, and second the response from my wife that I should get out more, and why don't I *'put the recycling out and weed the front border and do something useful for a change?'*

So, before I go looking for my gardening gloves, I feel it my duty to acquaint you with the result of my research, which starts with an impressive, if unlikely assertion:

'Bogie wheels are very interesting, and we owe them a lot.'

No, really. For those of you who have no idea what bogie wheels are – or couldn't really care less - I can tell you that they are the mechanism whereby a swivelling set of four wheels are attached underneath each end of a railway carriage, and in most respects, perform just like a supermarket trolley. I say *'most'* because generally speaking, the wheels on railway trains are a lot better behaved than many on a supermarket trolley, in that they nearly always travel in the direction the person in charge intends. The point is though, that by putting one set at each end and allowing them to swivel independently, the vehicle can be a lot longer, offering a smoother, faster, safer ride, and assist greatly in ironing out bumps by incorporating sophisticated sprung suspension.

'Well so what?' I hear you ask. The fact is, that bogie wheels also introduced an element into rail travel that remains firmly embedded in the psyche of virtually anyone who ever travelled by rail in the decades following the war – namely that evocative, mesmerising and, to many, soporific sound associated with rail travel. I refer, of course to the slow and hypnotic dee-dum, dee dum .... dee-dum, dee-dum song of the wheels on the track, so eloquently reflected in Mr. Auden's famous poem. Despite the modern introduction of continuous welded rails, I guarantee that the vast majority of rail travellers – and especially those of us currently drawing our old age pension - can still summon to mind that soothing sound that accompanied every journey. It was, after all, often the pleasant pre-curser to setting the elbow firmly on the window ledge cushion, the chin rested equally firmly in the cupped hand and the mind slipping almost imperceptibly into neutral, in order to gaze vacantly out of the window and watch the ever changing panorama of the world slipping by. Added to this, your by now lowering eyelids were perhaps also registering the constant rise, dip and swoop of that other graceful element of railway architecture – the trackside telegraph wires, strung for mile after mile like the waves on a tidy sea.

A familiar memory? A comfortable first stage before falling into a light but satisfying sleep – only to awaken with a jerk when your elbow slips off the cushion and you become aware that:

a) You have probably been muttering in your sleep as everyone else in the carriage is staring at you, and

b) The soft dee-dum, dee-dum of the wheels has been replaced by a much more strident, rapid and almost continuous ***diddly-dum, diddly-dum, diddly-dum, diddly-dum'*** *

And all this caused by bogie wheels? Well, yes. Consider the following:

* *It is a law of nature that you can never spot when the slow, soft and rhythmic 'dee-dum, dee- dum' becomes the strident 'diddly-dum, diddly dum, diddly-dum. Honest.*

As mentioned above, bogie wheels are essentially two pairs of wheels attached at either end of the carriage. As the first set crosses a join in the rails it makes the characteristic *dee-dum* noise. But as carriages are joined end to end, this means that the bogie set of the next carriage – either preceding or following, depending where you are seated - can also be heard. Thus we get dee-dum, dee-dum .... followed by a short gap before the next rail joint is encountered. If you are still not getting the picture, then perhaps the following diagram will help a bit:

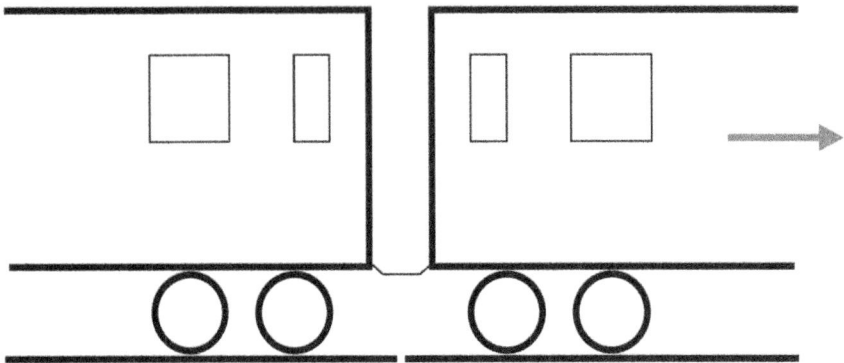

The first bogie set has crossed the gap, producing the first dee-dum. Passengers in both carriages now eagerly anticipate the second dee-dum of the following set in order to complete a most satisfying and entirely expected sequence.

If you consider all this to be a tad bizarre, consider the career of one Reginald Gardiner. This popular British actor had a successful career in films and on the stage, where his cut-glass English accent and impeccable dress sense meant that he was often cast as the typical upper class gent-about-town. He appeared in the Laurel and Hardy comedy *"The Flying Deuces"* in 1939 and in Charlie Chaplin's memorable satire *'The Great Dictator'* the following year. His career included stage appearances here and in the USA, as well as the early days of television. And what has all this to do with railways? Ask any child of the 1950's who listened to *'Children's Favourites'* on a Saturday morning, and they will tell you that a popular favourite would be one of Reginald Gardiner's records entitled 'Trains'. These were produced by Decca and recorded in 1937. To quote one of the many internet references to be found concerning this unique and gifted entertainer:

"...the records consisted of Gardiner, sounding slightly tipsy, reciting a monologue about steam railway engines (which he claimed were 'livid beasts') and impersonating both the engines themselves and the sound of trains running on the track. This latter he famously characterised as 'diddly-dee, diddly-dum' to mimic the sound pattern as the four pairs of bogie wheels ran over joins between the lengths of track."

These recordings were genuinely funny and very popular. They certainly appealed to a wider audience than just children – indeed, on one memorable occasion Gardiner was summoned to give a personal performance of this track (no pun intended) to the Royal Family at Buckingham Palace.

So - bogie wheels not interesting? You don't have to take my word for it – just go to YouTube and type in 'Trains' by Reginald Gardiner'... and listen for yourself!

The elegant Reginald Gardiner, whose unique talent was much loved by hoards of kids in the fifties.

It can be said therefore, that in the post war days before Lord Beeching wielded his axe, railways were an integral part of the backdrop to everyday life; they were always there, pottering around the country in their own inimitable and sometimes inexplicable way. The railway was just another element of the town - forever there and almost universally taken for granted. It was just a part of the *wallpaper* of the daily round, a rarely acknowledged element of the social fabric of life. The sound of an engine whistle, or the clanking of trucks being shunted in the station yard were once as much a part of the daily norm as the clinking of the milk bottles when they were delivered to your door – never specifically registered, and only noticeable if they ceased. So, if you can remember a time when people who travelled on trains were called '*passengers*' rather than '*customers*', when a carriage door slammed shut with a satisfying 'kiddely-CHUNK!' sound, rather than with an asthmatic hiss of compressed air, when you could still *open* a carriage window and get a healthy dose of black smuts in your eye, then I hope you will still be able to transport yourself back to the days when the soft *dee–dum, dee-dum, dee-dum, dee-dum* of the carriage wheels over the track was often the background to the excited chatter of children off to the coast for a seaside holiday.

And there you have it. Getting around on public transport in the fifties was surprisingly cheap and relatively easy. Mass car ownership only really took hold in the 1960's, and before that could happen, there was the Suez Crisis of 1956, something which we touched on in Chapter 3, and which resulted in some of the twentieth century's weirdest cars. And the railways? Well, by 1967 the far-reaching consequences of the 'Beeching Report' had been almost fully implemented. As a result, many areas of the country had their rail services closed, leaving some areas totally unprovided for in terms of public transport. The government of the day claimed that the gap created by the withdrawal of rail services would be filled by new bus routes, and so no community should be left 'unconnected'.

And guess what?

6 The 3 R's: Reading, Writing and Rubbing Out

I suppose it would be right to say that my formal education got off to a slow start – literally, as my first teacher at Bramble Road Infants was a certain Mrs. Slow. My mother didn't add to the need to up my game when she called our class as *'Mrs. Slow and her little snails'* - ho ho. Added to that, I was almost five when I started school: in those days, nursery schools didn't seem to exist, and things like play school had yet to be invented. My pre-school experience, unless you count Sunday School, was therefore practically zilch, and so as they say, kids like me we were 'blank canvasses' - or in my case, just 'blank'.

Not that I should have been at Bramble Road in the first place, as there was the infinitely more conveniently situated Highland Road Infants and Junior School just three minute's walk from home. However, this was the 1950's, when schools were administered by the Local Education Authority... chaps in suits and short sleeved argyle jumpers who sat behind desks and smoked pipes and exuded an air of confident paternalism and WITH WHOM YOU DIDN'T ARGUE BECAUSE THEY KNEW BEST. *Got it?* So, instead of undertaking a short walk to the school round the corner, my mum and I had a three quarters of a mile walk four times a day, as school dinners were not to be trusted. Worse still for my mum, I would often insist on undertaking this lengthy journey on my tiny two wheeler which I had not yet learnt to ride, but could scoot. As a result, my mum had to push it back home each morning and dinner* time. Awkward little soul, wasn't I?

* *The midday meal was always called dinner. As far as we were aware, only aristocracy had dinner in the evening, and that was obviously because they got up late, and had breakfast when the rest of us were having dinner. Consequently their meals slipped around the day in an oddly asymmetric way.*

I don't remember much about Bramble Road Infants except that it smelled of dust and damp, had a sandpit in the playground and I fell in love with Janet Hobbs whose Dad ran the greengrocer's on the corner next to the school, and who had nice sandals – Janet that is: I'm not entirely sure of the state of her father's footwear. I also have a distant recollection of spending an inordinate amount of time at the school rolling hard little lumps of sticky and much used clay into long worms, with a view to creating a coil pot – in imitation, no doubt, of early man's first attempt at producing crockery and thus avoiding the nuisance of having nowhere but his lap to put his half-eaten haunch of bison. Clearly, such innovative tableware would have been invaluable in allowing the happy owner to have then been 'hands free' when conducting a lively mid–meal debate with a neighbour on the pros and cons of sabre tooth tiger hunting. At least, that's the gist of what I got. I'm not sure I ever got as far as actually creating a pot of any recognisable form, as the lumps of clay were often brick hard, and what with that and the fact that our hands were often covered in sand from playtime, I found the experience dermatologically aggressive. Still, we all had nice clean hands at the end of the day.

Anyway, after what can only be described as the briefest of acquaintances with the world of academia, the time came for the class of 51 (and by that, I probably mean the number of kids per class, as well as the start date - the one thing you definitely can say of the Baby Boomers is that there were a hell of a lot of us) to move on to Junior school. So, with just a smattering of reading, and the ability to count to an impressive hundred or so under my belt I was sent to...guess where? Yes. Highland Road Juniors, three minutes' walk away. I was left in little doubt that this was the BIG step, and I really needed to brush the sand off my hands, wash the clay residue out of a my hair and GET A GRIP on doing some learning.

There was at least some consistency in the raising of us post-war kids, in that the underlying fact of being *well-hard* babies stood us in good stead for what was to come. For example, the name of my infants' school set the tone... I mean *BRAMBLE* Road? Who on earth thought that was a good name for a caring academic institution devoted to molly-coddling its tinies and gently setting them off on the path to educational fulfilment and glory? To be honest, naming the school after an aggressive botanical specimen whose sole purpose in life is to shred the skin of any human being who dares to pass within half an arm's length doesn't seem to be a particularly thoughtful move, does it? Where, may I ask, were the *'Hugglebunnies First Schools', or the 'Learningsfun Micro-Acadamies'?* About seventy years in the future, that's where.

But let's get back to my new junior school and step from the speculative to the well-hard realities of the early fifties. A good example is that all schools started at 9.00am prompt, and closed at 4.00pm, no ifs no buts. That was the standard school day, and if you didn't like it... then tough. Also, the basic curriculum was just that, basic. The core was the Three R's. Now, I have an issue with this. If ever the embarkation on an academic career was predetermined to founder at the first step, then calling the **R**eading, **W**riting and **A**rithmetic the three **R's** seems as close to stupid as you can get. If you really must take the initial letters to form something memorable, why not give it some degree of logicality and call it RAW, or even WAR? At least this would have been a more reasonable interpretation, and the way most junior schools were organised in those days, would have represented a pretty accurate description.

Anyway, like it or not, the Three R's is what we got, every morning, all morning, except of course, for assembly in the dusty school hall at ten past nine, regular as clockwork. At this point, Miss Porter and her staff herded us into tight packed lines in order to sing hymns. These were displayed on a flip over pack of very tired pillowcase-sized sheets of greying paper which were hoisted into the air rather like an aged washing line, and from which we little seven year olds were supposed to read and sing with enthusiasm. This was more of a hope than a confident expectation, as our particular hymn sheets had virtually no children's hymns and for someone who had only just got to grips with *Dick and Dora Green Book One,* trying to read – let alone sing – "*He who Would Valiant Be*" was a bit of a vain hope, especially when it got to the "*Hobgoblins nor Foul Fiends*" line. Had the hymn lyrics been more of the "*See here is Dick. ... run Dick run*" type, we might have stood a fighting chance, but it seems hymn writers were of a more ecclesiastical frame of mind. Had they tried something like "*See the lions... run Daniel, run!*" I think the response would have been a sight livelier.

So, like most kids we just listened to what the other nippers were yelling, and joined in, regardless of meaning. Thus the second line of "*All Things Bright and Beautiful*" was always "*All teachers great and small*" and there was almost an inevitability that the third line of "*Hark the Herald Angels*" was always going to be "*Peas on earth and mercy mild...*". Perhaps the most famous juvenile balls-up each Christmas was the really rather wonderful misinterpretation of the spiritually uplifting phrase given to Mary... "*Blessed art thou amongst women*" ... which became the sublime "*Blessed art thou a monk swimming*".

Once back in the classroom, it was down to the grind with our teacher Miss Grant - and boy, what a grind it was! Nowadays, children study 'Mathematics'. We didn't. We did the third R - Arithmetic.... no 'shape and space', no block graphs, no probability, no data handling.... just loads and loads of number work. Whether or not you had any idea of the workings of the number system, everyone had to learn their multiplication tables by rote. These were chanted by the complete class, in a "*once two is two, two twos are four, three twos are...*" sing-song fashion. Bearing in mind class sizes were large, individual children could get away with just miming for months at a time. Other popular avoidance strategies included lip reading bright kids then coming in a syllable behind, or making indeterminate noises which could quickly be mutated into another number when it came to the answer part eg *"nine sixes are six..fty sev..four"* . By such processes the hours flew by. No they didn't - it was a real drag, and left one hoping for a merry fire alarm or a visit by the nit nurse to enliven proceedings. That Arithmetic took up so much of our school day is due to the fact that this was all years before the arrival of the much easier – for softies only – metric system. We well-hard kids had to learn the imperial system of numbers, weights and measures, a system handed down over the centuries and based it seems as much upon the length of various regal body parts and the weight of a cannon ball, as it was upon logic. For a start, our tables didn't end at *'ten tens are a hundred'*; oh no. We went on to *"twelve twelves are a hundred and forty four',* an extension that contained such obscurities as the utterly useless **121** (11x11) and really quite vindictive **132** (11x12). Why on earth would anyone want to remember that? Anyway, we simply had to learn such bizarre number facts, because in our bonkers arithmetic there were **twelve** pennies in a shilling, and **twelve** inches in a foot. And twelves of everything were called a *dozen*, and twenties were called *scores*, and twelve dozen was a *gross*. Got it? Keeping up? *Well, you aint*, as they say*, seen nothin' yet.*

Money: Now as we have seen, post-war kids needed to be pretty good at money, as it was an essential requirement needed for the purchase of the very popular sweetmeats of the day, as well as when the demand *"fez plizz"* was made on the bus. And what a lot of it there was. I speak, of course, not of the quantity we had, but in terms of the range, value and size – not to mention weight - of the coinage in circulation. The coins were divided into two groups, 'copper' and 'silver'. Naturally, neither group was actually made of these metals, and this therefore was the first step put in place to confuse foreigners and children. There was also a coin which was half of something that did not exist – the **half crown** - in my mind putting it in a category of *'awaiting philosophical debate'*. Also there was another coin, the golden **guinea** which **a)** did not exist and **b)** was not made of anything now as we had run out of gold. All clear so far?

That's not to say that there were no advantages to our coinage; one very obvious one was that it kept us fit, because it was so bulkily heavy. Even a modest pocketful of copper had sufficient weight to set up a momentum of its own that could send you teetering off in any unwanted direction – not to mention its propensity to simultaneously rip out your pocket and pull your trousers down. Mind you, there were advantages to this fiscal bulk and weight: take, for example law enforcement.

Many a thoughtless 1950's bank robber would grab hold of a bag of cash whilst waving his gun around the counter, only seconds later to have his arm almost dragged out of its socket as the dead weight of the cash hit the floor with a resounding thud. Further flight from the scene might well then degenerate into an unbecoming and embarrassing matter of dragging the loot towards the open door, pausing regularly to regain breath and becoming totally shagged out before reaching the pavement.

Anyway, back to the classroom and pounds, shillings and pence... or '£sd'*. The smallest coin was the farthing, (or *four thing* as smug pedants were quick to remind us) which was worth a quarter of a penny, i.e. a d/4. I can only remember two things you could buy for a farthing in the 1950's, and they were both tiny individually wrapped

---

* *Now there's a case in point: **£sd**, we were told, was pronounced '**L**', '**S**' and '**D**', - not that anyone recognised the funny squiggly shape as an 'L' anyway - and it stood for **P**ounds, **S**hillings and **P**ence. Now, forgive me for being picky, but shouldn't it therefore be 'P' 'S' and 'P'? "Ah", but we were told "the '**d**' in £sd stands for 'dinari', the Latin term for a penny". Oh good. How perfectly flippin' logical. If the term 'it does my head in' had been invented then ... well, it would have.*

wrapped chews, one called a *Fruit Salad,* and the other a *Blackjack.* That is not to say that farthings weren't used to make up other amounts, and many's the time you would come across people in the street scratching their heads and puzzling over a handful of coins as they tried to work out the change from half a crown when they bought a quarter of Liquorice All-Sorts for ninepence three farthings. Any way, if you couldn't do the arithmetic, at least you could admire the impression of the little wren on the obverse of the farthing; it really was the best thing about it ... apart from, of course, its unique contribution to cycling.

I refer of course to that most bizarre form of transport *the penny farthing bicycle.* The name derives from the relative size of the coins, and the new nineteenth century word 'bicycle' originally refers to this peculiar form of the machine. Now you would have thought, wouldn't you, that given the poor state of the roads in the late

Guess what? (No prizes given)

nineteenth century, the last thing you'd want is to somehow launch yourself off on a rickety pair of wheels of vastly unequal sizes, where the likelihood of hitting a pothole and propelling yourself at speed over the handlebars was considerable. That's assuming you could get on the damn thing to start with, as mounting must have been an absolute nightmare – and I can think of no more certain way of separating yourself from your goolies than the no doubt frequent, unpremeditated and rapid ejection astride the back frame. So, that's the farthing for you – great for buying a small sweet, and a reminder of the gratitude we should have that modern cycling does not imperil your manhood quite so much – but not much else.In comparison, the half-penny (pronounced '*hay*–penny') was pretty self explanatory, and boasted a sailing ship design. It was quite a lot bigger than the farthing, but not nearly as big as the mighty penny, a virtual *discus* of a coin, and one which nobly bore the responsibility for being the foundation stone of our barmy monetary system. Don't believe me? Well, how many pennies do you think there were in a £? Ten? Fifty? Anything logical at all? Nope. There were **240** of the little devils!

"*Why?!*" I hear you exclaim. Well, there were twelve pennies in a shilling, and no less than twenty shillings in a pound, and if you'd been paying attention earlier when we were busy with the twelve times table, you'd have instantly worked out that twenty times twelve is two hundred and flaming forty. And don't forget that this means there were 480 ha'pennies in a pound, and a mighty 960 farthings. No wonder people got lost in a virtual blizzard of loose change.

I suspect the casual reader might be wavering in favour of putting the book down and wandering off for a restorative cup of coffee, but I would ask you to stay with it; come on – man up! We're fast approaching a truly memorable section of coinage that will leave you gasping in admiration at us tinies of the post-war years ... because we now come to the *composite* coins, those made up of a multiplicity of pennies, and the first of these was really rather exotic. Now, you'd be forgiven for expecting this first multiple to be a *ten* penny piece – but by now you might be erring on the side of caution, and beginning to suspect something far less logical would be the order of the day – and you'd be right. The coin was a *three* penny coin, known by all and sundry as the *threepenny bit,* and by the way, it was the only coin that wasn't round. It was a dodecagon. Really. It had twelve equal sides. I can only suggest that the inventor of coins thought to himself: '*How can I further popularise the use of the twelve times table and at the same time produce a coin that, if skilfully propelled along a hardened surface will make an annoying whirring sound?'*

I have no idea why this rather odd coin should have been marked out to be so different, and why it should have been called a '*bit*'... but then logic and connectivity were never much in evidence where the old monetary system was concerned. Such oddities do occasionally add to the rich diversity of life, and the threepenny bit did play an unintended part in our later sex education, at the point when we were starting to master the intricacies of rhyming slang. For those of you who can't see it coming, the early teen years were sometimes punctuated with the wistful '*Phwoaaar... bet she's got a nice pair of threepennies'*. Anyway, we jump ahead of ourselves – remember, we little seven year olds were still grappling with the mighty and totally weird arithmetic system - not to mention *Dick and Dora,* bean bags, plasticine and how far you could pee up the wall in the boys' toilets.

The next multi-penny coin was the first of the silver lot, and was the silver sixpence, a rather nice properly circular coin with a pleasing milled edge, which with due diligence and the application of the thumbnail at a particular angle, could be encouraged to emit a rewarding ripping noise ... nothing so gaudy as the threepenny bit's rough whir of course, but a modest and really rather refined addition to the coin-audio repertoire. For some unexplained reason, the sixpenny piece was always referred to as a *tanner.* This in itself was an unexpected blessing, the full appreciation of which requires us the fast-forward to 1960, and the introduction of ITV's famous soap *Coronation Street.* One of this programme's early stars was the lovely Pat Phoenix who played the buxom Elsie Tanner. As if you can't already see where this is going, let me remind you that **a)** two threepenny bits made sixpence, **b)** a sixpenny piece was called a tanner and finally **c)** threepenny bits were pubescent schoolboys' rhyming slang for a nice pair so amply displayed by the lovely Pat. Consequently, the comment that Elsie Tanner possessed *a nice pair* *of threepennies* had a happy circularity to it, and was commonly heard before much lascivious and broken-voiced laughter. Not that ladies of such dimensions appealed to just the young and speculative: older men were more sophisticated, as their much used observation *'bet you don't get many of those to the pound'* indicates... which brings me nicely back to the next thrilling episode in the Highland Road arithmetic saga – weights and measures.

These days we have grammes, kilograms, tonnes, millimetres, centimetres and kilometres, not to mention the odd litre or two. To be honest, their connection is pretty logical. In the fifties, as far as weight was concerned, we had *pounds** *and ounces...* but we also had *stones* and something called a *hundredweight.* Now, you'd have thought, wouldn't you, that the word *hundred*weight might have some direct bearing or reference to being a *hundred* of something, like a hundred ounces, or a hundred pounds. But by now, your suspicions will have been roused – and quite rightly too, because the dear old hundredweight was equal to **one hundred and twelve** pounds, (or eight stone, or one twentieth of a ton) for heaven's sake. Good grief. It's little wonder that we pre-decimalites either burst into tears or became devoted to thumb sucking and shutting our eyes in the vain hope that the horrible sums man would go away. In truth though, it was just a matter of hardening up to the realities of reciting in class for what seemed like hours on end:

> **'Sixteen ounces: one pound,**
> **Fourteen pounds: one stone,**
> **Eight stone: one hundredweight**
> **Twenty hundredweight: one ton**
> **Even though I'm only seven,**
> **I'm quickly losing the will to live'**

* That this unit bears the same name as its financial counterpart shows that juvenile confusion was in-built to the system. To be honest, trying to get your head around it was already complicated enough for the average seven year-old.

"Enough! Enough!" I hear you cry... but there's more: back to the cash register again. To be fair, the good old shilling was fairly inoffensive, even though it was made up of twelve pennies or four threepenny bits or a couple of tanners ... and if you managed to scrape together twenty of them you had a pound, so that's all pretty good. BUT...the remaining four imperial coins we have yet to meet extended in value beyond the shilling. *'OK'*, you might say, *'that's only to be expected'*. Agreed. However, the interesting thing was that of the four, the first was fairly normal but had a totally inexplicable name, the second was half of something that did not exist, the third did not exist (except at certain times when all you could do was get one and look at it; you couldn't spend it) and the fourth was made of gold, did not exist in any form whatsoever, but was used exclusively by very rich people, people who bet on horses, or were lawyers or Harley Street surgeons. All clear so far? Take a deep breath and try to stay calm.

The first of this mystifying quadruplet was the *two bob bit*. As the slang for a shilling was a *bob,* it doesn't need many of the grey cells to work out that this coin was worth twice as much. What was less comprehensible was that it was known as a *florin*. Why? Well if we were told, it must have been numbingly boring, because no-one I knew had the remotest idea or interest; it was just a flippin' florin, and in 1953 you could buy a fairly basic Hillman Minx Dinky Toy with it – OK? Just bear in mind that it was worth twenty four pennies, forty eight ha'pennies, or ninety six farthings, so pretty darn useful, I'm sure you'll agree.

The discerning reader will have noted that for the last few coins we have simply doubled up the value, in that two threepenny bits make a tanner, two tanners make a bob, two bobs make a florin. So, is this a logical pattern that's emerging? Is there the tiniest chance that the next coin will double up to a *four bob bit,* called something obscure like a Coronet? Come on! Get real! This is the imperial system! **Nothing** makes *any* sense! So it therefore won't come as much of a surprise that the second of the coins we're looking at is just a mere tanner's worth more than a florin... i.e. rather than being double our two bob bit, it has only got bigger by six pence. And it's called **half a crown**.... oh, and by the way, there's no crown (to speak of).

Although only a little more valuable than a florin, the half crown was physically quite a lot larger and heavier. Because of this reassuring size and mass, it somehow became the touchstone of schoolboy wealth in that it was weighty and large enough to be given as a present in its own right. Whereas the gift of a florin might be seen as the mark of a relation who was erring on the side of parsimony, the old *'half dollar'** was always seen as a welcome addition to the money box, where its weighty presence gave a reassurance rather in excess of its actual worth. Perhaps a little more to the point, it brought quite a lot more of the Dinky Toy range within the purchasing power of the lucky recipient, the Austin Devon Nestles delivery van with bright red livery and gold lettering being one, as I recall ... enough to turn a little chap's head, as I'm sure you will agree.

Now, even to a group of kids as unworldly and, to be honest, as gormless as us, it did cross our minds that, given 2/6d was *half* a crown, then it was fairly likely that the next coin to be inflicted on us would be the *whole* crown, fully complete, with no parts missing at all. And do you know what? We were right... except that there weren't any crowns. Well, there *were*, but only when someone became the Queen. Even then, you couldn't spend them, even if they did put a yellow Bedford Dormobile with Kodak advertising on the

* *Even though the half crown did not equate to half a dollar in value, we liked to call it that simply because it sounded American, and was therefore good. In the 60's we would have called such terminology being 'with it'. In 1953 we were so 'without it' as to be virtually naked..*

side firmly in within your grasp. So in reality, all the crown was good for was for looking at, and showing to your friends.

You will have noted that our journey through these last few coins has become increasingly bizarre, and so as not to disappoint you, I'm pleased to say that the final one does put us firmly and somewhat predictably deep inside Looneyland. This is because the **guinea** (or a 'golden' guinea as aspirant posh people liked to say) did not exist at all. It was a *notional* coin. Oh good, just what we kids at Highland Road Juniors needed. To be honest, before it was brought to our attention, you'd see many little groups of worried children putting aside their fag cards, untucking skirts from knickers and saying things like '*Yes, but what we really need is a bleedin' notional coin - let's hope someone invents one soon – especially if it's value is one pound and one shilling*'

And that's what it was: **twenty one** shillings. And the craziest thing of all? Even though the guinea never existed, it is still in use today, used principally to describe the value of prize money in horse races, and how much you have to pay a barrister for his services. No wonder we little kids sought refuge in playing *British Bull Dog*, picking our noses and throwing stones. So, with a sigh of relief let us leave, for the moment, the strikingly bizarre world of Imperial Arithmetic, and venture into the wider educative experience.

Afternoons, as I recall, were spent on rather more practical lessons, and centred a lot around yet more clay and rafia. Now, if you're not familiar with the latter, it's really akin to longish strings of a straw-like material, which can be quite gaily coloured – that is unless it's been used a hundred times before, whereupon it becomes **a)** noticeably shorter and **b)** rather more grey than vermillion or aqua-marine. Its main purpose was to combine it with a cardboard toothed circle (somewhat akin to an infant circular saw blade), on which had been wound green string in a rather pleasing bicycle spoke cum dartboard fashion. Now, what you had to do was to thread your piece of rafia on to a large needle (yes, a *needle*, one of those pointy sharp things which could so easily end up embedded in the wall, your desk or up your neighbour's nose) and then weave it in and out of the strings, starting nearest the central hub. After about three years, just before leaving school, starting shaving, and dropping an octave or two voice-wise, you might be fortunate enough to end up with a greyish brown disc of rafia that could then be triumphantly taken home and hidden by your mum beneath a teapot or large aspidistra.

Putting that questionable image to one side, and ignoring for a moment the horrors of a barmy number system, I do have to say that there were some compensatory benefits to being in 'the Juniors' in the fifties. For a start, we didn't get homework: that was for the big kids at secondary school. What we did get, though, was free milk every day in little individual bottles, heaved by the crate-load into the classroom each morning by a wheezing and ancient caretaker who would then spend the next few minutes outside the door giving an airing – if that's the right term - to his deafening, and possibly life-threatening smoker's cough.

Also on the plus side, we didn't have a school uniform, except for changing into plimsolls for PT, which stood for Physical Training (not *education,* notice) and was deemed to be good for us. Out in the dusty, walled in playground, we would be herded into rounders teams, or given some outdoor play equipment. The latter usually comprised skipping ropes (for girls, obviously – I don't think I ever saw a boy skipping, and if me and my mates *had,* well, questions might well be have been asked in the House), cane hoops, (remember, plastic was still brand new… and nothing BUT NOTHING was ever NEW at Highland Road Juniors, believe me) grubby rubber rings and bean bags. There were also a number of squared wooden skittles with a groove in the top, ready to receive a short piece of bamboo cane. The skittles *always* fell over with a surprisingly loud clonking timbery sound, so getting two of them to remain erect for a nano-second with a splintery bamboo stick perched bridge-like across both, usually took up at least 95% of the lesson. In any case the stick was knocked off straight away by the first lumbering and totally deluded idiot child who thought he or she might stand even the slightest chance of clearing the said cane with anything approaching athletic grace.

To ensure maximum health benefits, we boys had to strip down to our vests, but mercifully, not down to our pants, since this was in the years before Y Fronts. The girls were not so lucky, in that they were required to remove their skirts, but by way of preserving their modesty, would wear thick blue knickers apparently made to the same recipe as an army blanket, and were about as becoming. Indoor PT was not all that different in terms of equipment, but it did require children to get their first taste of gymnastics. Before a vision of lycra-clad lovelies doing amazing things on the parallel bars, or muscular young types performing the splits astride a pommel horse *and still smiling,* let me bring you down to earth – literally.

At Highland Road Juniors, gymnastics in the dusty old school hall required us to get out the mats. These were mainly of the very thin, black, crumbling at the edge variety, which by both smell and appearance had clearly been around since before the war – and I'm not sure I mean the (then) recent unpleasantness either. The other sort was the thick, coarse, apparently indestructible bristle mat type - much bigger, much heavier, and much more aggressive. So one type meant rolling around on a thin, disintegrating and dusty piece of crumbling rubber, or should you be required to perform on the other type, trying desperately to avoid contact with something that resembled, and felt like, an upturned pan scourer-cum-wire brush, and was rather better at sending you home with an unpleasant rash than it was at protecting you from the stickiness of the recently mopped wooden floor.

Not that we didn't welcome the chance to thrash about a bit in the school hall; on the contrary, at very least it was not one of the dreaded three R's, and secondly, one mat-based floor exercise provided an unexpected and much appreciated bonus. I refer, of course, to the *shoulder stand*. This involved lying on your back and raising not only your legs but most of your torso as high into the air as possible, supported by your arms neatly triangled into your waist. A particularly accomplished piece of gymnastics? A possible indication of early Olympic promise? Well, no, not really. But what such an exercise did give you was an unrivalled – if extremely brief - view up Miss Grant's skirt as she wafted fragrantly by to check and instruct more mobile and adventurous classmates. And I wasn't the only one, believe me. It may have perplexed our lovely teacher that so many of her little boys were bending over backwards (literally in some cases) to perfect their shoulder stand technique, but had she rumbled, one would like to think that she would have been at least a little mollified in that she could reflect that she was adding to our education in double measure – gymnastically and physiologically. In fact, looking at Miss Grant's legs became quite a popular and educative process in our class, although, in working so hard for the reward of the very occasional glimpse of stocking seams, you did pay something of a price in terms of aching shoulders and the dizziness caused by being inverted for lengthy periods.

Another brilliant idea, for which I claim a modest share of introductory credit, was *pencil sharpening*. Now, don't jump ahead of me here – it's got nothing to do with putting lead in your pencil. Like shoulder stands in the school hall, it was all a matter of *positioning*. As with all our teachers, Miss Grant spent quite a lot of time sat behind a high purpose-built desk from which she could survey the serried ranks of little kids all muttering '*See Dick, see Dora. Run Dick, run Dora*' or possibly '*twelve twelves are a hundred and sixorty fivfour*' etc. The bottom part of her desk, however, was completely open and the waste paper basket was always placed immediately in front of it. Thus, when you went to sharpen your pencil and happened to glance up, you were confronted with the view of Miss Grant's skirt-covered knees. Should she, at that moment, decide to cross her legs, concentration on pencil sharpening could be lost almost entirely... until you became aware that a) twenty minutes had passed since your arrival at the waste paper basket and b) you were not only knee deep in pencil shavings but had also succeeded in sharpening the end of your forefinger. Despite the obvious enquiry from teacher as to why your sharpening expedition had taken so long (and, no doubt, a question from the Headmistress as to why the number of pencils used in one class had suddenly shot up to a critically unsustainable level) it was a price worth paying, and one for which we would go to almost any lengths. And speaking of lengths, brings me somewhat tortuously back to the number system again, and the labyrinthine and mystic depths of imperial weights and measures.

Lest you think that my earlier reference to the use of 'regal body parts' as the basis for linear measure was just a throw- away remark, let me assure you that it really was the case. Now, which king we are talking about, I have no idea, but given the ferocious and egocentric nature of most of our royal ancestors, I strongly suspect that it was some bloke (e.g. *Ethelred the Measured*) who considered his place in history would be super-welded by making all of his subjects and their descendants forever after have to refer to his body whenever they wanted to get on with a spot of measuring. And that, of course, includes me, my classmates and the fragrant Miss Grant at Highland Road Juniors.

The obvious starting place is the ***foot***, i.e. the bit between the regal ankle bone and the kingly tippy-toes. Now, for those of you who have no idea what a foot looks like, (please don't fall for the obvious gag) it's a smidgen over 30cm, so we can assume that the bloke in question was either quite a big geyser, or was blessed with large feet.

This in turn presents something of a problem, in that even the dullest monarch must have been aware that a much smaller unit was also required, and thus a smaller bodily part needed to be identified. Now, before your imagination runs riot let me inform you that this role was taken on by the distance between the end of the royal thumb, and the first joint as you travel wristwards.... and was called the **inch.** And how many half thumbs do we think fitted into a foot? Before you whip off you shoe and start experimenting yourself – a practice which may elicit a raised eyebrow from anyone sitting nearby – let me tell you that the answer was, of course .... *12.* Not something nice and easy, like 10. No, it had to be 12. And so, we can lay the blame for us kids having to learn the 12 times table fairly and squarely - and in this case, quite literally - at the feet of *Ethelred the Measured,* or *Egbert the Length* or whoever the git was.

And it didn't stop there. The next bit was the **cubit**, the distance between the elbow and finger- tip, a rather baffling length as it seemed to have no relevance to any other body part, other than the fact that it was deemed to be half a yard, i.e. one and a half feet. Useful eh? I can only assume that it was the result of a *'seemed a good idea at the time'* moment, and perhaps only used by those seeking royal patronage and approval.

Not so the **yard.** If the cubit was consigned to a quaint backwater of history, the yard was a measure which had to be reckoned with, and came with a robust provenance in that it was directly related to the foot... and not just one of them either! Two? Five? Ten? Nope. The answer was, of course, THREE. Three feet, one yard. Obvious really. The yard was the length from nose tip to end of pointed forefinger when arms are extended in a **'look what a big fish I caught today!'** manner, and its introduction led to what can only be described as an avalanche of random measuring units... or perhaps a blizzard would be a better analogy since their introduction left most people completely lost and stumbling around the arithmetic maze.

Before we embark on the final exhausting part of this tortuous journey through the illogical, may I suggest a short break during which a stiff drink / lie down in a darkened room / creating an opportunity in which to reflect upon the deeper meanings of life is taken? ... because, to be honest, what comes next defies belief.

Having already visited the pretty damn useless cubit, our next port of call is the **chain**. Now, although it is rarely mentioned these days, this cumbersome unit is still in use today, for it is *the length of a cricket pitch*, and comes in at a baffling 22 yards. Presumably, the chain came about when our fun loving body-part monarch got really browned off at not being able to find any use whatever for the cubit, and picked up a stone and chucked it as far as he could with a petulant and unbecoming shout of *'There you are. I told you my forearm would come in useful one day. I think I'll call this new length a CUBITCHUCK'.* Mercifully, he was persuaded that 'chain' was far more regal, or perhaps he was threatened at being put in them if he didn't sober up. Anyway, there it remains, 22 yards of the best. As far as I am aware, this is the only use to which the dear old chain was ever put, so if cricket is not your game, or you have no desire to use the length of a cricket pitch as a means of estimating, say, the dimensions of a new hall carpet, or the distance between fruit flavoured yogurts and the checkout at your local supermarket, I regret to say it is likely to remain forever forgotten.

Surprisingly though, it does actually merit a far greater accolade, for it was the only unit of length to involve the use of **10**. Yes! Something ever-so-slightly logical at last! One can only imagine that this apparent aberration into common sense came about when the regal unit-maker, tired at the end of a long day trying out various body parts, decided that doing arm-stretches up and down the local cricket pitch was enough for the moment, and in a casual off the cuff remark to the recording bloke ready with his quill pen said – *'Blow this for a game of soldiers - just stick ten cricket pitches together and* *see what you get... I'm off to do some maiden chasing'.*

And the result? The ten chains stuck together made the **furlong**. At 220 nose to fingertips, (yards, in case you've forgotten), this was a bit far even for the best cricketers to slog the ball. Thus, a new use for this otherwise under-occupied unit was needed. I suppose one can imagine the desperate medieval *'bloke with the quill pen'* - aware that the meddlesome monarch would soon be back from his most recent session of maiden-molesting, and demanding to know to what good purpose the newly invented furlong had been put – saved his bacon by galloping off on his horse..... and putting the two together - voila!! A perfect length for horse racing. And so it remains today. And an added benefit? A use for the guinea... at last!

One might have suspected that, with the introduction of the logical 10 into recent unit derivation, the medieval pen-pushers might be anticipating further rational developments, especially as the all important mile was next. So, ten furlongs to one mile? .... but no, hopes were dashed when Ethelred the Length declared that one brief step into logicality was quite enough and that there should be just *eight* furlongs to the mile, making this most this important measurement a totally unmemorable *1760 yards*.

So there you have it. Miss Grant's classroom chant therefore was complete. Brace yourselves:

Twelve inches equal one foot
Three feet equal one yard
Twenty two yards equal one chain
Ten chains equal one furlong
Eight furlongs, or one thousand seven hundred and sixty yards
equal one mile.

And that's what we little kids spent much of our time trying to remember. I suppose it must have stuck after repeating it about two million times, and at least we were spared having to put in yet another barmy sub-division of length which was brought to our attention. Believe it or not, we were informed about this particular piece of linear insanity just *for our own interest...* which gives you a good idea as to what our teachers thought interested little kids, doesn't it?

Evidently, back in the mists of time, some complete twerp who ought to have known better came up with the idea that dividing a chain up into four bits would be a really good idea. Not only that, but this new unit would be called by not one, not two, but **THREE** names, **all meaning the same thing** … and all being equally useless. Thus was born those stars of the measuring world, the triumvirate of tedium, the triplicate of trivia, the five and a half yard ***ROD, POLE or PERCH.*** You could be forgiven for muttering '*Nah! Don't believe it! He's lost the plot'*. But I kid you not. It's right there in the OED under all three headings:

Rod / Pole / Perch: *A unit of linear measurement equal to five and a half yards; also called a Rod, Pole or Perch (depending where you're looking).* And why the names? Surely five and a half yards is too long for a fishing rod, and far too high for a clothes pole...and we couldn't begin to think of a bird cage large enough to accommodate such an enormous resting place for our feathered chums. To be honest, it made rafia work seem almost desirable. So why would anyone ever want to invent a unit so utterly bonkers that even *Eric the Length* must have done a double take and enquired of his mates: *'Five and a half yards? Three different names? You're having a laugh ainchya?!!'*

If Miss Grant didn't see it fit to come up with a satisfactory explanation, then that was good enough for us, and we could consign such flights of fancy to the waste-paper basket of history...and talking of waste-paper baskets, where is my pencil?

To say that our dear, dusty old Junior school was a centre of academic excellence might be pushing it a bit, but we felt generally quite happy to be there, and enjoyed the rough and tumble of the playground and the occasional frisson of admiration whenever the popular Miss Grant wafted by. In addition there were some really quite enjoyable forays into areas other than the Three R's. One such was Nature Study – not 'Natural Science' or even something as exotic as Botany, you will notice. Science wasn't done in junior schools, so the old nature table was as far as we got. This simple piece of classroom furniture became the home for various natural exhibits which were supposed to show the observant child how the seasons changed. Sorry to say most of this went over my head (as did so much else) but what we were really interested in was - *could you eat it?* With pussy willow and twigs covered in rose hips, this proved not to be the case, but evidently they were central to the process of producing new little plants for next year... as were conkers. Really? Obviously, conkers were primarily there to be used as missiles, for sporting contests or for bartering or for baking so that they were bullet hard if you were Barry Thorne's dad. Nevertheless, a little of nature's practices and processes did sink through the various layers of concrete surrounding our brains, and this was particularly so when it came to growing stuff. Now I don't want you to conjure up the picture of a school garden, with many a rosy cheeked child mopping sweat from a brow after carefully planting two rows of early season King Edwards, prior to picking a basketful of colourful sweet peas and plucking a dew drop encrusted rosebud to adorn Miss Grant's new lilac cardigan. What I am talking about is *beans and blotting paper*.

Contrary to every expectation, we were informed that you could grow a bean plant in a jam jar, simply by installing a suitable seed up against the inside wall of the jar, and securing it in place by pushing in a cylinder of blotting paper. Pour in half a glass of water, sit back and wait. Well, would you believe it? It worked - most of the time, and although it tried our patience a little in not springing up quite as high or as fast as that recorded by Jack and his giant chum, it was really quite interesting. Not only that, but we also got wet cotton wool and a few mustard and cress seeds, whose subsequent growth had the immeasurable benefit of being edible. So, as far as junior school science was concerned, that was just about it.

Predictably, of much greater interest and application for us tinies was the early inroads we made into the world of sport. Without exception, these were eagerly anticipated and much enjoyed. Like most others, our school arranged both cricket and football fixtures against neighbouring schools on Saturday mornings... yes, I did say *Saturday* mornings, which means that our long-suffering teachers were kind enough to give up part of their winter weekends to

A genuine 1950s photo of the mighty Highland Road Junior football team. On a clear-ish day, the team poses before covering itself in mud. Our popular games teacher looks really cheerful - considering it's Saturday.

allow a hoard of little boys to chase around a muddy public open space in search of an equally muddy football. As far as I was concerned, it was really a matter of just chasing the biggest group of kids in the hope that some errant boot might suddenly eject the ball in my direction, allowing me to at least get in an odd kick or two. All our after-school tactical lessons – e.g. *'try to kick it towards the other lot's goal for heaven's sake!'* - seemed to go out of the window, to be replaced by a junior version of mob rule that bore little resemblance to the beautiful game.

However, being in the team did mean that we got to wear a team shirt and team socks. These were owned by the school and by the look of them had been purchased immediately after the rules of Association Football had been agreed in the 19th century. To say they had an odd smell, and seemed to stand up on their own - and I'm talking about the shirts here – would be quite accurate, but nevertheless, we were proud to put them on, and to lace up our boots in eager anticipation of a crushing victory. Now when I say boots, the modern image of deftly crafted, ergonomically designed soft leather and multicoloured footwear probably springs to mind. Not so the 1950's. Yes, football boots were made of leather, but that's about where any similarity ends. These were enormous clod-hopping brown things which laced right up above your ankles, and had

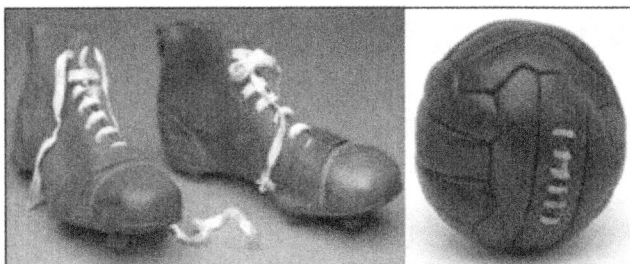

Well, this is what they should have looked like – but bear in mind all three were usually caked in mud and really HEAVY.

bulbous reinforced toe caps which allowed for no directional control whatsoever. You simply could not move your feet within what seemed like leather armour - but by way of compensation, you could not easily fall over, as the things were so stiff and heavy, as well as having at least six huge wooden studs nailed to the underside. These medieval looking additions meant two things: **a)** on hard ground you were at least another half inch taller and made a pleasing *clicketty –clack* sound when you walked across a hard surface, and thus were particularly important if there were any girls around, and **b)** in soft and muddy

And to prove the point, here's Robert Smith's left boot from the team photo.

conditions, we aspiring athletes became almost welded to the ground, and ended up either trapped or dragging around a couple of pounds of the finest corporation top-soil-and-occasional-dog-turd combo on each boot. Mind you, if you ever did get near the ball, you were lucky if it ever went very far when kicked, as it too was made of thick leather and weighed about ten times as much as the modern equivalent. What's more, it had a laced up section where the inflatable bladder went in, creating a knobbly and somewhat lethal raised section on the ball. Thus, if some super strong hooligan managed to get the weighty thing to leave the ground, going for a header was a risky business … you were as likely to end up with mild concussion as re-directing the ball towards the goal. Given all this, I suspect that our games lacked the cohesive fluidity and tactical finesse of the finely crafted modern game, but it did reinforce the view that, having been well-hard babies we were now becoming well-hard kids … and, of course, we were as pleased as punch to be involved.

Footy and cricket were a welcome distraction from the daily grind; so too, was rounders. This is, of course, a game in which both boys and girls can join, and was the only one suitable for our small, urban, walled-in playground. Bearing in mind class sizes were large, and we were always divided into two 20+ teams, there was a good deal of just standing about while you watched Susan Middlemist continually failing to connect the bat with the tennis ball so inaccurately thrown in her direction by Anthony Nabarro. Whereas the girls could spend their waiting time honing up their handstand skills, this hanging about for a good fifty per cent of the lesson was particularly hard on us little chaps as we had no other distraction.

Nevertheless, rounders was a game in which the whole class could enjoy, and thus allowed individuals to showcase their talents in front of all classmates. Clearly, the boys took such an opportunity to establish their pre-eminent place in the universal scheme of things, to reinforce their god-given destiny as hunter / provider / rounders champions. The inclusion of the girls was just tolerated as a necessary evil that had to be borne in order to at least get out of the classroom. Just occasionally, however, the boys would be surprised by the unexpected physical prowess of our female companions. One such was a lass called Theresa. Quieter than most of her contemporaries, she was a girl who looked radiantly confident in everything she did. She looked a very *together* sort of person - lithe, healthy and very, very fast. On the odd occasion that we had tag running races (rush across the playground, touch the opposite wall and return to your place) Theresa seemed to be there and back before the rest of us had barely screeched to an ungainly - often nose grazing - halt at the end of the first leg. She was good at everything like that, and could beat the boys at all athletic events, skimming with seemingly effortless ease over the canes, ropes and skittles which caused the rest of us so many high jump problems. When it came to that other preserve of the female athletic dominance – skipping – she was in a class of her own. Out-pacing all of her classmates she could run and skip *at the same time.* In defence of the boys, of course, I ought to point out that this was early evidence, even before the term had been invented, that boys cannot *multi-task* and thus were at a severe disadvantage when up against this particular challenge.

So, rounders, skipping, handstands, chucking grubby bean-bags about, tag races, tripping over ropes and canes suspended for that very purpose, was just about the extent of our outdoors physical education... but we loved it, and it did keep us together as a class, our unique not-so-little group of fairly grubby kids who actually got on pretty well together, both in and out of school. Despite the somewhat less than inspiring adventures of Dick and Dora *('See the dog. See Spot the dog. Leave my leg alone, Spot')* we usually enjoyed school and made good friends.

Why, it was during my time at Highland Road Juniors that I had my first proposal of marriage. Susan Watts was something of a rarity in that she always seemed neat and tidy, had a nice smile, and benefitted from the fact that her rather formidable mum ran a guest house round the corner from the school, and Susan was therefore in my book something of an heiress, potentially someone of substance. In addition, she was quite good at tables, was an early graduate on to *Wide Range Readers Book 4A*, and most impressively, always seemed to have brand new sandals, the rubber soles still white, the leather straps and toe piece brown and shiny, setting off to fine effect the whiteness of her freshly laundered ankle socks. I mean, with such provenance, such academic prowess, such economic potential, such clean footwear, how could a chap refuse? The proposal took place one Saturday morning when a group of us were playing in the lane behind her house,* and, in the short breathing space needed during a particularly energetic game of tag – which was fast descending into the giggling semi-riot that was Kiss Chase - she popped the question. Never being the type to quibble over the matrimonial etiquette of the girl asking the boy, I boldly cast aside such petty social conventions, and readily accepted. Our post-proposal celebrations lasted only a few minutes however, as I knew my mum wanted me home for dinner at 12.30 prompt, and I had a pressing engagement in the form of a marbles match booked with Geoffrey Hogg that very afternoon.

Speaking of marbles, the games played were a very popular and cheap source of entertainment. It now beggars belief that, given the amount of dog crap that all too often adorned public pavements and side roads in the 1950's, we played our games *in the gutter*. That more of us didn't die from the dreadful diseases we thus courted is a

---

* *Even as young as seven or eight we would often stray quite far from home to meet friends. This was seen as quite normal and in no way indicated a lack of parental care. It's just what kids of our generation did.*

matter of wonder. Perhaps, coming from an age where the very high standards of personal hygiene, and the modern means by which they are achieved were virtually unknown (and unavailable to the great majority of people) - made us more immune to such attacks.

Of more pressing concern was whether or not Geoffrey would be able to capture my favourite and newly purchased set of glass marbles, complete with the intriguing coloured centre, an enormous improvement on the old china ones - but still not quite as valued as that king of the marbles world, the ball bearing. These mechanical masterpieces could not be bought; they came from engineering workshops, or from dads who knew a bloke who had stripped a gearbox only to find re-assembly had left a few important parts left over. Regardless of the source and the means by which they came into your possession, ball bearings were very highly prized.

They were also an excellent commodity for bartering at school, where the game of marbles was just one of the many playground crazes that periodically swept through Highland Road Juniors, subject to a totally unpredictable and seemingly random timetable. As I recall, the only ones that were in any way date-predictable were conkers and the collection of used fireworks. The former speaks for itself, and despite having every intention of retaining a specially successful conker for the following year, it was inevitably lost/thrown away/eaten by the dog in the twelve months before the local horse chestnut trees cowered before the next autumnal assault. Thus we all started off the same, collecting our conkers, then trying to skewer them with the dividers from your older sibling's geometry set … just prior to visiting the newly accessible NHS emergency department to bandage up the wound caused by the said dividers. You then threaded your conker on to a piece of string and proudly took it to school... only to have it smashed to pieces in the first thirty seconds of playtime by Barry Thorne whose dad, if rumour was to be believed, had been baking his in the oven for a week… the conker that is, not his son. Used firework collection was really a matter of gathering together as many sticks from the tails of rockets as you could find, and then showing them to your mates at school. To be honest, this craze had limited appeal; once you had admired the recently scorched stick, perhaps compared its length with competing collectors, speculated on the colour of the display it had provided and made a few whooshing sounds to re-enact the exciting moment of ignition, there was not much to be done other than to use it as a rather poor substitute for a range of medieval weaponry.

Fag cards were keenly collected, and as their name suggests, were published by cigarette manufacturers and placed within packets in order to boost sales. The subjects were mainly footballers, and the collection of complete sets was the object. In the playground, however, we simply flicked them up against any convenient wall (with which Highland Road Juniors was uncommonly well blessed), and if your card overlapped your opponent's, then you claimed it as your own... the card that is, not the wall. This often resulted in unseemly disputes concerning what constituted an overlap and what didn't, and it wasn't unusual to see the ensuing disagreement settled by resorting to the use of the aforesaid medieval weapons.

A more peaceful – and perennial favourite – was the game of Five Stones. It is hard to believe that such imaginative and absorbing variations can be found in such basic equipment. Usually comprising just five little cubes of baked clay, the games were really a test of hand-eye coordination, and were of ancient derivation, having been played by none other than the Romans. Their equipment differed only in the sense that they called the game *Knucklebones,* hopefully coming from animals rather than being ex-parts of the less than fortunate conquered. I assume the participants in those far off times were still children; one can hardly picture J. Caesar Esq. settling down to a quick game of *Threesies* when there was so much invading to do, so many murders to arrange. Well, whoever they were, they did a good job in passing down through the generations a game that has really stood the test of time. The dexterity shown by some of our classmates and the endless permutations of the game were a source of delight. Well I can remember the tension building as an opponent neared the final *fivesies* round, a tricky manoeuvre requiring hands the size of shovels... only to hear the clanging of the playground bell right in the middle of the final throw. Since this signal required us all to shut up and stand up (*straight!*), to the keen competitors it was either a source of huge frustration or total relief, depending on whose turn it was. Hey ho... and so back to ye olde classroom, and the further delights of our crazy imperial measures or whatever else the lovely Miss Grant had lined up for us.

I've touched upon our forays into the world of creativity via the artistic prowess shown in our efforts at rafia weaving, but I have to say that there were at least two more ways in which Highland Road Juniors sought to reveal the budding Rembrandts among us. The first was powder paint. As its name implies, this medium came in a variety of gaily coloured powders which, with a little water added, transformed itself into a very easily applied emulsion, quite suited to the largely untrained and misguided efforts of young kids. Once equipped with a rather tatty old paintbrush and a sheet of kitchen paper, the aim was to dash off a couple of half decent portraits before a pressing game of kiss chase at playtime. Again, the theory somewhat outdid the practice, and I was not the only one who found that the powder paint itself had a tendency to gather in unwieldy blobs, whilst the rest of the mixture gave only the faintest watery hint of the intended colour. Thus my efforts at least, seemed to lack that certain something.... well colour for a start, and unless you were attracted to a portrait of someone who appeared to be suffering from acute anaemia but at the same time was irregularly pebble-dashed, the outcome was not always quite as envisaged.

But then, there was always papier maché. Now this stuff at least allowed a high degree of personal physical engagement – indeed, the term '*getting stuck in*' could have been phrased for that very purpose. In essence, modelling with this medium involved soaking strips of newspaper in stuff like wallpaper paste, then layering the result all together to create some kind of recognisable object. The final stage was to sit back, relax, and wait for about a fortnight for it to dry hard, prior to finishing the job with a coat of paint. I suspect you can visualise the atmosphere of barely contained mayhem that such a process unleashed: forty plus eight year old kids all tearing up newspaper and then immersing the strips in a bucket of gluey stuff prior to slapping it on to something or other to create a magnificent model of Nelson's column or an Egyptian pyramid. This was not a lesson undertaken lightly. If Miss Grant had taken a slug or two of something strong before embarking on such a risky enterprise, I for one wouldn't have blamed her. Nevertheless, and contrary to all expectations, a few talented children did produce some stuff that was as near as dammit, recognisable. The most advanced group was given an inflated balloon each, and around which the papier mache strips were layered. Once it had dried, the balloon was deflated, leaving the creative child genius with a hollow papier maché sphere which could become … well, anything you like, provided of course, it was spherical. Some children though, were too impatient, and popped the balloon before its newly acquired jacket of sticky newspaper had hardened… and the result? Well, it was the first time I had come across the term '*implosion*'. Never mind. You could always screw up the resulting mess and try lobbing it into the classroom waste paper basket… just a shame the latter was *yet again* filled with pencil shavings.

And what about junior school music in the fifties? Well, I suppose we did have some, but it was mainly of the '*let's join in with nice man on the radio*' type. True, we did have a few instruments, but not nearly enough for one each. Thus, if you weren't the lucky recipient of a warped tambourine, a tin full of noisy beads, or a triangle that seemed to have lost its little metal hammer, then all you were left with was the requirement to clap your hands and sing.

I have to say however, that it is to Miss Grant's eternal credit that as well as singing and percussion work, she did her best to teach us a bit about music theory. To do this she had a miniature tonic sol-fa 'staircase' which she stood on her desk, and as you might expect it went from bottom DOH all the way through the octave to top DOH. Having started us off at one of the steps she would then tap her little conductor's baton up and down the staircase, and we had to sing the correct notes. Were we enthralled by such an activity? Did it set us on the road to musical stardom? Well, probably not, but it was a lot better than *pounds and ounces, stones and hundredweights*, believe me. What we didn't then know, of course, was that our intimate knowledge of the tonic sol-fa put us in a truly advantageous position when, a mere decade or so later, the *Sound of Music* came out, and we *already knew* the essential words of one of its most famous songs.

But that was not all; in a further attempt to provide a bit of musical culture in her class, Miss Grant also tried to instil in us some basic understanding of musical notation. Now I have to say, this was a bold step, but well-meant. We were presented with four different types of notes – the basic golf club shaped **crotchet**, the double golf club *joined at the top* **quaver**, and the *golf club with a hole in it* **minim** ... and another one with a dot after it whose name always escaped me. Now these, we were told, showed just how long a musical note should last. She then drew a sprinkling of them on the blackboard* and we were required to clap out the rhythm thus recorded to the correct time.

* *All classrooms at this time – and for the next fifty years – were equipped with a chalk board, always called a 'blackboard'. It also came with a wooden blackboard rubber, handy for secondary school teachers to throw at miscreant pupils. Really.*

Now when I say clap, this had to be done in a very precise way: digit and second finger only, brought smartly down in the cupped other hand. Along with this fairly straightforward interpretation, we had also to chant **Ta.** So a bar's worth of crotchets would require four claps accompanied by the mantra **Ta, Ta, Ta ,Ta** . Not going too fast for you am I? Despite the fact that the humourists in the class were inclined to mutter *'Oh, you going somewhere then?'* at the conclusion of this brief performance, it says something for the dear lady's determination that we progressed to the other notes. Now the quaver, we were told, was twice as quick as the dear old crotchet, so it had to be digitally represented by a double clap, and accompanied by a rather more lively **Ta-Tay.** So a common bar's worth might now become **Ta, Ta, Ta-Tay, Ta** in a *'One, two, three-four, five'* fish alive type scenario.

And that's where it should have stopped. But no, flushed with her success, dear Miss Grant persisted in extending our repertoire into the dizzy realms of the minim – and riskier still, the *minim with a dot after it.* Bad news. You see, the minim is double the length of a crotchet…but you can't clap twice, because that would just sound like **two crotchets** wouldn't it? So, the answer was to make us little kids verbally interpret the minim as **Ta-aah.** But how do you clap an **aah** for heaven's sake? Well, what you do is this: one tap for the **Ta** bit, but then you remove your fingers from your cupped other hand, and in a rather languid manner, move your paired fingers in a graceful arc somewhat similar to the Queen Mother waving to the adoring crowds at Buckingham palace. Can you imagine it? And there was, unbelievably, worse to come. Evidently, the *minim with a dot after it* requires THREE beats… and therefore becomes – and I kid you not – **Ta-aah-aah.** And of course, the physical equivalent was to tap once, and then extend your paired fingers for **two** gentle waves to the side, as if you were stroking two cats: one sat next door and the other next door-but-one. In a crowded classroom, you can imagine the mayhem this caused. Dotted minims gave you the perfect excuse to reach across to the kid sitting next door but one, and give him a quick flick round the ear, and to wipe the nose of your next door neighbour all in one supremely fluid musical moment, accompanied by the angelic chant of *Ta-aah-aah.* And as if this was not a problem enough, there was always going to be an issue with left-handed kids, and being one of these myself, I speak from bitter experience. You see, while most of the class were ta-aah-aahing away like crazy to the right, me and a few others of the sinister persuasion were doing it to the left. In this way, the musical interpretation of the dotted minim led inevitably to an unseemly and often quite violent clash, occasionally requiring the said protagonists to reflect upon their wrong-doing outside the classroom door with their noses pressed firmly against the wall. Poor Miss Grant … and so much for our artistic and creative experience. Thus, and with a sigh of resignation, let us once more return to the world of academia.

Now, the keen observer will have noted that I have been a little light on references to the second of the Three R's – namely *writing*. This is probably because many of us did as little of this as possible, and anyway yours truly spent most of these lessons industriously pursuing my low level pencil sharpening/dreamy speculation hobby. However, when I did drag myself reluctantly away from the waste paper basket, I seem to remember ... well, not much about writing, if truth be told. But I suppose we must have done a fair amount of copying stuff, and been told to write a story or two, but nothing really comes to mind. That many of us were easily distracted was putting it mildly, but I was impressed by the efforts of some of the girls, who seemed so much better at writing than we chaps. The only literary milestone I do recall was a very important occasion indeed – *the day we got the ink.*

Considering its importance, I suppose you could call it a *red letter* day, but seeing the mess many of us made, perhaps a *blue/black* day would be more appropriate. All school desks in those days had a lid, and beyond this a groove to accommodate pencils, and at the end of this, close to the far right hand corner, a hole. For little kids this was an open invitation to roll marbles, dried peas, screwed up milk bottle tops – in fact anything spherical – along the groove and down the hole. But as we got older, a little china pot was put in the hole and filled with ink. Liquid ink. From a large jug. Stuff that spilled really easily, and stained even more easily. So it must have been with a fair degree of trepidation that our valiant teacher poured it out into our tiny pots, gave out the pens, and no doubt offered up a swift prayer.

As regards the pen, I expect you have in mind a shiny, brightly coloured plastic job, with at very least, a nice chrome piece screwed to the top to enable you to clip the whole assembly neatly into your top pocket. Forget it. Our school pens were just a piece of wooden dowel with a metal nib pushed on to the end. Unlike the much admired fountain pens produced by the *Platignum* company, they had no in-built reservoir of ink – hence the ink wells. Now, the nibs we were given were always of the scratchiest type, and didn't respond well to the heavy handed use we budding writers put them to. The end bit either separated and let far too much ink through, or more likely, took on the appearance of someone crossing their legs, with one bit firmly lodged beneath the other. So, the inexperienced writer would usually end up with blobs of ink all over the place, or with a hole in the paper resulting from an over enthusiastic application of a crossed nib. Some connoisseurs of the art even managed to combine the two problems, and ended up with a pleasing spatter design which could be expertly smudged to provide a design worthy of a prize entry for modern art.

To say our first step into the world where the third R (Rubbing Out) became an inevitable casualty was, to say the least, not without its challenges. Nevertheless, I suppose we must have eventually learned how to commit pen to paper without too much in the way of

+  +  = *TATE*

(Highly Commended)

spillage; some kids even got promoted to 'ink monitor', this enviable post being akin to the privileges granted to a trusty prison inmate and even outranked such lofty positions as beanbag or milk monitor. I have no recollection of aspiring to – let alone achieving - such giddy heights, and found the whole process a bit of a bind. What's more, it occurred to me that the ink wells were sited for the benefit and convenience of *right handed kids* and that we lefties were therefore at a severe disadvantage. I was enraged, and decided there and then to dash off a letter to my MP demanding Equal Opportunities, universal recognition of 'Left Rights', and generous compensation for the social and emotional damage inflicted by Highland Road Juniors, not to mention Repetitive Strain Injury sustained when reaching right across the desk every five seconds. And then there was the emotional damage caused by the sneering disapproval of the right handed and thus unfairly privileged non-sinister kids. So a sharply worded letter was required. Except, of course, this was the 1950's, and my writing was crap.

And I really needed to pull my socks up, for time, as they say, was moving on, and the threat represented by moving to secondary school was a growing cloud on the horizon. I say threat because, in those days, the move to secondary really was 'make or break'. The 1944 Education Act dictated that all children in their final year at Primary school would sit the Eleven Plus examination and the result would determine whether they went to a selective grammar school, or a non-selective secondary modern school. The fear that this exam engendered in even the bravest and most confident little soul was quite real, because the public perception at that time was quite unequivocal – the grammar school route meant success, the other... well ... goodness knows.

So all of a sudden, we were actually working a darned sight harder, the old pen nibs flying around the page, seven nines being as near as dammit sixty three every time, *Janet and John* sent packing (*'...see the hard questions. Run John, run!'*) not to mention those mysterious verbal reasoning questions of the type: '*tree is to root as dinosaur is to XXXXX*' etc. put to the test.

The pressure from siblings was also quite acute, the more so because one of our playground walls was the physical boundary between us and Southsea Secondary Modern School for Boys - and the sounds permeating through the wall only served to add to the scary stories spread by classmates such as:

'*When you goes to the Modern, you gets barred* the first day, then they takes you to the bike sheds and beats you up'*. Such warnings were generally taken as being gospel, for was it not true that all the Sec Mod kids were thugs, just doing their apprenticeship for the criminal world beyond? And, of course, they were all BIG BOYS to whom *barring* was a way of life! We all listened with wide-eyed incredulity, if not complete belief - despite the fact that many of us knew some BIG BOYS at that school, and they actually seemed quite nice, and not at all the type to engage in random acts of barbarity.

Nevertheless, the Eleven Plus struck fear into our hearts, and when we gave incorrect answers to likely questions set by anxious parents

---

* *This procedure allegedly involved putting a new kid's arms through the railings that surrounded the school and then pulling the limbs in question back through the next space, thereby squeezing the bar in the elbow joints. No one I knew ever saw it happen. It would have been a lot easier just to have stuck a kid's head through the bars. Never saw any of that, either.*

at home, it caused them palpitations of an extreme nature. Bear in mind that there was no homework for junior aged children in those days, but that didn't stop my mum from expecting me to be able to spell stuff like **grammar** and **school** and **success** (a choice more to do with subliminal associations than practical use I suspect).Thus she had the not unreasonable expectation that her son and heir, after four years at Highland Road Juniors, might just remember that, more often than not, seven eights *did* come to fifty six, and that '*swan* is to *bird* as *ant* is to **insect** you idiot!' Such domestic pressure inevitably provided yet another reason to dawdle on the way home and attributing the delay to a semi final marbles match with Geoffrey Hogg, *'now playing in a gutter near you.'*

So, the carefree days of perfecting the shoulder stand, of gazing out of the window to catch a glimpse of other kids lining up for rounders, of spending undue amounts of time on the way back from pencil sharpening to cast an eye over the jam jar containing dusty rosehips on the Nature Table, of having a quick look in the cupboard to see if last week's progress with the old rafia teapot/place mat was as colourful as you remembered, were fast drawing to a close.

Eleven Plus results day was fearfully anticipated. It was well known that fat envelopes meant success, thin envelopes meant failure. The misery of the children to whom the latter applied was awful to see, and for them almost impossible to bear amidst the glee of their more successful classmates. I kid you not. The remaining junior school time between results day and the end of term was for some a time of anguish, for others triumphalism, and for more than a few, disbelief. That there was an abrupt and irreversible change in our social cohesion as a class was undeniable.

And yet, looking back on those days of dusty school rooms, scruffy books, *Dick and Dora,* powder paint, sugar paper, rafia and scratchy pen nibs, there was a sense of well-being. Sure, the curriculum was very narrow by modern standards and the physical resources available at the school meagre indeed... but it was no different from the vast majority of other schools – and anyway, it was *our* Highland Road: the teachers were kind, they were patient, they were generous, and we were pleased to be there in our time. In addition, I suspect that the freedom we all enjoyed in terms of who we played with and, especially *where* we played at weekends and after school, depended a lot more on liberty and open choice than upon those issues which constrain children these days.

And suddenly, there it was: our last day as Juniors. That there were no school parties to celebrate the occasion shouldn't come as any surprise. And as regards discos - well, they hadn't been invented... and Proms? They were pathways along the seafront weren't they? That didn't meant to say that we weren't appreciative of our primary school years and of the friends and teachers we had met there, but this was the fifties and a big, nervously anticipated future awaited. I am sure that it was a comfort for many of us that there would be a good degree of continuity, in that many pals would be together again in September, for it was apparent that loads of kids had passed the Eleven Plus in 1958. Even I scraped through, and was pleased to find that plenty of my mates would be at the new school after the much anticipated long summer holiday.

It's extraordinary that few of us little chaps paused to consider that we would be moving on without the immediate company of the fair sex. Susan Watts and I never did get married. Despite our commitment to each other when we were both aged eight, we never over-publicised our matrimonial plans... in fact I am not at all sure either of us ever spoke of it again. True, every time I passed Mrs. Watts' well presented guesthouse, a little glow of anticipated inherited wealth would warm my heart, and I was always pleased to note the '*No Vacancies*' sign in the window, indicating that business was brisk, and thus the chance of my retiring to a life of consummate ease and indolence was that much greater.

I think quite a few of us bought our teachers a leaving gift. I was keen to offer Miss Grant my lately completed rafia teapot mat in recognition of my appreciation of her knees, if nothing else. However my mum vetoed the idea on the rather hurtful grounds that Miss Grant was probably 'sick of the sight of the wretched thing'. *'Not nearly as sick of it as me'* I mused, but then brightened at the thought that Christmas was only four months away, and careful storage of the masterpiece would provide me with a first class hand-crafted gift for my nearest and dearest at the festive season.

At the end of the summer term, it was with an outwardly carefree whoop and yell that we poured forth out of the Highland Road Junior School gate for the last time. I say 'outwardly' because I have no doubt we were all apprehensive as to what it was going to be like *up the grammar* in September. After all, weren't there loads of BIG BOYS up there too? And did the wearing of a blazer and a cap *really* preclude them from similar acts of outrageous and unprovoked terrorism on lowly first years as had been rumoured at the local Sec Mod? I guess we were all relying on a mental image of smartly dressed boys walking sedately around their playground deeply absorbed in a small book of poetry, or perhaps entering into a lively, but measured and respectful philosophical debate on the how many angels could reasonably be accommodated on the head of a pin... or perhaps just sneaking off for a crafty fag round the back of the bike sheds. Whatever. As to the immediate future, we were able to duck under the parapet of a five week summer holiday, pretending for a while that school did not exist and indulging ourselves in the almost limitless freedom that being successfully post Eleven Plus brought.

Looking back, the make or break nature of the exam seems not only cruel but also incredibly wasteful. It was quite apparent that some children who should have passed didn't, and vice-versa. There seemed to be no mechanism for children who performed badly on the day, or for the many thousands who were genuine late developers.

The 1944 Education Act enforced a rigid discipline of social engineering: if you passed, you were academic... if you failed you were not, and therefore destined for lower positions in later life. It seems brutal. It *was* brutal. It condemned some children to a lack of choice and opportunity. Furthermore, the courses offered in Secondary Modern schools did, for the most part, reflect entirely that limited vision of the likely outcomes for the children they taught. If ever there was a self-fulfilling prophecy, this was it. Thus, the parting of the secondary school ways was reinforced by what you studied. Although much was made by those who still had pretensions of transferring to a grammar school two years later – the so called Thirteen Plus – I don't think I ever came across anyone who had actually done it.

But what I did come across in later years, was a quite substantial group of young people who, despite going down the Sec Mod path had, by sheer determination and extraordinary application - and perhaps with the help and support of sympathetic teachers who recognised individual talents - achieved notable academic success. And what a struggle it must have been, and what tortuous paths they had been forced to take to convert their RSA Certificates* into something more meaningful. Also of note, is the fact that at the end of the 1950's, it was still possible for children to leave school at the age of fifteen and I remember a few local kids who, dissatisfied with their lot at school, did just that.

It would be unfair and incorrect to imply that Secondary Moderns were schools that only had children who regarded themselves as failures. Clearly, many did benefit from their time there, and went on

* *Some Secondary Modern children were awarded Royal Society of Arts certificates. These helped in providing a focus but they lacked the clout of O Level GCEs taken by children at selective schools. By 1965, RSAs had been replaced by CSEs: the Certificate of Secondary Education. Later still, with the coming of Comprehensive schools, CSEs and GCEs were combined to become the GCSEs we still have today.*

to enjoy the world of work happily and successfully. It just seems such a shame that the straight jacket of the curriculum taught, and of the expectations – or lack of them – that such courses imposed, meant that many a talent may have never had the chance to flourish. Heavy stuff, but rather like the way in which the immediate the post-war government set about providing for disabled people, this was just another blunt instrument... and with hindsight, it is easy to be critical. In doing so, however, it is really necessary to set such developments in context, and thus to give full consideration to the sort of educational experience and opportunity available *before* the war. Just a brief study of the inconsistent and seemingly haphazard way schools for the vast majority of ordinary children were organised in the 1930s, makes the 1944 Education Act seem a great step forward. And I suppose in some ways it was: just a pity that it left Ann Johnson in tears, and Dave Wheatley saying that he didn't care, and that his dad would get him a job anyway, and he hoped we'd all miss the bus on our first day at the grammar and get the cane. So there.

Truth is, it didn't need Dave to scare the life out of me; wearing the new uniform was one thing; catching two buses with an awkward change in the middle to a school over three miles from home was quite another. Always keen to find some sand in which to bury my head, it was a good job I didn't have to think about it until September! In the meantime, there was the seashore, Auntie M's beach hut, the old woolly bathing trunks, stones to throw and girls to impress down the park, plus of course, keeping a weather eye out on how the bookings were going throughout Mrs. Watts' busy summer season.

7   In Sickness and in ... Bed

To be honest, for the majority of the time, I used to quite enjoy being ill. For a start, I was lucky enough not to catch anything much beyond the normal childhood illnesses of chickenpox, measles, mumps, colds, flu, unidentified tummy pains and, of equal importance, that well-known childhood illness - swinging the lead.

That being said, you have to bear in mind that in the 1950's, there weren't nearly so many diseases or conditions to choose from. Such exotic things as Aspergers Syndrome, Dyslexia, Attention Deficit Hyperactive Disorder and Repetitive Strain Injury were as yet totally unknown ... and as a result, we didn't get them. So, quite obviously, we were a lot healthier. As far as I am aware, cholesterol had not been discovered, and so we didn't need to bother about 'good' or 'bad' extremes of the substance; as far as I can remember, we didn't even have a cholesterol that was simply 'mildly offensive'. So, in our ignorance of the whole range of illnesses we were missing out on, we just got on with occasionally feeling poorly.

For me, being ill meant one thing: Lucozade! The unvaried sickness routine in our house comprised my mother telling me I was not very well, and then sticking a thermometer under my tongue (*'don't bite on it, you'll get glass in your mouth and mercury in your tummy - and it's poisonous!'*) Great start there then: a possibly lethal implement inserted in my body, and I've not yet even laid my fevered brow on the nearest pillow.

The next part of the routine was to be sent back to bed while my mother rushed round to the local chemist's shop to get all that was needed for her ailing offspring, chief amongst which as far as I was concerned, was the aforementioned fizzy drink. Now, you have to understand that in the 50's, fizzy drinks for most kids were still something of a rare luxury, so the arrival on the bedside table of a brand new bottle, *all for me*, was a moment to be relished, and its opening keenly anticipated. That it was a medicine, and therefore good for me was beyond doubt as it was wrapped in yellow cellophane which squeaked when you held it, and the bottle had a raised dimple design on it, which put the product in a class of its own when it came to restoring an ailing, but quite excited child. Added to this was the extra attention I was getting: my mum would re-make the bed, while I stood looking dramatically pale and wan on the cold lino, before tucking me in. This she seemed to do with unnecessary relish - so much so that I could hardly move, and it's just lucky that I suffered from no respiratory complaints, as I might have expired there and then through lack of oxygen.

All things considered, however, it was at this point that the luxury of being ill and in bed kicked in. With the lethal thermometer firmly back in the bathroom cabinet, the Lucozade within easy reach and the warmth of the huge pile of bedclothes seeping through, the sounds of the day started to intrude, chief amongst which was the sound of the *other kids going to school!* I could even hear the playground in the distance, and could picture exactly what was going on. This always produced a feeling of smug security and comfort especially as in the next few minutes, all my classmates would all be sat cross-legged on the dusty hall floor mouthing the words of '*He Who Would Valiant Be*' before filing off to get to grips with stones, pounds and hundredweights, not to mention the latest thrilling episode in the long-running saga of *Dick and Dora*, or the equally dopey *Janet and John* (*John is ill today. See the spots! Run Janet, run!*).

Of course, sometimes things were a little more serious, and rather than cart me off to the local surgery, my mum would call for the doctor to come on a home visit. In the 50's this was a common practice... it was as if, having been granted the luxury of a National Health Service in 1948, everyone wanted to try out its bountiful and generous services, and these included a high proportion of home visits by your local GP. Now, this may seem an excellent thing, but there was a slight downside to it as far as we sickly kids were concerned. Doctors were regarded by everyone with a respect which bordered on hero worship, and so when a visit was about to take place, your house, home and patient had to be displayed in the very best light. So, my mum would spend the intervening time rushing round the house making sure that the doctor's route to my sickbed was clean, tidy, free of any speck of dust, and that I was looking my best... hair brushed, teeth cleaned, pyjamas pressed, any accidental gaseous emissions wafted out of the window, Lucozade bottle favourably positioned and so on. Dr. Dixon, the epitome of the new, efficient and totally free NHS would arrive in his shiny Ford Consul (one of the first cars I had seen that was not black, and with chrome that still shone), and would breeze into our house in businesslike fashion, stethoscope, black doctor's bag and trendy ginger moustache all ready and brimming with positive diagnostic anticipation. Usually his examination would take but a few moments and would generally include the placing of a cold stethoscope on my hitherto warm chest, being asked to say 'aaaah', after trying not to be sick when what appeared to be a length of timber was stuffed half way down my throat, and offering my wrist so that my pulse could be taken. It is quite possible that the good doctor might have been a bit disappointed with me, as I never (and thankfully) seemed to have anything of particular note wrong with me, but that didn't stop him from prescribing – or even whipping out from the depths of his bag - a bottle of medicine. This was always **a)** pink **b)** horrible and **c)** sealed shut with a tiny cork that was really hard to get back in; it may have been, in fact, a punishment meted out to those he considered to be *wasting his bloody time*, as he always seemed to be in a rush to get out, even when tempted by my mother's offer of a cup of Nescafe and a biscuit from the plate of *Petit Beurre* artfully displayed between the Lucozade and the Allenbury's Blackcurrant Pastilles and specially brought out for the occasion. Still, it was an exceptional service, and proof positive that the NHS was, like an increasing number of its patients, alive and well.

And much needed. The state of the nation's health prior to its introduction was pretty grim, and there is plenty of evidence to support this view. Take for example, archive footage of the soldiers evacuated from Dunkirk in 1940. Film of the troops cheerily giving thumbs up signs and waving from crowded carriage windows showed the appalling state of dental hygiene – or lack of it. Everywhere, there was clear evidence that many people put up with ill health simply because they could not afford appropriate treatment. It is therefore unsurprising that the NHS was so heavily utilised. Free Doctors, free medicine, free hospitals, free dentistry, free glasses.... what more could you want?*

But, of course, such philosophical considerations did not really impinge upon us kids. All we knew was that doctors drove nice cars, smelt of antiseptic and, besides shoving a piece of wood down your throat and giving you nasty stuff to drink, were really nice people. Furthermore their visit would often recommend an extended period of staying home from school. Such a delightful prospect, which even with my mum's predilection for making beef tea and serving up boiled white fish in a pallid and frankly unappetising greyish sauce, made any slight suffering or temporary discomfort well worthwhile.

Another side benefit was the opportunity to also brush up on your acting skills. This usually occurred when your doting parent, having observed your obvious progress and appearance, would move in the direction of suggesting that an earlier than anticipated return to

* *Before we get totally carried away with all this apparent state sponsored largesse, it should be borne in mind that the new NHS was free for all 'at the point of need'. To meet the cost, those in employment paid a National Insurance levy which was usually deducted from weekly wages or monthly salary.*

school was on the cards. At such a juncture, hearing the approaching parent hammering up the stairs was a moment to shove the comic under the bed clothes, shimmy down a bit so that the eiderdown came up to your chin, and take on a suitably pallid, listless and clearly-in-need-of-further-bedrest attitude. To seal the deal, I found that a slightly husky voice added to the scene's authenticity, and making rather more than was necessary when reaching for a sip of Lucozade usually made the outcome pretty much a cert. The only slight fly in the ointment was that at that point, she might reach for the trusty thermometer again to see if indeed the beloved offspring really was still a bit poorly, or was in fact hamming it up to the level of an Oscar nomination.

Now, I have a problem with thermometers; in addition to being quite delicate and filled with poisonous stuff as mentioned earlier, they are almost impossible to read, and generally require at least a half an hour of standing by the window and twizzling the spindly glass number round and around in the vain hope of seeing just where the hell the mercury has got to. And even then, the numbers you got didn't make any sense. In those days, of course, we only had Fahrenheit degrees, and even as a tiny, I was assured that my temperature should be 98.4 degrees. I always thought that seemed rather a lot, but then reflected that Fahrenheit degree numbers were utterly bonkers anyway. I'm pretty certain that the good Mr. Fahrenheit was a pleasant enough bloke, but to be honest, the numbers he gave to the top and the bottom water temperatures (boiling and freezing) would even have had *Eric the Length* and *Ethelred the Cubit Maker* speechless with admiration. I mean, come on! The freezing point of water? At the risk of me approving something continental, wouldn't '**0**' be a fairly good choice? But oh no! Mr. Fahrenheit chose *32,* that's what! Yes! *Thirty bleedin' two!* And what's more, after what one may assume to be a fairly lengthy interval during which I suspect he may have taken the opportunity to knock back another pint or two of something intoxicating, he came up with the boiling point of water at a truly staggering **212** degrees.

Well, no one likes a joke more than me, but I have to say that the intervention of Mr. F and his crazy temperatures were often what made the difference between me spending another few days luxuriating in the comfort of my own bedroom with this week's copy of *The Beano* for company, or being turfed out back to the harsh realities of the eight times table. What's more, I'd have to resume feigning a genuine fascination with *Dick and Dora* as well as competing with classmates over who had the hardest conker. So all in all, having extra days off won the argument hands down.

There were, however, downsides to such a strategy; even such an unenthusiastic student as me would recognise that having so much time off school would put one yet further behind, and the odd snatch of shouted conversation caught from a couple of my fellow eight year old classmates on their way home after a hard day grappling with the world of academia might set me wondering... e.g. *'... yes but do you really think the introduction of the subjunctive clause merited such a deep analysis in Troilus and Cressida? No? Neither did I. Give us a go with your yo-yo....'* Better just bury my head in the sand, reach for the comic and see if there were any Allenbury's left in the tin.

Sometimes, of course, we were genuinely really pretty ill, and the public at large was fearful of an outbreak of, for example, scarlet fever or serious diseases such as diphtheria. Above all at that time, was the threat of polio. This appalling disease seemed to affect youngsters in particular, and in the 1950's there was no effective remedy. Children were sometimes so incapacitated that they had to be put into an 'iron lung' to enable them to breathe. This fearsome contraption enclosed the body right up to the neck and though no doubt, it saved many lives, the machine was a terrifying prospect. As the decade progressed, intensive work notably in the USA, brought the first of the vaccines, and thereafter the fear of this terrible complaint started to diminish.

On reflection, the application of statistics puts the disease into perspective; polio certainly killed a lot of people, but not nearly as many as, say, influenza. Nevertheless, it was still feared a great deal more than its common counterpart. There was a feeling I suppose, that lots of people got the flu, and most recovered...probably a better bet than getting something much rarer but which appeared to kill at random. All heavy stuff, but it made us all the more accepting of the fact that if a vaccine was available, you had it regardless. Many of these, such as the one for smallpox, were administered at school. At Highland Road Juniors we were only told a few minutes before the dreaded application of the needle – presumably because we were more or less a captive audience, and couldn't easily escape even to the relative safety of the toilet block at such short notice. So we would line up at the bottom of the Headmistress's staircase, and creep up one step at a time... all the time watching the kids who had already been done coming down. That some were in tears didn't help, and neither did some of the comments from the more sadistically minded *'It's a blooming great needle, big as a drain pipe'* or *'Margaret Simpson has fainted – 'spec she's already dead!'* etc. etc. Nearing the top of the twisting staircase brought you within range of the antiseptic/disinfectant tainted aroma that always seemed to accompany medical people – so different from the familiar smell of wet exercise books and dust that wafted around our venerable and very aloof headmistress, Miss Porter. The only saving grace was that she always had a big and colourful sweetie jar into which we were invited to plunge our hands to collect *'just one mind'* of the sticky contents on completion of any painful procedure. So, finally, there we were, next in line for the whispered assurance from the rather stern lady with the needle skilfully concealed behind her back who purred *'just a little scratch'* a microsecond before a massive stinging and burning sensation shot through your arm, and you had to use your one remaining good hand to dash away the tears so that you could see if Geoffrey Robinson and co had left any of the red sweets behind, greedy gits. Most kids, of course, would have had no trouble picking out the red one on any occasion, tears or not, and this was because the newly created NHS was also pretty keen to get to grips with the nation's eyesight. As a result, NHS glasses were suddenly *everywhere*. Picture the thin framed Harry Potter type articles, but make them smaller, rounder, more flimsy and with spindly metal arms that ended in a flexible curvy bit that went over your ear ... and you have it. Oh, and add a thin layer of snot and sticky finger prints which adorned *every* pair of children's NHS glasses that I ever saw. That these kids ever managed to find *anything* was a veritable source of wonder especially as these were the days of the **'lazy eye'**.

Now quite why so many children's eyes had given up taking regular exercise and keeping themselves in tip-top condition, I have no idea. As it was normally only one eye of each pair, we can only assume that one of the little blighters had been taking it easy and letting the other do all the hard focussing stuff while putting its feet up and not concentrating on anything much beyond the end of the shared nose. However, these little toe-rags got their come-uppance with the new NHS, oh yes. Once confronted with the old reading chart, the game was up. As a result many children were informed that they had to get their lazy eye up to standard, to get this optical miscreant to do some of the work, to redress the balance. And the treatment? Well, to achieve this desired aim, the good eye, the conscientious, hard working, diligent and taken-for-a-ride eye would get a justly deserved compensatory rest. As a result, NHS specs were provided with the lens in front of the good eye covered over with white (i.e. opaque) sticky tape. It must have come as quite a shock to many a lazy eye, happily idling its time away behind the cover of the adjacent bridge of your nose, to suddenly find out that the game was up! It was now *its* turn to spot *everything*! Goody two-shoes was on holiday, and wouldn't be offering any help at all until Mr. Lazy came up to scratch and promised to forego its idle ways, and put in a full day's looking!

Thus children blessed with this diagnosis were condemned to wearing a blank white patch taped over half of their NHS spectacles. As a look, it wasn't great, and bear in mind that the lazy eye, lulled by perhaps several years of putting its feet up, was really not up to speed with the current requirements of the job, and so there was a lot of blundering about to start with, normally accompanied by the cries of *'No, I'm over here Barr*y'. Some children thus treated showed commendable spirit by fighting back against the inevitable taunts of *'Hey Nelson – seen any ships lately?'* etc., and by far the best way to do this was to draw an eye on the white tape. This resulted in a rather off-putting and frankly quite scary monocular and unblinking mad stare – made all the more weird as it was entirely unsynchronised with its partner lazy eye, which was of course wandering about all over the place in its vain search to see something...anything!

I suspect that the birth of the NHS led to a rush of enthusiasm to detect and treat anything within reach, and the ophthalmologists were as keen as mustard to do their bit. Not being one to miss out when there was something going free, my mum took me to the opticians to have an eye check as one of my eyes seemed to ache a lot. I put this down to too much mental arithmetic at school, but she would have none of it. So in we went – and hey presto! I was diagnosed as having a 'slight squint' in my right eye, and was duly prescribed some new bendy NHS glasses. I was mortified. A squint? A ruddy squint?? You must be joking. The likes of the wonderful Ben Turpin had a squint – surely I didn't look like that, did I? Once we got home, I shot off to the bathroom and examined my eyes in the mirror. Nothing obvious there... when I looked straight ahead, there was no particular sensation of the right hand side of my nose appearing in the picture. ... so it was obviously quite a sneaky sort of squint, that needed to be caught in the act. As a result, I tried looking to the left, then all of a sudden, when my squinty right eye was least expecting it, looking straight ahead in an attempt to catch the errant optic guiltily sliding into place a second or two late. Well, that didn't work. And then it struck me: if lots of kids had a *lazy* eye, then perhaps my condition was a *suspicious* eye! Not sure of what its partner eye was up to on the other side of my nose, it was continually trying to check up on its competitor's progress. Taking this diagnosis a stage further, it occurred to me that those eyes that wandered off course on the opposite direction, like Marty Feldman's, were neither lazy nor suspicious – they were just plain *bored;* being fed up with the general field of vision right in front, they were inclined to wander off to see if there was something more interesting off to the side. And who could blame them?

Now that's what I call a squint. The great Ben Turpin at his best.

So there we had it: the new NHS had inadvertently provided me with the incentive to scientifically analyse a whole new area of ocular diagnosis: eyes could be *normal*, *lazy*, *suspicious* or *bored*. So, I didn't need glasses – all I needed was to reassure my right eye that it was OK, that lefty was in no way better and really wasn't being given the best views ... and if that didn't work, I could simply resort to telling it to *just stop being so paranoid!*

But if I had sorted out my supposed eyesight problem, I definitely had made no progress at all with dentistry. To all of us kids, the dentist meant one thing: *pain*, and again, school was often the place where such a spine-chilling prospect became apparent. That the school dentist was installing himself in the headmistress' study generated not just horror, but was responsible for a few damp patches in the trouser area of the more sensitive children. Once again, it was up the old creaking staircase, and because there was no actual treatment this time, just recommendations to your own local dentist – *there were no sweets*. The only thing you could hope for was that the school dentist was also suffering from a lazy, suspicious or bored eye and wouldn't spot the obvious decay in your less than pearly molars. Unfortunately for us, this was relatively unlikely as tooth decay was really quite prevalent in the fifties, and the associated toothache was quite common.

Now, to set this in context, you have to understand a number of things. First, up until 1953, children had been denied a lot of sweets because they were still rationed. So when rationing came off, there was a surge of unrestricted sweetie buying, and similar surge in sweetie manufacturing to meet the demand. Thus to find children stuffed to the gills with sticky sweetmeats was very common. The second factor was that teeth-cleaning was not particularly popular with us tinies, and despite the first TV advert *ever* being for *SR Toothpaste* in 1956, such hygienic dental practices still did not appeal. Electric toothbrushes hadn't been invented, and the bewildering array of dental products available today was only a pipedream. Well, to be honest, they may have been a pipedream to dentists and manufacturers – to most kids, having to give your teeth even a cursory flick over with the toothbrush, like washing behind your ears, something to be avoided. Those dental products that did present themselves were largely unappealing; the Gibbs company still produced a product called Tooth Powder which came in a little flat tin. As far as I could make out, it was really an abrasive powder, the dental equivalent of Vim or Ajax sink scourer, and seemed quite aggressively uncompromising.

The next nail in our proverbial dental coffin was the fact that our parents generally encouraged us to eat lots of sweet things. Now this may sound odd, but again, the effects of the recent war have to be considered. Throughout hostilities and for a good many years afterwards, rationing meant that nearly all food was hard come by; some was very scarce, and some non-existent. For example, having been born in 1941, my sister didn't see a banana until she was four years old, and then didn't realise it had to be peeled before it was consumed. Now, this was not because my mum hid them from her in order to facilitate some kind of weird banana fettish – it was simply that bananas were not imported throughout the war. An additional factor that had a pronounced effect upon the adult mind was the pre-war spectre of their children being under-nourished and thus growing up with complaints such as rickets - the result of a lack of the calcium normally provided by drinking milk - or diseases and complaints brought about by a lack of vitamin C. So, after the war, a third of a pint of milk per day was provided free at all schools – right into and including the secondary phase of education, and National Orange Juice was provided for all young children. Perhaps it is therefore not so surprising that our parents were keen to put as much as they could on the dining table, to fill the biscuit barrel with Custard Creams and the like, and never to let us turn our backs on a chocolate Bourbon. I can remember being allowed – perhaps even encouraged – to make myself a *sugar sandwich*, and supper often comprised a few more biscuits and the almost mandatory hot chocolate drink. The fact that children started to fill out was therefore unsurprising, but was seen as a kind of status symbol, and the bulging extremities of overfed offspring fondly described as 'puppy fat'. To add the final layer in this tale of dental woe was the fact that there was apparently no understanding of the qualities of fluoride, and its protective provision in public water supplies had to wait many a long year.

Given all this, it is surprising that we had any teeth left at all – but we did, and those that survived were frequently in need of the tender care bestowed by the NHS dentist. I can well recall climbing the stairs up to Mr. Svensson's surgery: that his practice was on the top floor of an ordinary terraced house just down the road made it all the more sinister. That he was Swedish and had a ginger moustache that bristled scarily close to my face as he prodded shiny pointy things into my mouth made the whole experience completely terrifying. But worst of all was *the drill.*

This medieval piece of machinery was driven by a series of thick metal wires attached to a motor. It made a lot of noise – perhaps purposely generated to hide the screams of the patient - and by modern standards was very slow. The drill bits themselves seemed to

A bit scary. Like the shadows?

be quite large, and I'm almost sure Mr. Svensson used to hold them right in front of my eye line as he selected the most knobbly and blunt one he had. At times like these, I almost wished I had a couple of lazy eyes to prevent seeing what I was seeing. Perhaps it was his way of making you grateful for the next horror - the injection. Anaesthesia at the dentist was, fortunately, pretty freely available, and it came in two forms: cocaine and gas. The former was delivered via a syringe the size of which would have made a horse inclined to bolt, and the latter came via a rubber mask. The first caused panic, pain and more panic, in that order. It then left you with a numb half face for the rest of the day, such that bitten lips and half chewed cheeks were a common after effect. Like many patients, it seemed I rarely became properly numb until I got home again after fleeing from my tormentor's eager administration of the dreaded needle, and spent the rest of the day mopping tea stains from my shirt over which I had dribbled copiously for a number of hours. True to his profession, Mr. Svensson was keen to get to grips with the drilling about one nano-second after you had just about survived the hideous pain associated with having your gum punctured by something that seemed the size of a knitting needle. Cranking up the old pulley system of the drill, he would approach with that manic stare which immediately took me back to the Gestapo interrogator in the film *'Carve Her Name With Pride'*, just before he says *'Vee heff vays of making you talk; resistance is futile ... now, vhere ist der radio transmitter?'*

Instead what he invariably murmured was *"Let me know if you feel anything"*, to which I should have replied: *"Excuse me, but isn't the sole purpose of you shoving a bloomin' great needle almost through my neck and out the other side, to make sure I don't have any pain whatsoever?"* But of course, I didn't for two reasons: first he was the one holding the drill, and second, by this time my mouth was so full of pieces of ironwork, I could not move my tongue or lips to formulate anything that even remotely sounded like a comprehensible word anyway. So, cocaine had its downside.

Gas, on the other hand, was relatively painless, as it put you completely out. I suppose, therefore, it was a *general* anaesthetic, although we never really thought of it in that way. I suppose also that, like all 'generals', there was a degree of risk associated with its administration. Not that we cared... just to get away from the sight and sound – not to mention the vibration - of ye olde drill as it ground through your decay at approximately twenty two rpm, was enough.

The only problem with gas - apart from the small issue that you may never wake up again - was that if you *were* fortunate enough to survive it, it left you disorientated at best, or in more extreme cases, severely deluded for the rest of the day. My wife tells me of a fairly typical post–gas reaction that she had following the removal of a tooth in the early sixties (the date I mean, not her age). On coming round in the recovery room next door, she became convinced that the dentist had removed the wrong tooth. After several attempts to get back through the surgery door without meandering off course and reeling into the adjoining wall, she burst into the surgery and in floods of tears yelled at the somewhat startled dentist:

"You've taken out the wrong fool, you tooth! ...and stand still while I'm talking to you ... both of you!!"

Inevitably, this sort of dental experience filled the likes of us with all sorts of good resolutions to clean our teeth thoroughly and regularly, and to forego the luxury of a night time sweetie award when the lure of sticking your wettened finger into a paper bag still half full of luminescent lemon crystals was almost undeniable. But the road to the dental surgery was, like so many others, paved with good intentions, and so Mr. Svensson was, no doubt, quite secure in his chosen profession. On reflection, the fact that to this day I still have nearly all of my own teeth, implies that he was also a very good dentist.

But, putting inter-visit dental neglect to one side, I wouldn't like it thought that we fifties kids didn't take at least some responsibility for our own physical well-being. In particular, as the sixties loomed larger on the horizon and TV advertising took a real grip, even scruffy little boys began to think: *'perhaps I should just occasionally give the old ears a more than cursory wipe with the flannel ... and may be just a bit more attention to the state of my knees wouldn't go amiss'*. Added to this growing awareness of the need to keep ourselves marginally presentable was the increasing pressure to look like the people on the telly. They were generally pretty clean, looked nice, and had white teeth, shiny shoes and glossy hair, so all in all, a lot to live up to.

Rather more to the point, and coming as something of a rude awakening, we suddenly became aware of the need to guard against... **B O** (Body Odour). There was a TV advert for Lifebuoy Toilet Soap which must have been the first tentative trickle in the tsunami that was to become the deodorant business. In the ad, a bloke at a party keeps approaching others only to be shunned within a few seconds of proximity... and whilst the people he has approached don't exactly drop to the floor in a swoon or stagger about clutching their throats and throwing up all over the place, it is pretty obvious that his proximity is causing something of a problem. Luckily, the hostess of the party – a kindly soul – spots the problem and, taking a deep breath, and suppressing the temptation to hold her nose, sidles up to the perplexed bloke and breathes the two magic letters in his ear: *"B O!"* I can't remember if she also whips out a bar of soap from her handbag and shoves it in his pocket, but suffice to say that we are left in no doubt that the lucky recipient's malodorous days will soon be a thing of the past; successful party-going complete with sparkling conversation and equally sparkling armpits is assured.

I am sure that very few of us knew what B O was or stood for until it was explained in a whisper by our slightly embarrassed parents. But once the secret was out, there was certainly a good deal of extra scrubbing going on in the bathroom. That BO had to be avoided at all costs was underlined by the fact that it also became a good weapon to use against anyone you didn't like. Shouting: *"Oi!! –anyway, you've got B O!"* was as good a way as any other to conclude an argument, especially if the target was a bigger kid and you were near enough to skedaddle down the street before running into your house and slamming the front door tight shut. Sophisticated we were not.

Also, of course, as we progressed towards the end of the fifties, nature was making itself felt in other ways. Sex education didn't really exist in any recognisable form at that time and certainly not for primary aged children, and *especially* not for boys. Nevertheless, we all had a growing appreciation of the female form, and even the dullest git at the end of his junior school years must have noticed that girls seem to be changing a bit, and that *Kiss Chase* was upping its popularity even against such stalwart playtime rivals as *British Bull Dog*.

And then, of course, my pal Doug brought a nude book into the playground one morning. He told us that he had found it in the front garden of a house he passed on the way to school, and said we could all look at it (boys only, of course) at playtime. The rush with which we little fellows gulped down our third of a pint of milk and the alacrity with which we smartly *'sat up straight'* in order to be the first to be dismissed to the playground, must have surprised our unsuspecting teacher. Suffice it to say that thirty seconds later, half the class were crowding around Doug and gazing with rapt attention at the exposed breasts of the young ladies disporting themselves on the tatty pages of a much used and very old monochrome copy of *'Health and Efficiency'*. Actually, not much was said. I'm sure many of us had never seen naked breasts before, and it had a strange – and not unwelcome - effect. I can well remember a slightly anxious voice piping up and enquiring of all the others, *"Here. Has your thingy gone stiff?"* Well, in a number of cases, yes it had. Later less public investigation revealed quite conclusively that few, if any of us had even the remotest inkling of an idea why our thingies had gone stiff, but it was generally agreed that it was not an unpleasant feeling.

Although usually way down the list when it came to educational prowess, I was unexpectedly just a shade ahead of some of my mates in respect of the female form. True, like many others, I had never seen a book like *'Health and Efficiency'* before, but my education in this respect had received a helping hand from a totally unexpected quarter a few months before. To explain:

In the hope of bringing me up to be a good clean-living lad and regular churchgoer, my parents had bought me a '*Children's Illustrated Bible*' the previous Christmas. To be honest, I was not that elated, and would have much preferred the desirable '*Coles Twenty Ton Mobile Crane*' that the Dinky Toy company had just produced to supplement their 'Supertoys' range. Nevertheless, I accepted the proffered volume with as much good grace as I could muster and quickly flicked through the volume which confirmed that yes, there were a number of coloured plates inserted at intervals to enliven the scriptures within. *Now, where's that Atom Blaster water pistol I was hoping for? The one made from bright orange clear plastic complete with rubber bung and Easy-fill instructions?* You might imagine that it was some days before I picked up the Bible again, thinking I'd just check out the nicely coloured pictures, although I was pretty sure there wouldn't be a huge amount there to interest a growing lad. Wrong. You can imagine my surprise when, in the chapter on Exodus, which devotes much of itself to Moses and his adventures, there was a picture of him as a baby being discovered amongst some convenient bulrushes at a presumably crocodile- free location on the banks of the River Nile. And who was doing the discovering? Some curvy maidens, that's who... and fortunately for me, baby recovery must have been strenuous work on a pretty hot day, as they appeared to have left their blouses behind. Strewth! Although never mentioned, I suspect my parents must have been impressed by the keen interest their dopey son took in poring over his illustrated bible throughout the ensuing weeks.

So, accidental, unofficial and entirely rumour-ridden sex education had begun. One rumour I remember in particular was from a little fellow in our class who proclaimed with the authority only invested in the truly ignorant that ...'*when you gets married, something inside you changes, and you can have babies . It's like a*

- 172 -

switch; so before you gets married you can't have babies! Know what I mean?' Well, no, not really.

Sex ed in any primary school was still way over the horizon, in the late fifties. Looking back I have the vaguest recollection of our lovely teacher seeming to rush over a couple of innocent enquiries when the class was gathered around the Nature Table. Since this was of the type *'Where do tadpoles come from then Miss?'* and the fact that she seemed ever so slightly flustered when showing us the stamen and stigma of a pussy willow twig, the likelihood of us getting any real information was non-existent, and of course, was the perfect environment for misinformation of the most bizarre type, invariably peddled by those least qualified to give it.

Nevertheless, the combination of our slowly increasing maturity, the powerful influence of advertising, and exposure to unheard of influences through the new window on the world that was television, became a powerful influence on our lifestyle. Inevitably, there was a real shift in attitude towards the fair sex, and this took the form of not only trying to tidy ourselves up, but for the first time to become just a little bit *trendy*. And the late fifties was a good time to do it.... because, for the first time ever, there were *teenagers*.

Prior to the 1950's, people in the thirteen to nineteen age bracket were... well, just youngsters who hung around waiting to become 'grown-ups' and looking like gawky versions of their elders. They had no distinct identity, no individual fashion and, beyond the accumulation of unsightly acne and a propensity for grumpiness, no real group distinction; teenagers simply hadn't been invented. And then came the Teds.

Even before the final abolition of rationing in 1954, a new teen culture was starting to emerge as a direct result of the coming together of a number of factors: almost full employment, giving rise to increased spending power; the blossoming of post-war enterprise to create and drive forward a new consumerism; new versatile materials to be processed by cheap and efficient manufacturing processes and the need for the country – and probably the whole world - to break free from the cloying depression of the immediate past. Most of all, there was a new sense of optimism and progress...and all of this gave youth the right for its own *teenager* label ... and to be *different*.

Prominent in the queue to be so entitled were the Teds. Now you might have thought that the first move towards a new identity might have been a trifle tentative, that the initial steps towards the teenage revolution to come might have been rather more 'toe in the water'. Not so. It was full on. The obligatory uniform for the Teddy Boys was a knee length light brown or tan drape coat with a black velvet collar, a white shirt with black bootlace tie, tight black drainpipe trousers ending significantly above the ankles to reveal day-glow coloured socks which in turn accentuated the massive proportion of the brothel-creeper footwear. These were large brown suede boots which perched panther-like on inch thick black crepe rubber soles. So, there you have the sartorial elegance of the new Edwardians, from which they derived their name. But the final flourish was not to be found at the local clothes market – it was to be styled at the barber's shop.

For a Ted to be a proper Ted, he needed to have a thickly Brylcreamed blow wave which was constantly attended to when out strutting with his mates through the regular application of his plastic finger brush. Typically, the well greased coiffure could be attended to on passing any reflective surface, and shop windows were perfect for the job.

Now, to think that we little chaps suddenly turned into teddy boys once we reached double figures would be a step too far. For a start, our mums wouldn't let us, we had no separate income to provide the necessary, and besides brothel creepers were no good for kiss chase as they were too heavy and inclined to set up a mono-directional momentum all of their own, so you'd probably miss Susan Watts altogether, leaving her in the lecherous clutches of a more suitably shod competitor. And besides, by 1958, wasn't the Teddy Boy look starting to look just a *little bit dated?* So, where could we junior age kids go to embark upon the road to popular fashion? Taking the only cue we could from the Teds, we headed to the local barber for a first ever update on the hair-style.

Although my own barber was just along the street from the dentist, a visit to Mr. Ransom's wasn't accompanied by any of the fear and dread that having your teeth drilled absolutely did. To be honest, it was just something you had to get done and Mr. Ransom would occasionally provide old comics for junior clientele to peruse whilst waiting. It was either that, or trying to swing your legs fast enough to create a draught that would send the fine collection of recently snipped hair which adorned every surface into little eddies and swirls all over the lino.

Hair dressing for boys was a straight-forward ritual. You sat in the chair, and Mr. Ransom shook the previous customer's hair from the cape onto the floor before wrapping it tightly around your neck. He then proceeded to give you a *short back and sides.* There was no choice in the matter, and it never occurred to anyone to ask for anything else – mainly because we didn't know there *was* anything else. I don't remember any word being spoken throughout the entire five minutes of the barber shop experience; the only sounds were the buzzing of the electric clipper which was sent lawn-mower like up the back of your neck to quite close to the crown. Sides and front were done using a pair of very sharp scissors which flashed backwards and forwards from Mr. R's breast pocket with amazing rapidity. On completion of the cutting, he would get two large brushes and in a movement not dissimilar to a boxer providing a punch-bag a good pasting, give your head a thorough two handed brushing from brow to neck. This was done with such vigour that it caused your head to thrash about quite violently in a back and forwards motion, and for your eyebrows to ascend to abnormal heights – almost as if they were trying to climb over the top of your head. As a result you were left with a very surprised expression which took about half an hour to subside... and a sneaking suspicion that perhaps the good Mr. R might have had his ambition to be a boxer unfairly thwarted at some point. Or, of course, it may be that perhaps he just didn't like little boys.

The final flourish to the performance, however, was the liberal administration of the brilliantine. This liquid smelly stuff was housed in a thickly dimpled bottle on the counter, right under the adverts for *Erasmic* ointment (*'to quickly and easily stem the blood flow from razor cuts'*) and something or other which older blokes could buy in packets of three (*'...something for the weekend sir?'*) The neck of the brilliantine bottle was plumbed into a rubber tube which itself ended in a lemon-sized rubber bulb, a somewhat larger version of the apparatus used to power water pistols. Mr. Ransom would then circumnavigate your head liberally spraying the recently shorn area as if his very life depended on it. With a final sweep of the hands very similar to that epitomised by our bull-fighting chums, he would create a mini blizzard of recently cut hair by whipping away the cape with one hand and holding out his hand for the 1/6d fee with the other: it really only wanted a Spanish *'OLE!'* and perhaps one red rose between his teeth to complete the theatrics.

So, back on the pavement one paused only to try and scratch away the remaining bits of hair inevitably stuck down your collar, before running like the wind in a vain attempt to outpace the lingering sickly sweet and all pervading smell of the brilliantine. The resulting short back and sides was something the modern reader might identify as rather North Korean in appearance, but the fact that we all went home sporting what nowadays might be called the Kim-Jon Un look didn't enter our heads. And that was the way things were... that is until some time in1958, when Paul Stoneham turned up at school with a *brush cut.*

Being born and brought up in a naval town, we were well aware that many of the American sailors who visited our shores sported *crew cuts.* This was seen as something really quite exotic and therefore not for us. However, when Paul turned up with the crew cut's more hirsute cousin, the brush-cut, it was seen as something extraordinary, a real pioneering act of undreamt proportions. In our class, it simply hadn't occurred to anyone else, but here was perhaps, the perfect opportunity to become just a little more *individual* in the eyes of the ladies. That is of course, if you could convince first your mum - that it was desirable, and second Mr. Ransom - that it was in any way, shape or form possible. Well, some managed to do it, some a little more advisedly than others. Given that the style was the result of cutting your hair all over to about one inch in length and then applying Brylcreem to make it stand up on end, it suited some more than others. One kid in our class for example, was a very red redhead, and thus his newly acquired brush cut gave his head the appearance of being permanently on fire – so much so that it may have prompted a few classmates to reach for the odd crumpet and toasting fork in his presence. Others of course, looked pretty good, and the overall effect was to induce in all of us a growing self-awareness, and that we too could start to develop our own individual style. That the path to such an ambition was full of pitfalls, misguided choices and fashion statement cul-de-sacs did not deter us at all. Although Mr. Ransom made us all aware that he did not agree with *any* new style, even he had to bend with the new hurricane of teenage fashion, the first gentle breeze of which was reaching the unpromising nursery of pre-pubescent boys in the late fifties.

Another indication of our growing self-awareness was the fact that even the most unobservant among us became aware that cosmetics were playing a greater and greater role in our lives. Before this, the fact that the local chemist displayed tins of talcum powder and shinily wrapped bath cubes produced by the Max Factor company was about as far it went – and then only at Christmas time or just before Mothers' Day, when such purchases became essential. Oh, and there was also a lot of pink soap wrapped in cellophane and ribbons which also fitted the bill. However, once our awareness of Brylcreem came on the scene, and the need to avoid being labelled as a repository of the dreaded B O became apparent, there was a growing appreciation of the need to attend a little more purposefully to our own presentation. That such a move was closely linked to our appeal to girls, made even the most relaxed little git take note with a rather more determined air.

For my own part, and knowing there was no way on earth my mum would agree to a brush cut, I boldly asked Mr. Ransom for a 'Boston' next time I went for a haircut. Although hardly a radical move - the style required hair on the back of your head being left a little longer, and terminating at neck level in an abrupt line, rather than diminishing into nothing as before – this was seen pretty much as sacrilege by the good Mr. R whose somewhat predictable response was '*A Boston! A Boston? What do you want one of those for?!*' After a good deal of wheedling and reminding him that he had done the same for Clive Weston just two days ago, there was a grudging 'Hrmmph!' and lo and behold, yours truly was able to hold his head high at school the next day – quite literally in fact, as showing off your smartly terminated hairline-at-neck-level needed a good deal of inventive contortionism to display to full effect. I think I might even have forsaken continued improvement of my by now quite famous and accomplished shoulder stands in favour of doing some press-ups, in order that Miss Grant could get a full eyeful of the new and impressive hairdo.

So, with coiffure suitably re-modelled, the chemist's shop - hitherto a place of absolutely no interest at all - started to become yet another focus for our growing self-awareness. There also started to develop a positive interest in being the first to get some of the new stuff on offer; when *Olde Spice After Shave* hit the shelves, and the famous boxer Henry Cooper was telling us on the telly to *'splash it all over'*. Well, who were we to argue? And splash it all over some did, even though we were well short of the need to take up shaving. The stuff smelled nice, the girls seemed to go all a-twitter when it was worn, so why not follow Henry's advice? Some boys took this to such a liberal and generous extent that such administration resulted in red and streaming eyes. Just lucky those kids with the lazy eye patches could at least cover one of the reddened eyeballs - perhaps the only time when being so afflicted put them at an advantage.

Not that any non life-threatening accident or illness was without its attraction, for by now, we were all fully aware that if you had a problem, the nurses at the local hospital would look after you, and you might even return to school with a heroically bandaged arm, or better still, something in plaster! The school nurse was one thing, but she was no match for the glamorous ladies *'up the hossie'* where it was all starchy whiteness, offset by matching blue uniform with cute little cap whose attachment atop the sophisticated hairdo one could describe as 'pert'. But best of all was the *upside down watch*. This latter item was attached to the uniform at chest level, and was installed in an inverted manner so that the lovely lady could hold your wrist with one hand, and measure your heart rate by observing the watch on her chest whilst taking your pulse. It occurred to many of us that perhaps by pursuing this invariable procedure, the readings obtained from boys might have been much higher than was normally the case; having a lovely lady in striking uniform tenderly holding your wrist, and giving you a cast iron excuse to look closely at her chest area was doubtless, responsible for many an inaccurate reading.

Not that we needed any encouragement. The reputation and standing of the medical profession was at an all-time high, and not only because of its amazing cost-free undertaking to look after every little bit of you: it was now a glamorous occupation, for was it not on the telly? Enter ITV's *'Emergency Ward Ten'* and *'Dr. Kildare'*.

The former was an early soap which, just before the closing credits, established the *'end of programme crisis'* formula to ensure your continued attendance at the next broadcast. Not that it really needed such persuasion in the early days for the programme's huge popularity had already established a dual effect upon the newly gawping TV audience. First, making its debut as early as 1957, it was instrumental in setting the pattern for soaps for generations to come. Second, it had the subliminal effect of confirming the central place that global health care had in our lives: it was the weekly embodiment of the Welfare State, and the extent to which it would go to make you...yes YOU...better, regardless of your state of health, social or financial standing. Powerful stuff.

'Dr. Kildare', on the other hand, was really a romance, made all the more so because its eponymous hero, played by the suave and good-looking Richard Chamberlain was a real sex symbol... and he was also American! What more could a girl want? Each week with the immediate prospect of the lovely Dr. K flashing his perfect smile and heroically saving lives, it was time for many a housewife to shove the *Quix* washing up liquid back in the cupboard, turn the telly on to start its three minute warm-up time, get the washing in from the clothes line, turn off the gas under the kettle, make a cup of Ovaltine, get a couple of *Rich Teas* from the biscuit barrel, whip off the flower printed pinny and matching turban headscarf, plump up the hairdo, light up a *Park Drive* and still be in time for the opening theme tune.

'Dr. Finlay's Casebook', on the other hand, played a very different role. Its format generated a cosy familiarity far removed from its sexy American counterpart. Based in the fictional Highland locality of Tannochbrae, Arden House was home, surgery and epicentre of the good doctor's practice, and the jangling candlestick telephone,

Perhaps Janet is asking Dr. Finlay 'You'll have had your tea?' In the meantime, has Dr. Cameron spotted a likely horse in the 3.30 at Cheltenham?

always answered by the dependable Janet with her up-tilted Highland accent clearly enunciating *'Arden Hoose'* was the frequent opener to many an episode. What made the series so popular was that it was set in the 1920's, well before the birth of the NHS. As such, it presented a touchy dimension to the drama – *whether or not the patient could afford to pay for the necessary treatment.* In addition, there was the good-natured but nonetheless present tension between the modern Dr. Finlay, and his senior partner, the dependable and elaborately bushy-browed Dr. Cameron brilliantly portrayed by Andrew Cruikshank. Other characters fleshed out the rest of the highland medical environment – principally Mistress Niven, the starchy and inquisitive district nurse, and Dr. Snoddie the local authority's Health Officer. This thin grey person was about as far away from Dr. Kildare as could possibly be imagined; he seemed to have a permanent head cold which blended beautifully with his ability to pour cold water on just about anything the adventurous and oh-so-modern Dr. Finlay wanted to try.

Underwriting all of this small screen medical entertainment was the immensely popular *'Doctor in the House'* series of films starring Dirk Bogarde which got off to a tremendous start in 1954. Not only were these films very funny, they were also in colour! Hard to believe that, in the early fifties, there were still a lot of monochrome films around, and the innovation of such colourful wizardry to be found in developments such as *Technicolor* was much admired and sought after. That the 'Doctor' film genre continued for sixteen years right up to *'Doctor in Trouble'* in 1970 speaks volumes on the popularity of medical drama; it was something with which we could all identify – after all, we all got ill didn't we?

I can't remember which of the films made me laugh the most – but one scene remains firmly lodged in my mind. Played by the formidable James Robertson-Justice, Sir Lancelot Spratt, the acerbic senior surgeon at the hospital is making his rounds surrounded by the usual coterie of nurses, junior doctors and students. He comes to a bed occupied by a patient played by the worldly-wise Arthur Haynes. *'And what's the matter with you?'* booms Sir Lancelot. *'Well,'* replies a clearly embarrassed Arthur, *' It's my…. you know… down there…'* he mumbles, indicating the lower abdominal area with his eyes… *'It's my er…'* Clearly impatient and exasperated, Sir Lancelot yells out what he considers to be the conclusion of Arthur's sentence: *'Rectum?'* he yells.

'Well, it certainly didn't do 'em any good did it?!' comes Arthur's quick reply.

And of course all medical entertainment whether via TV or films provided oodles of information with which to impress the neighbours: details of new up and coming illnesses, gruesome symptoms by the score – just a smattering of knowledge of these provided the dedicated viewer with sufficient information to regurgitate it in an alfresco way any time, any place, anywhere. Such newly discovered and highly questionable expertise was great for **a)** diagnosing and **b)** frightening the next door neighbour half to death when contemplating the cause of his latest discomfort. In the 1960's, Tony Hancock brilliantly played on this newly popular pastime of amateur - and completely misguided - diagnosis in *"The Blood Donor"*. Take for example, his exquisite description of the circulation of the blood around the body. After a naïve enquiry by fellow patient Hugh Lloyd as to *'what blood was for'* Hancock replies:

'Well you've got all those veins, haven't you? And you've got to fill them up with something! There's no point in the heart banging away all day with nothing to pump around, is there?! If your heart didn't pump the blood around, it would all sink to the bottom. It would be very uncomfortable… a bit like walking around with a boot full of water!'

As was often the case, comedy writers such as the brilliant Ray Galton and Alan Simpson spotted such human weaknesses quickly, and scripted the ensuing behaviour to great effect. In this case, ignorant amateur diagnosis of the ailments afflicting clueless friends and neighbours was – and remains – a popular pastime.

In a way, the introduction of the all-encompassing NHS was like providing us with a new and free sweet shop: loads of interesting and varied new complaints to fall ill with, loads of resources with interesting shiny bits of equipment to be put to use, and loads of people keen to make even the most enthusiastic hypochondriac well again. Not only that – the range of different types of hospital was quite remarkable. I remember once being plagued by a continual watering of the eyes. Now, I hadn't been sticking my head out of my dad's Morris Eight in an unadvisable manner (not that this particular car ever got up to a speed sufficient to cause ocular problems), neither had I been experimenting with sticking my head in a load of frothed up washing up liquid to see if you could breathe bubbles - and so the cause was unknown. As a result, my mum whisked me off to the doc's, and he said that I should go to the Eye and Ear Hospital, a specialist facility with which Portsmouth Health Authority was blessed. Now, I was most alarmed at this totally unexpected development. I had assumed that the doc would simply give me something in a bottle to swig down or at worst, recommend a new pair of NHS specs. I made no secret of my disquiet, to which my mum expressed some surprise, reminding me that the Eye and Ear hospital was pretty much brand new.

OK, I freely admit that thus far, I had not been the most attentive little chap either in school or indeed anywhere, and of those things that didn't completely pass me by, there was a quite measureable group where, if it was at all possible to get hold of the wrong end of the stick, I was a prime – and I must say in all modesty, - quite spectacularly good candidate. Thus the spoken term *Eye and Ear* was immediately interpreted by me as the **Iron Ear** hospital, where, surely complaints and treatment must be at the same level of gravity as those requiring an iron lung?? I suspect my mum was a bit disappointed in the lack of courage shown by her offspring who grizzled continually all the way back from the doctor's, and claimed thereafter that his eyes had dried up entirely, and anyway, what did ears, metallic or otherwise, have to do with watering eyes?

Suffice it to say that after some rather caustic comments about *paying attention in future,* the subsequent expert diagnosis of blocked tear ducts didn't exactly rank high on the list of life-threatening, or indeed, even vaguely interesting complaints. However, I was very relieved that this tiny procedure was successfully performed at the hospital without recourse to any dramatic equipment - and that I never saw any indication of the presence of chrome-plated ears. Mind you, coping with the embarrassment of my late discovery of the identical sounding Eye and Ear / Iron Ear was quite enough.

'How could you have got it so wrong?' asked my mum, in a tone which I found just a tad below the sympathetic. *'It was written up all over the hospital ... and the words Eye and Ear aren't difficult to read are they?'*

Easy for her to say... she didn't have watering eyes to contend with.

8   Pre Bop-A-Lula

It's hardly conceivable now, but when we tinies were running around in the early 1950's, we did it unaccompanied.

Let me explain: I don't mean unaccompanied in the sense of being chucked out into the street to find our own amusement – although we did have a lot more freedom to do just that than kids do these days. What I do mean is that whatever we did, we did it without the continual and incessant accompaniment of pop music. And why? Because pop music hadn't been invented, that's why – and neither had the means to carry it with you wherever you happened to be. Honest!

Although skiffle groups set up an early momentum, the birth of Rock and Roll in the UK didn't really happen until the end of 1956, when Bill Hayley's *'Rock Around the Clock'* burst forth upon a generation. Such innovation demanded something different, something slightly rebellious, something their parents would absolutely hate: Rock and Roll was it. Prior to that, popular music mainly comprised a number of crooners who tried to emulate the stuff pouring out of the USA, but from 1952 onwards it became clear that an alternative to sentimental ballads was needed. As mentioned above, the void was filled in part by the growing number of home-grown skiffle groups – and more of their important contribution anon. But for the real Rock 'n' Roll, Bill's song certainly started the ball rolling, to be followed in short order by more extreme songs such as Elvis Presley's *'Hound Dog', 'Heartbreak Hotel'* and *'Long Tall Sally'*. It was these that set the 1956 pulses racing. But great though these songs were, in the opinion of many, the number that really seemed to strike a chord and typify the revolution in music, was by another American called Gene Vincent. And the title? It was:

'Be-Bop-a-Lula'.

Quite why this particular record had such a lasting and profound effect upon Baby Boomers in general - and boys in particular - is hard to fathom. It may well have been that when Gene toured the UK with his song, he delivered it wearing a tight-fitting black leather suit and performed it in a manner which years later Alvin Stardust made all his own – just ever-so-slightly menacing. The term 'macho' wasn't around then, but I guess Gene would have qualified. The song itself was really quite basic, but it had a strong, simple, earthy and repetitive beat; its lyrics were blunt, unsophisticated to the point of being barmy, and well, just *forced* you to join in. For blokes especially, it was near impossible to prevent yourself from singing along and elaborately embellishing the original with your own hip-swivelling and highly stylised rendition.

I don't know why the song had such an effect... I *still* don't, but just try asking a group of old blokes to sing you a number that typifies the birth of Rock and Roll and like as not some old guy will come up with a highly personalised version of the song, and throw in a few geriatric hip swivels whilst miming combing the memory of his long-gone blow wave back into its Brylcreemed perfection.

But Gene, Elvis and Bill only appeared on the scene two thirds of the way through the decade. *'So'*, you must be asking yourself, *'what did Baby Boomers do for their entertainment in those oh-so-quiet pre-Bob-a-Lulan days? Surely there must have been record players and radios around to tune in to?'*

Well, no, not really. Even if pop music had been invented ten years earlier, there was nothing much to play it on: don't forget, these were the days *before* vinyl, when things such as your own record player or personal radio were just distant dreams. Living in a world without wall-to-wall music is difficult to imagine these days, so permit me to shed a little light on a time before continuous entertainment became the norm. Yes of course there was music in the early fifties, some of which was popular, (although not readily available), but it was not what we would now call now call *pop*. Of course, radio sets were fairly common, (often still referred to as 'the wireless') but were usually quite enormous, being housed in a large and highly polished wooden cabinet. Because of this they were anything but portable, and were regarded by many families as a treasured and expensive piece of furniture to be displayed as a status symbol in the sitting room, where they were lovingly polished at regular intervals. The dial was usually quite large, honey coloured, and packed with useless information. Considering all we really had to listen to was the BBC, and there were only three stations to choose from – the *Light Programme*, the *Home Service* and a little used third station which, with a stroke of imaginative genius was called *The Third Programme* - I could think of no reason why our trusty PYE radio dial boasted such stations as *Stockholm*, *Hammerfest*, *Oslo*, *Helsinki* and so on. And why the concentration on Scandinavia? It's not as if the post-war population had a burning desire to catch up on the state of the herring fleet, or how to knock up a tasty smorgasbord in place of the usual Friday night fish and chips. Furthermore, tuning in to the useful tips covered in such northern delights as *"101 Things to do in a Snowstorm"* or one of their very short programmes: *"Where to look for the Northern Lights"* lacked immediate fascination.

Mind you, with the amount of whistling, farting and screeching static interference that most radios picked up from poor domestic

Huge, shiny and imposing. Ours was full of static farts, probably caused by dodgy 1950's domestic wiring.

electrical connections all the time, it might as well have been in Norwegian, for all the sense it made. Nevertheless, we did tune in as best we could, in the hope of picking up any programme that might be interpreted as '*light entertainment*'. As mentioned, most radio sets were anything but portable being huge and heavy; even the smaller sets were still powered by lots of valves mounted in a sturdy metal frame and which could be seen through the fretted back panel of the set glowing dimly in the hot and dusty confines of the cabinet. And, of course, they were powered from the mains, as battery technology was pretty much languishing in what seemed a protracted infancy and appeared to comprise either heavy accumulators full of appallingly dangerous acid - fine for submarines perhaps, but not great on the living room lino - or the little *Ever Ready* jobs that were sufficient only to let you down after ten minutes in the front lamp of your bike. So, the family radio had to be near a mains power plug... and in the average 1950's household, there weren't many of these. If you were fortunate enough to find one close to your radio, it would invariably be made from heavy brown bakelite and blessed with just *two* pins.

I emphasise this because it may underline the fact that the added safety feature of a third earthing pin had not yet been introduced – at least, not in our house it hadn't - and the few sockets we did have tended to have added adaptors so that other implements could gain their supply from just one outlet. Bear in mind also, that plastic coated wires were still to come; in terms of insulation, wires were still covered in a kind of brown woven braiding which had a nasty habit of becoming somewhat scorched and either disintegrated or unravelled close to the terminals. So, electric points often took on the appearance of slightly singed Christmas trees, and were rightly regarded with some caution: plugging in an appliance was always something of an adventure, and it was not unknown for my dad to take a little involuntary leap backwards when turning the switch on, in anticipation of the not uncommon flash-bang, which preceded a trip to the fuse cupboard under the stairs. It also led to some downright dangerous practices – the sort of things that would have today's health and safety conscious consumers requiring the immediate application of smelling salts. The chief culprit was the habit of using pendant type light sockets as power points in their own right. What you did was:

a) take out the light bulb and **b)** insert what I suppose today might be called a 'splitter' – i.e. a dubious inverted Y shaped contraption which plugged into the light socket but provided at its other end *two* bayonet type outlets. Into these you could then plug other items, the most popular of which was the electric iron. Thus, you had the iron cable trailing from the ceiling, and although the second part of the splitter could accommodate the displaced light bulb, it was quite often used as the power source for yet another implement, a popular contender being the radio. Thus was born the quaint but adventurous hobby of *'ironing in the dark to music'*.

So, you can see that what with the appalling interference produced by valve radio sets, the inherent danger associated with plugging in the damn thing in the first place, and the fact that quite often the only broadcast you were likely to be able to hear was the shipping forecast from Helsinki, you will appreciate that listening to the radio, though immensely popular, was not without its challenges.

With this in mind, my own parents took the decision to get rid of our beautifully veneered, highly polished but almost completely useless valve radio and in its place rent a pair of radio receivers from a company called *Radio Relay*. It seems almost inconceivable that in those days *renting* a radio set was common. I had

Sexy they were not

- 189 -

mixed feelings about it, having to offset the anticipated thrill of actually being able to hear whatever the three BBC services were dishing out without the crackle, whistles, screams or farts characterised by our outgoing set, against the fact that the new receivers were decidedly utilitarian. They were, after all, not much more than a basic speaker with a single volume control attached via a cable to a little selector box on the wall which had but three positions: *Light, Home* and *Third.* To be honest, they were far from glamorous ... but at least we had two of them, and so could now choose to be seated for our listening pleasure either in the dining room *or* the sitting room. Pinch me! I must be dreaming!

And it was in the latter where, as a five year old with time on my hands, I was idly gazing out across the pavement in front of our house - perhaps to see if Ben Parsons was creaking by on his invalid trike - when the Home Service delivered some information which even I thought of as perhaps quite important. I duly ambled up the passage to the kitchen, pausing only for a quick slide on the polished lino, following which I delivered the message to my mother who as usual was extracting some jam tarts from the oven: "*Hey mum! The King's dead*".

So the date must have been 6th February 1952 - and the fact that I had heard this important piece of information unaccompanied by the usual cacophony of static, underlined the fact that Radio Relay was here to stay... well for a while at any rate.

It was quite common to invite friends round to listen to the radio, and as a result Geoffrey Hogg and I would listen together for anything remotely entertaining. *Children's Hour* had been started after the war, and featured items such as "*Jennings and Darbishire*" and "*Toy Town*". The latter was, as its name suggests, based on the rather less than exciting adventures of a number of townsfolk who were a somewhat bizarre mixture of humans and animals. The main characters were *Larry the Lamb* who insisted on rendering his lines as a mixture of bleating and speaking – a sort of '*bleatospeak*' if you like – and his sidekick *Dennis the Dachshund*, who always spoke with a strong German accent. This I found rather an odd choice since **a)** he was pretty hard to understand and **b)** bearing in mind the huge range of national stereotypes to choose from, why select one with whom we had recently had six years' worth of fairly serious disagreements? Surely '*Sammy the Scottie*' or '*Lionel the Labrador*' might have been a little less controversial? Nevertheless, we tuned into the Home Service to hear the latest, and to be blunt, pretty tame escapades of bleatospeak Larry, *Mr. Growser* the grocer, *Ernest the Policeman, Mr. Mayor* (no idea what he did) and the faithful Teutonic canine, Dennis. Anyway, the signature tune '*The Parade of the Tin Soldiers*' was nice.

By contrast, the adventures of *Jennings and Darbishire* were something with which we could more readily identify. After all, weren't these audacious schoolboys altogether decent chaps (pronounced '*cheps*') whose adventures at their prep school were a lot nearer to home? Well, probably not... Jennings' dad was a stockbroker, and Darbishire's, a Church of England clergyman. Added to this you had to throw in such school-based posts as 'Housemaster', 'Matron' and Mr. Topliss who... '*teaches shooting once a week in the shooting range behind the gymnasium*'. Leaving aside the wisdom of going behind the gym with a bloke carrying a gun - if we're not back in the land of make-believe again, we're certainly a hell of a long way from Highland Road Junior School and the common lot of most kids in the fifties, I can assure you.

Saturday morning's '*Children's Favourites*' (the forerunner of Ed Stewart's *Junior Choice*) was, as its name implies, very popular with us littlies. It's interesting to note that its host, 'Uncle Mac', was none other than one Derek McCulloch, a well known radio broadcaster whose repertoire also included *Larry the Lamb*. Small world, wasn't it? Bearing in mind this was before the advent of pop music, the range of musical offerings for youngsters was really quite limited - but you have also to consider that not being surrounded by music 24/7, we heard such presentations infrequently, so their inclusion in Uncle Mac's programme was always welcomed. Hence such classics as *'The Laughing Policeman', 'How Much is that Doggie in the Window?'* and even *'The Teddybear's Picnic'* were always well received, and Danny Kaye's *'The Ugly Duckling'* was a right laugh.

If the antics of an outcast duck were not enough, there was always the truly bizarre adventures featured in *'Sparky's Magic Piano'*, in which a kid who is having obvious difficulty in tickling the ivories in anything approaching a cogent form, finds that his piano is alive! It speaks to him in a singularly metallic manner, and rather than slamming the lid shut and running screaming from the room, Sparky finds this enormous fun, not once reflecting on the fact that he's learned absolutely nothing, and still can't play a note. Hey ho. Better, I think to rely on good old *'Tubby the Tuba'* (whom I took to be a distant cousin of Dennis the Dachshund) who elicited enormous sympathy in that he was always overlooked by the other instruments in the orchestra. These comprised the brash trumpets, the bellowing trombones and of course the French horns whose behaviour, to be frank, was really quite unbecoming, and did much to harden the view that we should always be wary of continentals. That is, until the day when Tubby hit upon a short series of notes of such melancholic poignancy that it stopped the rest of the orchestra dead. Jolly good too – well done Tubby, say I.

Another fifties favourite bore the unlikely title of *'You're a Pink Toothbrush'*. Sung by Max Bygraves, this was the romantic story of how a lonely blue toothbrush meets the love of his life by the bathroom door. Quickly identifying the pink newcomer's availability (not to mention gender), the blue toothbrush bristles with almost unseemly desire and steers this steamy liaison towards an early marriage. To be honest, the pace of this relationship did leave the perceptive listener querying the depth of genuine affection one toothbrush might have for the other – or whether or not there were more serious moral implications in their rapid betrothal. Nevertheless, the relationship seemed solid enough, as they agreed to ever thereafter use the *'same toothpaste'*. Anyway, Uncle Mac didn't seem to mind, so who were we to question such a moral dilemma? Bearing in mind this was not a request show, surprise was all important, and as mentioned earlier, 'Trains' by Reginald Gardiner was a very welcome, novel and non-musical inclusion on the playlist.

The songs on *Children's Favourites* were interspersed with popular and stirring orchestral classics such as *'Coronation Scot'* the *'Dambusters' March'*, *'The William Tell Overture'*, and *'The Devil's Gallop'*. These last two were particularly well known as the latter was the theme tune to the really exciting and cutting edge radio drama series *'Dick Barton, Special Agent'* (where the dialogue was frequently of the ***'There!*** [sound of thumping]***Take that, you foreign swine!'*** variety), and the former, the theme tune to an early American TV series entitled *'The Lone Ranger'* (***'A streak of white, a flash of light and a cry of Hiiii-Yoooo Silver!'***) All stirring stuff for kids on a Saturday morning which often had juvenile listeners acting out these images *like anything.*

For teenagers in the early fifties, there was very little opportunity to listen to what might be described as more popular music on the radio. Request music shows (and you can't really include *'Housewives' Choice'* each weekday morning in this: Doris Day's thigh slapping rendition of *'The Deadwood Stage'* might have been some ladies' cup of tea, but it was hardly pop) were more or less non-existent. Apart, that is, from a special programme broadcast once a year... yes ONCE a year. I speak of the week long *'Radio Show'* from Earls Court.

Greatly anticipated, this programme featured all that was brightest and best in the radio and (as yet) infant TV world. The majority of the daily visit seemed to deal with the host wandering around the various commercial stands – household names such as Decca, Bush, HMV, Phillips and so on – and interviewing the reps who were keen to describe their latest offerings. Bearing in mind TV sets were still relatively rare and very expensive, there was quite a lot of talk about

Nice sound - but big and expensive

radiograms – the inordinately large and highly polished pieces of furniture which combined both radio, gramophone and storage for all one's large 78rpm - and thus highly breakable - record collection. So, most of it went over our heads as there was nothing much to capture the attention of the younger generation. This was a shame in a way, because I'm sure there would have been considerable interest in practical items such as *'how to tune your radio to get anything other than the fishing forecast for Hammerfest'*, for example. But no. Clearly an opportunity lost. However, there was one part we really did look forward to, and this was the *daily request spot*, when visitors to the show could test the range and variety of the BBC's extensive Gramophone Library. For the 1950's this was almost unbearably exciting, and took the format of the host conducting a brief interview with a visitor, at the conclusion of which he or she was invited to test the BBC's mettle to the nth degree by asking for a record – *any* record - to be played. We were given the impression that once the request had been made, a host of BBC employees would hurtle off into the dimly lit archives of Broadcasting House to locate, retrieve and wipe the cobwebs off some dusty 78rpm record, completing their task with a breathless dash back the awaiting turntable. What fun... and don't forget this was the 1950's, and skiffle groups were suddenly becoming all the rage. So, there was a slim chance that one of the interviewees might step aside from the normal (boring) requests such as Alan Breeze's '*I've Never Seen a Straight Banana*' and ask for Lonnie Donegan's skiffle group playing '*Rock Island Line*' or '*Freight Train*'.

Although still not exactly 'pop', skiffle was new, exciting, and most of all, it was OURS. It was different, 'jazzy', easy to sing along to and almost totally reviled by our parents' generation – perfect! It was also very accessible because the music was pretty simple, and it was cheap. The growing number of skiffle groups needed only to gather together three musical instruments: a guitar, a tea chest, and a washboard. The guitar is fairly easy to explain, but tea chest and washboard? *Musical instruments?* Let me explain. Until the 1960's,

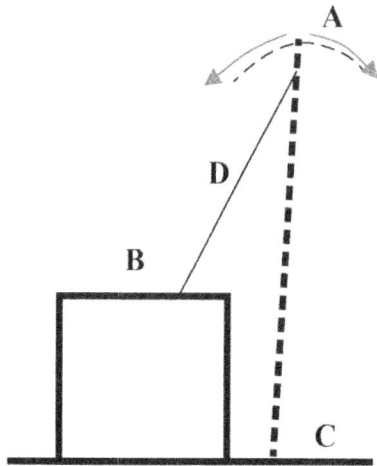

The theory:

1. *Grasp broom handle at A;*
2. *Place one foot firmly at B;*
3. *Place other foot firmly at C;*
4. *Check for hernia;*
5. *Tension string as per arrows;*
6. *Pluck string at D;*
7. *Listen to melodic G# result as chest vibrates*
8. *Apologise as group wanted E#*

tea was imported from foreign parts in wooden boxes. These took the form of large plywood cubes, strengthened with metal edging, and lined with a type of tin foil to keep the tea dry. Now, I've no idea who discovered the musical characteristics of said tea chest, but if you turned the empty box upside down having first pierced the bottom and threading through a piece of knotted string, you could pull this up tight and attach it to the top of a broom handle. OK so far? The other end of the broom handle was placed firmly on the floor alongside the tea chest, and by pulling its top the string was tightened; plucking it then produced a slightly muffled musical note generated by the vibration of the tea chest. So, you had your guitar strumming out some basic chords, and an upturned wooden box-cum-broom handle double bass – all you needed now was the percussion section. A drum set was expensive, so best look for a local solution. And if a discarded tea container could provide a substitute double bass, then surely something equally prosaic should be readily available to provide the missing toe-tapping beat

A sink plunger perhaps? How about an ironing board... or maybe an upturned coal scuttle and pair of old corsets? No. The answer was a *washboard and thimbles*. Obvious when you think about it really. Even in the 1950's, washboards were going out of use: a hand held wooden frame enclosing a corrugated metal sheet upon which clothes were scrubbed with soap was really becoming old tech, as increasingly available washing machines (albeit twin tubs) and local laundrettes were the more fashionable alternative. However, just like the little rolling threepenny bit, the humble washboard could be made to emit a strident whirring sound when your fingernails were whipped firmly across the corrugations. Unfortunately, repeated and enthusiastic application quickly resulted

The Railroad Bill skiffle group. In the fifties pop fashion was 'a work in progress', so many bands still dressed quite formally.

in very sore fingers, and so a more durable solution was needed. And where better to look than in the sewing kit, containing as it did many thimbles. So, grab a handful of these (quite literally) and Bob's your uncle: your percussion section is complete and raring to go.

The early fifties found thousands of skiffle groups all over the country banging away on these bizarre instruments... and in all likelihood many more thousands of housewives looking into their sewing boxes and muttering to themselves *'Funny, I'm sure I had at least four thimbles'*. Now I'm not saying that the music was particularly refined - what do you expect from a discarded tea chest and a geriatric soap scrubber? But it was fun, and what's more, it was seen as being uniquely owned by the young: it was all ours. The majority of the older generation didn't like it, and better still didn't understand it, and this made aspirant teenagers feel a difference, almost an *independence* from the world of our parents. Well, with songs like *'Does Your Chewing Gum Lose Its Flavour on the Bedpost Over-night'* and *'My Old Man's a Dustman'* how could you not fail to be part of this brave new world?

And so it was with eager anticipation that we tuned into the request spot from the annual Radio Show. Would the interviewees disappoint by asking for Gracie Fields shrieking out *'Salleeeey, Salleeeey, Pride of Our Alley'* for the ten millionth time, or would they go for *'Don't You Rock Me Daddyo'* or *'Cumberland Gap'* by the great Lonnie Donegan? Not only was teenage liberation expressed in the wild beat of the music, but the lyrics of many – though incredibly tame by modern standards - were a challenge to the staid and stuffy status quo of the time. Bearing in mind that the BBC would not be forced into introducing its own pop-devoted radio station for *over a decade* (Radio One in 1967), getting the Light Programme to play such irreverent and ground-breaking music was a bit like getting the vicar to admit to farting. *'Cumberland Gap'*, for example, had lyrics we thought really quite racy:

I've got a girl,
Six feet tall,
Sleeps in the kitchen
With her head in the hall...

And again:

Two old ladies
Sitting in the sand,
Each one wishing that
The other was a man

OK, sophisticated it was not, but to get the BBC to play it was something of a triumph and although it might have been in my imagination, I'm sure I could pick out the slight air of embarrassment that accompanied the Radio Show presenter's comments that book-ended the record, e.g.:

'Well, I expect 'My Old Man's a Dustman' may take a few moments to find in the record library – let's hope it's not already been put out for the refuse collection!' And all the time you could bet that he was thinking *'Why the hell can't you choose Mario Lanza singing something nice from 'The Student Prince', you moron!'*

Although it's easy to be critical of the BBC's rock solid 'we know best' establishment and its obvious reluctance to even acknowledge the onset of a totally new cultural development, it *did* keep us entertained. For example, there can be few Baby Boomers who were not brought up with *'Two Way Family Favourites'* of a Sunday lunchtime, with hosts Jean Metcalfe and Cliff Michelmore. Quite apart from their somewhat gushing enthusiasm for each other (they were brought together by the radio programme, then called *'Forces Favourites'* after the war, and were married in 1950), the programme was incredibly popular because:

a) It was Sunday lunchtime, and thousands of families were together for the big meal of the week;

b) Dad was back from the pub/church/both, and therefore in a good mood;

c) Ye olde valve radio set had been coaxed into providing something other than *'How to build an extension to your igloo'* in Norwegian... and most of all...

d) *'Family Favourites'* was a *record request* show, so people got to hear what they *wanted* to hear, not what the BBC thought was good for them.

And after a satisfying lunch, why not settle down (as millions did) to listen to *'The Billy Cotton Band Show'* whose rousing cry 'WAKEY WAAAAAKEY!!!' from the man himself preceded a rather eclectic mix of music dotted with familiar landmarks - for this was the age of the catchphrase.

These dated, no doubt, from the popular wartime show *ITMA,** whose favourite line: *'Can I do you now Sir?'* became a beacon of humorous familiarity and hope in those desperate times. Like many other post-war radio shows, *'The Billy Cotton Band Show'* built in its own catchphrases, chief amongst which was an interlude when Billy was yelled at by an American who cried: *'Hey You! You down there with the glasses!'* which preceded a bit of transatlantic banter. Often this would be followed by a related piece of American music, or by resident singer Alan Breeze who would often launch into ballads such as the pathos ridden *'Bless This House'* with the same gusto as his spirited rendition of *'When is a Sausage a Sausage?'* or *'I Can't Do My Bally Bottom Button Up'*. Rather appropriate for post Sunday lunch, don't you think? Comedy shows then filled the airwaves, and *'Life with the Lyons'* and *'Meet the Huggets'* set the pattern for the decade to come when programmes such as *'The Clitheroe Kid'* and

---

* *'It's That Man Again' was a very popular wartime radio show featuring Tommy Hanley. Its great strength was its homely humour which took the style of slick talking rather than the out and out hilarity of, say, 'The Goon Show' of later years. In a sense it was familiar rather than funny, but ITMA gave comforting reassurance when it was most needed.*

.

'The Navy Lark' became so embedded, that by the dawn of the sixties, they were regarded as an essential ingredient to the weekend ritual.

The late fifties saw a move in radio comedy from the comfortably predictable and simple humorous style of programmes such as the aforementioned *Huggets* and *Lyons*, to the beautifully crafted and full-on comedy of the likes of 'Hancock's Half Hour' and Kenneth Horne's 'Beyond Our Ken' with its later variation 'Round the Horne'. The developmental route was taken via a number of memorable programmes which became more specifically comedy oriented, such as the long running 'Take It from Here' with Jimmy Edwards and a young June Whitfield, and 'Educating Archie'. The latter was most extraordinary in that its central character, the eponymous Archie, was actually a ventriloquist's dummy, in the firm control of one Peter Brough. But this was the **radio**, and bearing in mind the whole art of ventriloquism is entirely visual, it makes one wonder why it was so popular. Nevertheless, it had high audience appeal and the cameo appearances by Max Bygraves whose catchphrase 'That's a good idea.....SON!' was always welcome. Also featured was Beryl Reed, whose Brummy character *Marlene* always said 'Good evening, each!' in an accent so thick you could stir it with a stick. Looking back, you could say that this was an early introduction to regional dialects which were virtually unknown on the BBC at that time. 'Educating Archie' had a big following, and the same was true of 'Take It from Here', which included a very popular weekly feature concerning the life of 'The Glums'. Had dysfunctional families been invented in the fifties, the Glums would certainly have qualified - with June's character, the bright but wistful *Eth* nicely balanced by her gormless fiancé *Ron* played by Dick Bentley and the unscrupulous and conniving *Pa Glum* portrayed by Jimmy Edwards. Thus radio comedy developed into a high quality product, full of memorable characters, catchphrases and a considerable amount of quite risqué innuendo in shows like '*Beyond Our Ken*' - very daring for the period.

But the one radio show that was in a class of its own was, without doubt '*The Goon Show*'. Created and written by the unique Spike Milligan, its large cast of characters were brought to life by Spike himself (as *Eccles, Minnie Bannister, Count Jim Moriarty, Miss Throat* etc). Supporting him were Harry Secombe as *Neddy Seagoon* and the multi-talented Peter Sellers as nearly everyone else: *Bluebottle, Major Dennis Bloodnok, Henry Crun, Hercules Grytpype-Thin, William Cobblers* etc. Strikingly original, the Goon Show went where no other comedy programme had been before, and left the BBC establishment completely bemused. That it was broadcast at all, shows the persuasive power of Milligan. The dear old Beeb was like a rabbit caught in the headlights: it had no idea what to do next, but thought it ought to do *something*. Apart from providing a very tentative and nervous green light to putting the programme on air, its sole contribution was to provide a title. That it came up with the astoundingly unimaginative '***Crazy People***' says a great deal about the distance between creative innovation on the one hand and the establishment's view of what a 'proper' light entertainment programme should be on the other.

But we jump ahead of ourselves; whilst the Goon Show and Hancock were indeed creatures of the mid to late fifties, the standard daily radio offerings on the Light Programme and the Home Service were far more conservative. As far as I was concerned, the weekday routine started off after the morning news with '*Housewives' Choice*', heralded by its distinctive and surprisingly catchy theme tune. The programme itself was about er.... *housewives* and their *choices* ... so at least there was just a micro–chance that Mrs. Stevens from West Bromwich might choose something a bit jazzy, or even humorous. The audience was of course, huge, as in the 1950's most mums, and a surprisingly high proportion of unmarried women stayed at home while the menfolk went to work. The next programme in the morning schedule was the rather pious –but thankfully short - *'Five to Ten'* religious broadcast. Starting as you might expect at 9.55, it was always introduced by the announcer's solemn voice: *'It's Five to Ten'* followed by a chorister giving it what-for from Durham Cathedral or somewhere similar. Just five minutes later, light relief in the form of the ever popular *'Music While You Work'* hit the airwaves.

Although targeted much more at keeping factory workers happily engaged at their work benches, it was also attractive to the many thousands of housewives who were busy buffing up the lino or mangling the bed linen* in a steamy kitchen. This essential task was completed just prior to chopping up the remains of Sunday's veg ready to make that night's Bubble n' Squeak, and trying not to break the little key which was the one and only way to get at the contents of a tin of Fray Bentos corned beef. ** It was also another brilliant example of unimaginative programme titling, and in similar vein it came as little surprise when the weekday lunchtime broadcast for

*In the sense of extracting water from wet fabric by squeezing it between two heavy rollers you understand – **not** ruining it by inattention or lack of ability.

** For reasons unknown, corned beef was packed into cans which were cuboid in shape. As such, a conventional tin-opener was redundant. Instead, to open the can, a small key was provided which was supposed to engage with a lug on the side of the can. You then turned the key which had the effect of winding itself around the can, pulling with it a section of the container, the complete circumnavigation therefore separating the top of the can. That was the theory. The practice was very often quite different. If you lost the key, broke it, or put it on upside down, you might as well chuck it all in the bin. Even if you made it all the way round, the key - now wrapped in multiple layers of very sharp tin - often refused to detach itself from the can. Struggles to get it to do so usually resulted in **a)** a hopelessly bent can; **b)** the can contents unexpectedly making a bid for freedom and landing with a fatty 'splat' noise on the kitchen floor or **c)** a visit to casualty. Even if you were entirely successful with the key, getting the tight-fitting corned beef out of the main body of the can was another challenge, and the use of knives, skewers, lollipop sticks, bent forks and violent shaking to extract the meat without getting it all scrunched up is a subject of further debate … and quite beyond me.

factory workers was almost inevitably called *'Workers' Playtime'*.

Of a slightly different format, this was an outside broadcast variety show from the canteen of some factory, and as such featured not only the compulsory singers and instrumental pieces, but comics as well. In keeping with the current trend, each would come with his trade mark catchphrase, and the humour was mainly of the *'Oh what a cheeky chappy I am!'* type. I seem to recall contributors such as Tommy *'You lucky people!'* Trinder, Arthur *'And now before your very eyes...'* Askey and Max *'No!... here!... listen!'* Miller fulfilling these roles, as did Cheerful Charlie Chester. To me, the programmes were OK-ish ... but perhaps only just that.

Into the afternoon, *'Listen with Mother'* was still going strong, with its pastiche of well-hard songs, rhymes and unlikely tales. Next on the Radio Times list was *'Woman's Hour'* which seemed to go on forever, and was about... well, women I suppose. That it persists right to the present day is testimony to its broad appeal... but for a little boy?

Another programme which deserves mention was *'Mrs. Dale's Diary'*. Broadcast twice a day, this short programme followed the life of the good lady who was married to Jim Dale, a country doctor. I'm assuming he was a GP – to be honest, I didn't listen all that closely, and once the rather tedious piece of harp music which constituted its introduction was registered, I would slope off to look for an interesting piece of string, or gaze in a vacant way out of the front room window to see if the boy next door-but-one had come back on his BSA Bantam motorbike. Suffice it to say that Mrs. Dale seemed to be in a perpetual state of anxiety, as the opening remark from her *Diary* always seemed to be *'I've been very worried about Jim lately'*. Well, I could have told her not to worry: Jim seemed destined to go on forever and a day as far as I was concerned - it was all there, in the Radio Times.

The same was true of another early soap: *'At the Luscombe's'*.

Based in a fictional part of the West Country, this programme too had what seemed to me to be an oft-repeated opening line where an equally anxious Mrs. Luscombe would cry to one of her six children: *'Dot? Dot! Where are you Dot?'* As you can imagine, this was not entirely gripping for the average junior school kid – except to say that:

a) The head of the Luscombe household had a small building firm described as *'H. Luscombe and Son, Builders and Sanitary Engineers'*. Now, the inclusion of the less salubrious part of that title in a BBC radio broadcast was quite surprising: reference to anything to do with toilets was virtually unheard of... and

b) The actress who played the sought after Dot Luscombe was Aileen Mills... and Aileen Mills lived in our town! And my dad delivered groceries to her house! And he might one day even see her! How exciting would that be? Well, probably not quite exciting enough, as once the theme tune and the opening querulous enquiry had been made, my juvenile brain tended to lapse back into its customary torpor and the attraction of trying to swat flies in the garden before *'Children's Hour'* started, usually won the tug of war as to where my attention would wander next.

Like most news and current affairs programmes, those provided by the BBC at 6pm were of little interest to the average nine year old, and the next radio stop was at a quarter to seven (*never*, you will note, *6.45*, and not in our wildest dreams *18.45*, not in our house at any rate: we didn't hold with messing around with the time; what would the neighbours say?). I digress. But at a quarter to seven it was time for our daily dose of *'dumpty-dumpty dumpty-dum'* – as the familiar theme tune of *'The Archers'* filled the house. As it was my mum's favourite programme of the day, I had no choice but to listen – indeed I think it might have been compulsory in those days to be up to date on the comings and goings of Dan and Doris and all the regulars at The Bull in Ambridge. My own favourite character was, of course, Walter Gabriel. Even to a little lad, he seemed like a complete loony, a fact emphasised by his insistence on calling everyone '...*me old Darling, me old Beauty'*. The only downside as far as I was concerned was that his voice was rather husky, and therefore just a little bit reminiscent of Ben Parsons.

The '*News' and 'Radio Newsreel'* programmes at 7.00pm were another arid area for me; that the Suez crisis was in full swing, and Anthony Eden was so deep in the brown stuff that he might have had good reason to call upon the sanitary services of Harry Luscombe and Son, was completely lost on me. What I was waiting for was the 7.30 – 8.30pm time slot which hosted the main comedy shows. Alright, you might have to put up with a bit of '*Have A Go'*, an early quiz show in which Yorkshire host Wilfred Pickles would invite people to do all sorts of odd things in order to win prizes dispensed by his wife '*Mabel at the table'*.

There was also the highly regarded '*Letter from America'* flawlessly presented by Alistair Cook. Now you would have thought that such a serious programme would have been of no interest to a little air-head like me, but you would have been wrong. First, as you might have spotted, it was from *America,* and as far as we post-war kids were concerned, America was where all good things came from; it was the land of Roy Rogers and his famous horse Trigger, and they also had bubble gum, flashy cars with lots of chrome and very white teeth – the people that is, not the cars. So, what's not to like? Second, as my dad pointed out, Alistair Cook never once stuttered or stumbled in his presentation. It was as if he had never heard of the words '*er'* or '*um'* or ever felt the need to cough or – dare we think it - fart during his presentation. So, I *had* to listen, didn't I? Surely one of these days a wasp would fly up his nose, or he'd drop his script with a resounding thud on the studio floor, or get an unreachable itch in his scrotum? But no. He was perfect... and he continued being perfect for the next forty eight years, eventually finishing in February

2004, making *'Letter from America'* the longest running spoken radio programme ever. But I didn't know that in 1956, did I? And I was sure he'd slip up one day. Some hopes!

So, apart from the radio, what else kept us amused on these Pre Bop-a-Lulan, pre- television, days? Well, quite a lot, actually. For a start, going to *the flicks* was very popular. Cinemas were big business, and there were lots of them, bearing a whole variety of names ranging from the pretentious, through the enticing, via the incomprehensible to the vulgar. Names such as The Roxy, The Palace, The Empire, The Essoldo, and The Gaiety vied with the more ubiquitous Odeon and Gaumont. What's more, colour films were now quite commonplace, and there was the fantastic 3D *Cinerama* which came, circus like, on a visit to *'a town near you'*, where you could buy special tickets to go and sit in an enormous blue tent and watch the spectacle of the Niagara Falls etc. as if you were actually there. What excitement!

Ordinary cinema programmes always included two films, with a travelogue/news item between. The supporting, or B film, would quite often be monochrome, and either a rather tired western with grey cowboys shooting at grey Indians whilst circling their grey wagons and telling the grey womenfolk to *'Hush your hollering and fetch me some vittles!'* Regular alternatives to the 'also rans' menu were American gangster films featuring a fine array of pre-war cars with running boards wide enough to accommodate several villains firing tommy guns, and adventure stories which seemed always to have the hero flying an antiquated plane through a torrential rainstorm whilst at the same time trying to placate the entreaties of the heroine who was sure they were about to come to a sticky – and fairly immediate - end.

The ones I liked the best were the space adventures; if you think that the props and scenery used in the later TV series *'Crossroads'* (and brilliantly sent up by Victoria Wood in *'Acorn Antiques'*) were bad, then you have just an inkling of how awful these films could be. But, of course, that was at least half of the attraction. The fact that the bloke with a goldfish bowl on his head was walking past a Martian crater that wobbled every time his silver sprayed wellies went anywhere near it was all part of the fun, as were the death ray guns made of red plastic and silver paper that were *sooo* much like a stretched water pistol.

Nevertheless, the main feature films on the programme were often very good, and played to packed audiences night after night. A roll call of films for 1956, for example, details some pretty memorable stuff including '*Carousel*', '*A Town like Alice*', '*1984*', '*Moby Dick*' and '*Around the World in 80 Days*'. My favourites for that year were '*Reach for the Sky*', the story of Douglas Bader and the Battle of Britain, and the biblical epic '*The Ten Commandments*'. The former had us little boys rushing out of the Odeon with arms outstretched making aeroplane, machine gun and explosion noises – never a subtle combination – whilst the latter gave the old dressing gown/tea-towel combo normally reserved for the annual Christmas shepherd extravaganza an unexpected extra use. All we needed then was a stern look, a big stick, a few bits of stone and a piece of chalk, and we were away. Oh, and a burning bush and the ability to part the waters of the Canoe Lake would have been an added advantage.

But these cinema presentations formed only a small part of the average kids' movie diet; of much greater significance was *Saturday Morning Pictures*. Looking back, I can only feel sorry for the poor souls who had to provide this entertainment: it was really complete mayhem from start to finish. The idea was that the cinema should provide a couple of hours of mixed cinematic entertainment for the dear little children living in the neighbourhood, thus allowing their doting mummies and daddies a spot of time to themselves each Saturday morning. That was the theory, but a nano-second of reflection indicated that such lofty ideals were very much a hope rather than an expectation. If you put hundreds of kids in a darkened room, provide them with sweets which double up as a source of nourishment/tooth decay *and* a useful missile, plus you have only a handful of harassed adults to keep order, what do you expect? The menu was as follows:

With the lights still up, the manager of our cinema, Mr. Layborn, would come and stand in front of the huge and gorgeously draped curtains to start the show. His opening remarks characterised the expectations that the management had of likely outcomes, as they were an unusual amalgam of welcome and threat. At the end of this, all children were required to sing a communal song. In order to ensure the success of this choral masterpiece, Mr. L would shout, *'Sing up, and follow the bouncing ball!'* At this point the verses would appear on the screen, and a little ball would bounce along underneath the words to ensure the tempo was maintained. In reality, the outcome frequently bore little resemblance to the intention. Despite Mr. Layborn's threats not to meddle with the lyrics, a number of junior wags would do just that. Often the chorus to the ever popular ditty *'Over the Mountains, Over the Sea'* tended to degenerate from the given lyrics which were ...

I see the moon, the moon sees me,
Through the branches of the old oak tree
Please let the light that shines on me,
Shine on the one I love

...into something far less salubrious, which went along the lines of:

I see the moon, the moon sees me,
You're a bleedin' liar 'cause the moon can't see
Please let the light that shines on me,
Shine on me as I pee

So, having got off to a cracking start, with just a few kids ejected for not following the bouncing ball - and an apoplectic Mr. L beating a hasty retreat towards a nearby bottle of aspirins - the cinema would quieten down (a relative term, you'll understand) ready for the first item, the cartoon.

It's hard to understand that in the 1950's, cartoons were almost the sole preserve of the cinema. Relatively few people had a TV, and before the introduction of ITV in 1956, such programmes as there were did not include such frippery. Instead, we were given such oddities as marionette shows in the form of *'Muffin the Mule'*, *'Andy Pandy'* and *Bill and 'Ben the Flowerpot Men'*... all very tame, all in very precise and clipped English (apart I suppose, from Bill and Ben who danced up and down on their very visible strings uttering incomprehensible sounds that seemed to be an endless repetition of *'flubba–lubbalub...little weeeeed'*) and all in glorious black and white. So, when Saturday morning pictures showed *'Bugs Bunny'* or *'Tom and Jerry'* it was to a huge roar of approval; the cartoons were noisy, they were in colour, they were funny... and they were *American.*

After this there might be a short B film, which could well be a very old and amusingly jerky silent movie, such as the Buster Keaton classic *'Steamboat Bill'* complete with the famous falling wall sequence, or the nail-biting antics of Harold Lloyd climbing up a sky-scraper and desperately hanging on to the giant clock in *'Safety Last'*. Others were less entertaining, and their popularity could be gauged by the number of sweets-cum-missiles which were launched at this point in the programme. An interval followed offering the chance to dash to the loo and to re-arm at the sweet stall, following which the big picture was screened. Again, this might be an old British comedy such as George Formby's *'It's in the Air'* but by far and away the most common was the western. The vast majority of these followed the same formula, and nearly always featured a gunslinger who could shoot the middle out of a silver dollar tossed into the air half a mile away, and whose horse was usually white and obviously the *GTi* model, as it could outstrip all other equine contenders with contemptuous ease. Our hero could also catch a runaway train, grapple with a villain on its roof, and head off a stampede of three thousand cattle as they thundered towards an unprotected homestead where the heroine was busy wringing her hands and pointing her usually formidable bosom in the direction of the impending disaster and crying:

'Oh Rocky, please hurry, we're about to be crushed by the cattle, the injuns are firing flaming arrows into the shack, the baby's fallen down the well, there's a grizzly bear in the barn, and I've got a hair appointment at 2.30 sharp – so hurry... HURRY!'

Another favourite scene featured a Wells Fargo stagecoach which was always being chased by either a gang of bandits, or by a large group of ferocious injuns. We must have seen this played out hundreds of times, and the drama *always* followed an entirely predictable path vis... one of the stagecoach crew lies on the roof and fires his Winchester rifle at the pursuers – one or two of whom obligingly fall off their horses with the customary expression of surprise (*'aargh!'* does this very nicely). In the meantime, the coach driver takes up a most earnest stance on his violently swaying seat and slaps the reins up and down whilst shouting *'Heeeaaah!!! Heeeaaah!!!'* at the horses, and in order to make absolutely sure the poor beasts have got the message that he would be most obliged if they could gallop just a little faster, he also lashes out with his cracking whip. Such behaviour always seemed entirely counter-productive to me; horses are intelligent animals and it won't have escaped their notice that just hanging around with a load of heavily armed mal-contents in hot pursuit isn't a particularly good idea. Thus one supposes that being shouted at and whipped by someone who is supposed to be *on your side* must therefore have pissed them off terribly. Would it not have been much better for the driver to have yelled: *'Hey fellas – if only you'd put on just a bit more speed, there's an extra bag of oats in a stable of your choice just a mile down the road plus a couple of hot fillies just gagging for it !'* It will come as no surprise that raising such a point with one's rowdy chums at Saturday morning pics was a fruitless exercise, however.

So, there you are: a heady mixture of make-believe, cartoons, cheap sweets, old films and the chance to improve your throwing skills... and the pleasure of watching poor Mr. Layborn trying to cover up the fact that of all the things he liked in the world, children came nowhere close - that was Saturday morning pictures for you. And of course, the final feature would dictate the manner in which the dear kiddies would *erupt* from the cinema at noon, and I use the word advisedly. It was not just the rush to get out before the National Anthem,* although that played a significant part. What spurred us on was the thought of the charge home assuming whichever role had been dictated by the main film. Thus it was that, more often than not, we'd take to the streets at the gallop, slapping our own hind quarters, and emptying imaginary six shooters into Mr. Chandler's carefully arranged tobacco and confectioners display in the shop over the road. Equally, of course, anyone in the immediate vicinity could be speared with a lance or chopped down with a sword, and it was not unknown for many a hand grenade to be expertly lobbed into the front gardens of Festing Road, or for Ben Parsons' invalid carriage to be peppered with machine gun bullets.

Back in the now empty cinema, you could picture Mr. Layborn and his staff breathing a collective sigh of relief and beginning the arduous task of sweeping up the generous precipitation of popcorn and other tasty projectiles. Perhaps they were imagining their little customers busy gunning each other down in the local streets as they headed pell-mell home for dinner which might well be mashed spuds

* *All cinemas played the National Anthem at the close of the performance. The audience was supposed to stand in respectful silence Didn't often happen, especially on Saturday mornings.*

and spaghetti hoops. And don't forget that all of this palaver was merely in preparation for the delights of Saturday afternoon.

In the fifties, there was a marked seasonal difference in how the post-Saturday lunchtime period was enjoyed: either there was a proper (professional) football match, or there wasn't. It was therefore most definitely a summer and winter thing. Throughout the decade, if you were a keen football supporter - and most boys were - you supported your local team. To follow the fortunes of a team based elsewhere was virtually unheard of. Everyone – and I mean *everyone* – supported their local team. For us, this meant a trip to Fratton Park to see 'The Royal Blues' (aka Pompey, or more properly, Portsmouth Football Club) achieving a surprise win/ dismal draw/a right thrashing by the visiting mob.

I recollect that there were an awful lot of the latter and not many of the former. Even so, that didn't stop us from leaving at 1.30pm each winter Saturday afternoon in order to get a standing place at the front, right up against the low wall surrounding the pitch ready for

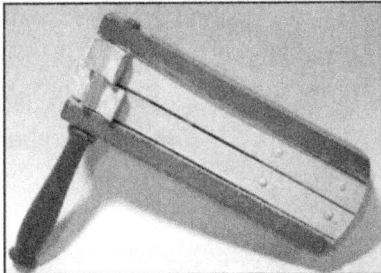

The football rattle: like many things of the 1950's, subtle and sophisticated it was not.

the 3.00pm kick off. If you couldn't get to the front, little lads like us couldn't see anything of the action, as the crowds in those days were massive. So, dressed with blue and white bobble hat, blue and white scarf, blue and white rosette pinned nattily to our lapels, and wooden rattle in hand, off we'd go. For those of you unfamiliar with the rattle, let me assure you that, young as we were, this was not the piece of equipment commonly tossed out of prams by the youngest members of society – even we were not *that* unsophisticated. The football rattle was whirled above your head so that the flexible wooden slats would be vibrated by the revolving cogs. The noise was appalling, but evidently embodied all that was needed to show the players that their efforts were appreciated, and to offer further encouragement. So thus equipped, we would head for the turnstiles, pay our 1/6d, pause briefly to fork out a few pennies on a bag of curiously bright red and green sweets which looked and tasted like sweet cardboard, and then rush down the terraces to claim a premium spot right at the front... only to wait there for well over an hour as the terraces filled up behind us. But such a position was worth the wait: we were close enough to smell the embrocation, view the thigh strapping and observe the gum chewing of players required to take a throw-in. So the pitch level view was good, but we were right at the bottom of the sloping terrace in front of a large section of a huge standing crowd, the majority of whom had no benefit of the randomly placed leaning bars. Nevertheless, the thought that we were packed in tightly against an immoveable three foot wall and were therefore prime candidates for getting squashed never entered our tiny minds. To be honest, I can't remember any incidents of crowd surges, of bad behaviour, of intimidation of opposing teams, of foul language, or indeed anything you wouldn't want your mum to hear – well, almost. Crowds seemed to be generally good natured, and the terraces provided a magnificent opportunity for humorists to offer their comments in the breathless hush that followed a catastrophic event, like the opponents scoring a goal. At such times, remarks addressed to the defending goalie might be:

"Oi! The idea is you use your 'ands to stop the ball, not just wave them about! I thought you were measuring up for a pair of curtains!" etc., etc.

Of course, there was comment aplenty, much of it of an advisory nature, and a great deal very amusing. Oddly, the one occasion that really sticks in my mind, and so fully typifies the gallows type humour of football crowds, occurred a few years later when I had stopped regular Saturday attendance, as other weekend focussed interests had started to take its place. On this particular occasion however, the *other interest* had been persuaded to accompany me to Fratton Park to see a particularly important fixture. The match was not going well: it had been one of those tense, hard games when what little skill our team possessed had been noted only by its almost complete absence. The crowd had grown quiet and uneasy. Encouraging cries of **'Come on the Royal Blues!!'** were having no apparent effect. My only delight had been at one particularly quiet point in the second half when I heard, distinct but incomprehensible, a familiar voice cry out:

'C'mon da Rarny Bewn!! Seddem alight da Roysaah!!

The interpretation is as follows:

'Come on the Royal Blues!! Set them alight the Royals!!'

For those of you who recall Chapter 5, the recognition that our bus conductor friend was spending a little of his well earned free time enduring the unedifying spectacle of the local team gamely pursuing its sporting destiny with what can only be described as lemming like zeal, what follows may bring a little light relief to this sorry tale.

Pompey had endured a hard game, with the team desperately clinging on for a draw and with about four minutes to go. Given the lacklustre performance that afternoon, there was no credible likelihood of a deciding goal in our favour and so the crowd, with one eye on the clock, was anticipating gathering the meagre outcome as consolation for a largely wasted afternoon. Picture, therefore, the home crowd's growing anxiety as one of the opposing team gathered the ball deep in his own half, and with a determination similar to that displayed by the legendary *Roy of the Rovers*, started a single handed assault on the Pompey line up. A neat swerve put him past the first line of defence, a feint to the right left our centre half with the puzzled *'Where the hell did he go?'* look on his face, and by now well into the left wing of Pompey's half, the crowd fell silent. There was now only one defender left between an increasingly anxious looking goal keeper and the huge likelihood of a last minute disaster! True to form, the predatory attacker swept past the Pompey's left back by tapping the ball neatly between his legs and leaping around his splayed feet; one could almost hear him going *'nyaa-nyaa de nyaa-nyaa'* as he did so. Had we had the time in that breathless moment to complain to the defender so ignominiously defeated, I daresay he would have burst into tears – either that, or be busy searching for a pen with which to scrawl his resignation letter on a convenient shin pad – but no! All eyes were glued on the forthcoming disaster. With the ball at his feet, sweeping in to be lined up on the right hand post and only eleven yards out, I don't suppose that in the excitement of the moment, the shark-like attacker even had time to register *'Blimey! I'm only two rod, poles or perches away from immortality, a winning goal bonus and a fresh bar of soap in the team bath'* before placing his shot in the back of the net. As you may imagine, Pompey's goalkeeper was by now in an extreme state of agitation, and quite possibly wishing that he had taken the afternoon off and instead spent a happy hour choosing a book on flower arranging at the local library. Instead, of course, he did what all goalkeepers in similar circumstances do: without taking his increasingly widening and fear-filled eyes off the approaching disaster, like someone suffering from St. Vitus' disease, he was continually leaping from one foot to the other, whilst at the same time touching the near goal post as if to ensure that it hadn't suddenly vanished into thin air, or that this was real, and not just a bad dream. The ground was silent... ten yards to go... the near goalpost just a couple of feet to the left, perfectly placed for a right-footer... the goalkeeper shitting himself, along with most of the crowd. The attacker's right boot was drawn back, and then with athletic poise, shot forward to administer the *coup-de-grace* ... the ball sped forward at a terrific rate; right height, right speed, just *wrong direction!*

Instead of the confidently expected gracious curve to the left, the ball simply went straight ahead, missing the near goalpost by a good two feet, and embedding itself in the arms of an understandably surprised spectator two thirds of the way up the Milton Road terrace. No one could believe it – especially the goal keeper who couldn't believe his luck and hoped that his recent sanitary difficulty would not be noticed. The attacker sank to his knees and stared with incredulity at the ball's final resting place, before proceeding to beat the turf with his fists...and the crowd, having just watched a full minute of approaching disaster, was absolutely silent... until one voice popped up from deep inside the terrace to yell ...

"Oooooh, hard luck mate… good try!!"

You had to be there to appreciate the deep and perfectly aimed irony of the comment. It brought the house down. So, football, or at least what passed for it at Fratton Park on a 1950's Saturday afternoon was an important part of our weekly entertainment. It made those of us who proudly wore our ancient Highland Road shirts imagine the roar of approval – and perhaps disbelief - from the Fratton terraces

Saturday evening saw the publication of the 'Football Mail'. The front page had this cartoon sailor indicating what the result had been that afternoon. I guess we saw the one on the right a little too often.

as we slotted home the winner against Wimborne Road on a muddy Southsea common.

Although most schools boasted a cricket team, competition with other schools never seemed to reach the same level of excitement as did footie: perhaps it was because the summer saw other pastimes such as tennis and swimming, and we were a little less keen to give up our Saturday mornings to spend a lot of time sitting on the grass watching other people play, awaiting our turn to go into bat and face hurled cricket balls which were rock hard and BLOODY HURT when they hit you. Even though Highland Road Juniors had an assortment cricket pads, which although generally grubby and often mismatched (much like the players) did at least afford your legs some protection, there seemed to be an awful lot of body exposed to the wild bowling of the kids from the other side; a ball could just as easily come whizzing past your ear one minute, whilst the next delivery might be crashed into the pitch just a few feet in front of the bowler. Some deliveries never even made it as far as the batsman, whilst others were so wide that they would startle the occasional pigeon which was exploring a dry crust of bread just beyond silly mid-off.

So the yearly sporting round continued. Once a foothold in the vast and carefree expanse of the five week summer holiday was established, thoughts turned away from team games to the lure of the beach, where in our mind's eye we expected to rush down to a bright and sun-drenched shoreline, ready to dive with athletic grace into the foaming surf like a junior torpedo. Reality was somewhat different. For a start, Southsea beach was very stony; you couldn't rush anywhere, and so progress towards the wet bit was really a sort of protracted hobble, interspersed with cries of 'Ouch! Bugger!' - and sudden unanticipated lurches to the left or right depending on which foot was hurting the most. Also, the English Channel is pretty damn cold, so even when your bruised feet had managed to transport you to the wave-break line, the numbing shock of the first wave was just that, and caused many a brave athlete to abandon the immediate goal of launching himself headfirst into the briny. Another slight flaw in the plan was that quite a lot of us could not actually swim. Lessons in the noble art of propelling yourself with lithesome ease through the water were not provided in any junior school I knew. If you wanted to learn, you had to get your mum to take you to the baths where several fearsome ladies patrolled the pool edge shouting, pointing, blowing whistles and advising you in the strongest possible terms to *'let go the steps and strike out across the pool, you quivering little git!'* Well perhaps not in quite so many words, but that was the gist of it.

So, most of us just floundered about in waist-high water at the beach, and after what seemed forever, managed a few strokes of doggy paddle. Given time, constant practice, and the understanding that seawater tasted horrible, some even managed to become reasonably competent swimmers. As may be imagined, self-taught swimming styles were something to witness, the most popular variation being what might be described as 'vertical thrashing', where the trainee achieves a small measure of buoyancy by constantly beating the water to death in a windmill-like fashion, whilst at the same time swivelling his head from side to side in a manner better described as *sheer desperation.*

1. Insert penny. 2. Pull back lever. 3. Watch ball disappear into 'lose'

But the beach, of course, had other attractions. One of these was the proximity of the other sex, which was of growing interest, and another was the inevitable array of promenade entertainment, much of it in the form of slot machines which would happily consume your proffered penny. Seafront arcades, and Pompey had a fine example on South Parade Pier, comprised an odd collection of skill based games, such as the mechanical grab and vertical bagatelle, but they also had what might be termed animations. Such was '*The Laughing Policeman*', '*The Drunken Sailor*' and '*The Haunted Castle*'. All very lurid and much enjoyed, especially if you could look over the shoulder of someone who had been rash enough to fork out the necessary loot to get the thing working in the first place.

The pier, like so many of its kind in the fifties and sixties, also had a quite lavish theatre where seaside entertainment, usually featuring some slightly faded celebrity from the world of entertainment who was ensconced for the summer season. Nevertheless, in the days before the mass entertainment of the TV really took hold, such extravaganzas were eagerly anticipated and were, I suppose, the final embodiment of the *Olde Time Music Hall* variety acts

The pier also was the location for a very special summer entertainment: the weekly firework display. Now, you have to bear in mind that fireworks were not nearly as common then as they are today, and were generally only seen each November, and then only in your back garden. Thus, having a big (ish) display on a balmy summer's evening, free of charge, was a very big deal indeed. Whole families would gather on the seafront in the gathering dusk - which to young kids was excitement enough – well in time to get a good view of the proceedings. To be honest, I don't suppose the whole display lasted for more than fifteen minutes, and consisted mainly of rockets being fired out over the sea, which reflected kaleidoscope-like the multi coloured sparks and magnified their crackling detonation. OK, it was only a pale imitation of the magnificently choreographed and multi-layered displays which are provided nowadays; sophisticated it was not – if you listened hard enough you could almost hear the blokes at the end of the pier cursing as their matches prematurely and inconveniently blew out - but sixty years ago it was an event of some significance, much anticipated and enjoyed: it was an integral part of our summer routine.

And there you have it in a nutshell. Life at that time – and for a decade or two afterwards - was much more *seasonal*. Whereas these days, you can get pretty much anything you want whenever you want it, this was certainly not the case back then. Summer stuff like holiday firework displays, strawberries, calamine lotion and new sandals were for the summer time only – they were not to be had at other times. It simply wouldn't be right, my dear – what would the neighbours say?

Although the onset of autumn meant the inevitable return to school to see how poor old Dick and Dora were getting on (see the embrocation – run Dick, run!) it too had its traditions to anticipate with some excitement. Right up front was the conker season, when the local horse chestnut trees received their annual barrage of sticks and stones tossed up by scores of children who had little heed of where such missiles would land, provided the largest, hardest and most deadly conker was delivered to an outstretched hand. Also at this time, there was an opportunity to visit the local bombsite to see who could accumulate the most scratches in the annual hunt for wild blackberries, as well as collecting anything combustible for November 5th. I have to say that an excessive and often fruitless amount of time was spent on this latter activity. For a start, we lived in a very built up area where there was no room for the sort of mega-conflagration most children had in mind - plus the fact that searching for combustibles on a *bomb site* might not have been a very good idea in the first place.

Getting your fireworks was the subject of much discussion and a degree of anguish as weekly budgets mainly came from small pocket money sources. Whether to get a sedate but colourful *Roman Candle* or a brilliant *Mount Vesuvius* - or to blow the lot on penny bangers and *Jumping Jacks* was a question which demanded a great deal of careful consideration. For those of you unfamiliar with *Jumping Jacks*, they can most accurately be described as *anti-personnel ordnance.* Once lit, they were thrown on the ground near a group of girls who were required to scream as loudly as possible while leaping about in a most rewarding but erratic manner as the firework farted, fizzed and banged its way around their feet - living out its short life by exploding in a totally unpredictable but entertaining way.

The majority of actual bonfire parties were very local affairs and were held with friends in people's back gardens, much to the consternation of the fire brigade. Once it started to get dark, the tin box in which all your fireworks had been carefully stored for what seemed like months, was ceremoniously gathered up by your dad who would then proceed to the garden. Much hammering and

The ad on the left was the one we loved. It epitomised the pyrotechnic fun we were going to have with immense bangers, whooshing rockets and dizzy Catherine Wheels. The fact that reality was often very different didn't seem to matter much... and we never NEVER had anything like the number of fireworks this lucky little chap has got his hands on.

banging then took place as Catherine Wheels were nailed into place... then nailed again when it was discovered they wouldn't spin, then nailed a third time when after an experimental spin they fell out onto the (wet) ground. An empty milk bottle was always buried in the ground – this the launch site for the '*Starburst*' or '*Golden Meteor*' sixpenny rockets you had painfully purchased. You will no doubt be thinking *'Hmmph! A milk bottle doesn't seem a very safe or well designed pyrotechnic lift-off facility to me! Surely the ensuing conflagration will crack the glass, and added to the fact that the neck of this container hardly passes as a guidance system, is it not entirely possible that the bottle might tip sending the rocket in a rather more horizontal trajectory than had been anticipated?'*

Well yes, of course. This was the late fifties for heaven's sake. Health and Safety hadn't been invented, and the fire brigade had every reason to be quite nervous. Even so, most of us had the presence of mind to close the upstairs bedroom windows. All in all, firework nights were eagerly anticipated, and apart from the few people whose houses burnt down, were much enjoyed by all. Post

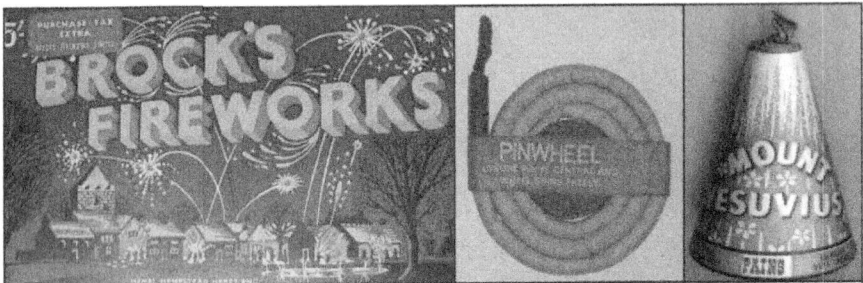

Brocks, Standard and Pains were the companies which were most popular, and their clever adverts excited most feverish anticipation of the big event. Mount Vesuvius and others with extravagant names raised our expectations, and most Catherine Wheels roused our dads to the challenge of getting the damn thing to spin – or at least fizz convincingly – in the first place. Unlike the multi-coloured, star bedecked rockets shown in the adverts, most just went 'WHOOSH, leaving an all too momentary sparkly trail – and a scorched stick.

display, dads would come back into the house wreathed both in the aura of a job well done and the distinctive but pungent aroma of burnt sulphur and other explosive substances. They were also quite often given to wiping the last traces of a rocket smear from their faces where at least one *'Crimson Comet'* had decided all on its own to lean on the other side of the milk bottle – in a fresh attempt to finish off the job on our back wall that the Germans had failed to complete in 1941. Apart from readily accepting a restorative bowl of Heinz tomato soup, most dads also spent just a little post-display time applying soothing ointment to their hands after the noble attempt to get the damned Catherine wheel to spin had been suddenly and painfully thwarted when it spluttered into life, stuck solid, then suddenly rotated sixty degrees before wrenching itself free from the afore-mentioned nail. Hot pursuit had menfolk all over the country chasing its sparkling and highly dangerous form as it spluttered, coughed and farted across the lawn. Bit like our dads, really.

All good unsophisticated and home-spun fun, but very much ours - and that was true of all the seasonal events which we looked forward to. It was as if the very anticipation was as much a part of the event as the occasion itself, and I suspect that with the ever present on-demand nature of such things these days, something of the excitement has been lost- as well as the seasonality of our yearly round.

An oddity which sticks in my mind occurred on the one and only occasion when I was unwell during the first week of November. Making sure my parents were in no doubt as to how much their enfeebled and disease-ridden son was going to be missing out on the massive celebrations everyone else would be enjoying - whilst he, *all alone,* would be tearfully sipping a lukewarm cup of Bovril - I managed to get them to promise to *'see if they could think of something'* to compensate. Result!   Well, they certainly did come up with something – the like of which I had never seen before and never seen since – INDOOR fireworks!

Now forgive me from mentioning it, but hadn't the Fire Service been on the local radio warning people to keep their windows shut tight, their curtains drawn, their pets and elderly relatives safely corralled indoors? And here were my nearest and dearest bringing fireworks *inside... to my bedroom, to my sickroom, to a room full of Vick Chest Rub vapours, a room full of highly combustible candlewick bedspreads and nasal decongestants, and what's more to a room with quite new shiny green lino!*

I needn't have worried. Indoor fireworks were the decidedly odd. Brought up to my room on a tin tray, these strange little packages were set alight. Yes! With real matches – in retrospect the best part of the display. The result of the application of a lit match was what can only be described as the product of a very reluctant toothpaste tube, whose aperture is only about the diameter of a cocktail stick. This allowed only the long-winded escape of some thin brown stuff. Some came out in straightish lines, others curled around in a somewhat sensuous way... to be honest it was all a bit suggestive and really rather unappetising, especially for a poor invalid child, barely able to raise himself up off the pillow.

Well, these two might have been amused but I definitely wasn't... I'm with Queen Victoria there. Thin brown stuff escaping like reluctant worms didn't do it for me: ungrateful little git wasn't I?

So, that was firework night for you. I suppose the only thing I wasn't allowed to do was, at the end of October, to make up a scruffy pile of old clothes to look like a guy, and deposit it on the pavement in a busy street before besieging passers by with the strident request *'Penny for the Guy, mister?'* This was the traditional way for children to raise the additional cash to finance their firework fantasies. There were two problems with this, however. The first was that few, if any of the so-called and home produced guys looked anything like even a human being - let alone bearing a striking resemblance to the famous seventeenth century arsonist after whom it was named. The second, and perhaps greater flaw was that, should you be fortunate enough to con someone into parting with a few coppers, the temptation to spend it immediately by getting an older mate to buy you a banger to let off at the bomb site a few minutes later was almost irresistible. I suspect it was for this reason that parents withdrew their support for the old Penny for the Guy routine. Shame in a way, as it was the only historical connection most kids had with an event which loomed very large in our legend.

In contrast, I have little recollection of Halloween. I knew of it, of course as me and my folks attended church, and Halloween was just described as All Hallows Eve, the day before All Hallows Day. In fact I was not aware of any special way in which to mark the event – and there was certainly no such thing as *Trick or Treat*. As far as I can recall, this American custom didn't really start to take hold until the mid to late seventies. Prior to that, total incredulity would have been the response if anyone had come to your door suggesting you might like to give them some nourishing comestible simply because in doing so, you would nullify the certainty that evil would result in the form of the noisy removal of dustbin lids, or the decoration of your front window with a skilfully thrown raw egg.

Well, such a proposition in those days would have been credited with either: **a)** the ready provision of a flea to be taken home by the aspirant blackmailer firmly lodged in his ear or **b)** the reply… *'No, mate, I think you'll find Bob-A-Job' week* is next month: clear off!*

*Each year the Cubs raised money by offering to do household chores for a 'Bob'(a shilling, now just 5p). Generally speaking, this went down well with the community, and errands were duly run, or front paths swept etc. It was also popular with the children concerned and provided the opportunity to wear the uniform around the neighbourhood. Like many of my pals I did it for several years. Bear in mind there were no CRB checks or guidance as to what was/was not acceptable - but I was never asked to tarmac a driveway, or to completely redecorate a sitting room... neither was I spoken to inappropriately as far as I can recall. Mind you, being a bit gormless and naive, it would probably have gone over my head anyway

Once into mid-November, the signs that Christmas would soon be upon us were starting to emerge. This might sound a bit tardy for these days, of course, when those who leave such advertising for anything later than September 1st may well be considered to have taken their eye off the ball and left everything hopelessly and irredeemably late. Believe it or not, I am writing these words on 25th July – and have just checked my email in-box and guess what? Yes – the first advert for Christmas, promoting a Festive Supper Dance with the opening words: *Yes, we know it's still five months to go, but Christmas Party Nights are selling out fast!!*.... point proven, I think.

As you may have gathered, I was not the most observant of little chaps, but even I became aware that after Bonfire Night, it wouldn't be long before the fat bloke with the sack would be hoving into view in the not too distant, and there would be a surfeit of robins, holly and snowmen appearing on advertising bill-boards and in my mum's magazines. Thus, I became a little more sensitive to other signs: on the radio, Dan and Doris Archer started talking about how the turkeys were *'fattening up nicely for the season'* and *'Housewives' Choice'* would more frequently play that catchy seasonal jingle *'Sleighride'* recorded by the Boston Pops Orchestra. I suspect that for me and many others, this was the first incident of the word 'pop' being used in the context of music, because by 1956 things were starting to change.

For a start, my sister was asking for records for her Christmas gifts, and was making noises about having her own Dansette record player – at that time still a very expensive piece of equipment at about thirty guineas (remember them?) and so beyond our pocket. It would be another two years before we even had a telly for heaven's sake, and we were by no means alone. Playing her precious 78's on the family gramophone was OK, but clearly lacked the trendy image she wished to promote; trying to dance with her friends on the front room lino with a nosey little brother sidling round the door to gawp at the flared skirts, tight belts and lavishly applied lip-stick was not the sort of ambience a budding pop-diva wanted to create. Of special irritation was the need to change the needle of the gramophone every so often. Whilst newly produced record players had a sensitive and delicate stylus pick up, old gramophones such as ours had a detachable needle which after a while became blunt. Once the sound produced had become so muffled as to be almost unintelligible, you had to unscrew the damn thing, open a little drawer in the gramophone housing the needle storage tray and then to select and screw in the new one. More often than not, of course, the drawer was either empty or had a number of slightly rusty needles which could best be described as 'seconds' - or more accurately 'knackered'. No wonder my sister longed for a Dansette. By now 'Rock Around the Clock' by Bill Hayley had been around for a few weeks, and with other catchy numbers like 'Shake, Rattle and Roll' and early Elvis hits such as 'Hound Dog' the stage was set for the Rock'n'Roll revolution. Well it was in some houses, but despite my sister's best efforts, it had to wait a while yet in ours. Like thousands of other frustrated teenagers, my sister and her pals simply didn't have the means of buying – let alone playing - such offerings, as the broadcasting of early pop on the BBC was very limited indeed. If you wanted to hear music of this type, short of forking out for a concert performance or a ticket to the nearest dance hall, the local coffee bar with a juke box was about the only reliable source of the new Rock 'n Roll available for many.

So, while pop music was going through its gestation period, Christmas 1956 was busy in the preparation... blissfully unaware that this was probably its last truly 'pre-bopa-lulan' manifestation, for after this, the media played an increasingly significant part in the seasonal festivities.

As far as I was concerned, the arrival of a very large Christmas tree in the Guildhall Square was enough to set the pulses racing. Having just achieved double figures age-wise, I was now allowed to go into the city with my mates, and the Christmas tree was quite a big draw. For a start, it had coloured lights. Seems preposterous now, doesn't it? ...but back then, the dressing and especially the illumination of a publicly displayed tree was a big deal. In addition, the mid to late 1950's also saw the department stores in the city centre entering more fully into the Christmas spirit by putting up what seemed to us very imaginative seasonal displays, complete with the much anticipated Santa's Grotto.

I suppose such commercial progress was a reflection of the country at last shaking off the remnants of Austerity Britain. With rationing finally disappearing in 1954, commerce and industry was now really getting up to speed in responding to the national feeling of optimism and gleeful anticipation that was now prevalent - the first ripples of what would become the huge wave of bubbling confidence which would sweep over the whole country in the early sixties.

But, first things first: Christmas at home 1956 style was there to be enjoyed. We were on holiday, the dreaded Eleven Plus was still a good year away, Dan and Doris were pleased with the way the turkeys were coming on in Ambridge – and it was time for dad to get up in the loft and heave out the old suitcase containing the Christmas decorations... what's not to like?

Now, when you think of Christmas decs, your mind no doubt conjures up images of miles of sparkling and multi-coloured fairy lights with which to bedeck and garland every surface; a free-standing and gaily illuminated reindeer gracing your front garden; beautifully packaged coloured pendants of subtle and creative design just ready and waiting their artistic and colour-coordinated suspension from the superbly groomed branches of an artificial snow-encrusted Christmas tree. Well, if our home was anything to go go by, it was a bit different back in the fifties.

For a start, hanging baubles were made of a very thin – and very sharp – material which nearly always broke where the wire loop attached them to the thread. So you were not off to a flying start. The bigger decorations, however, were made of coloured paper, and were often stored folded. So, it was with what might be described as fearful anticipation that these venerable items were taken out for their yearly showing. The little metal clips would be released in the hope that the elderly decoration might still open up rather like a stiff old door on creaky hinges to reveal in a concertina-like manner its dusty tissue- paper heart.

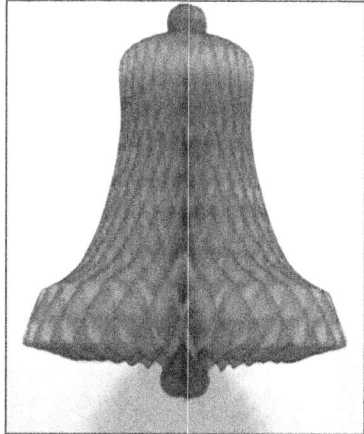

This one looks pretty good... for a start it is symmetrical, and has no rips or the remains of last year's vain attempt to sellotape a new plastic Santa to the pseudo clapper.

Does all this sound a bit over-dramatic? Well, yes, but these decs were quite near to being family heirlooms, and their storage since last year had been up amongst the spiders and cobwebs in the loft. Added to that, some of them were pre-war, and so it's not surprising that they had taken a bit of a beating over the years. Nevertheless, they were dusted off, repaired as best we could (thank the Lord for the all new SELLOTAPE), and positioned with the grotty bits facing the wall. Bell shapes were popular, as were stars, snowmen and lanterns. Together they formed a perfect backdrop for the wonderful paper chains that me and my classmates at Highland Road Juniors had spent many a laborious hour sticking into little sugar paper links. Given that in all the excitement we sometimes forgot to put the links *together* before sticking (and there's a limit to how many dull individual paper rings even the most forgiving household can absorb) it was a real achievement to end up with two or three feet of rather grubby and somewhat worn paper chain. But were we downhearted? Yes, quite possibly, but it was Christmas, and the tree was about to be put up in the front room. There was the usual frisson of excitement as to whether or not the old lighting set would again leap into life, or my dad would similarly leap when he found out that the black insulating tape so lovingly applied last year had unravelled in the ensuing twelve months, thus exposing him to a merry belt of the old 240 volts.

Let me just put 'lighting set' into some kind of perspective here. These days, we are surrounded by light decorations of the most absorbing and multi-coloured designs, of complex construction with innumerable programs, sparkling strings available in vast lengths to be hung inside and out, to include mega-sized illuminated Santas, jocular penguins, animated herds of reindeer and so on. Sixty-or-so years ago you got a string of about a dozen lights shaped like a bell, and illustrated with nursery rhymes. For example, ours had these two inch bells (5cm to you – but remember, the decimal system was for foreign people only in the 1950's, and Christmas, as we all know, was British to the core) decorated with the following festive motifs:

1. Cat and fiddle
2. Cow and moon
3. Dish and spoon

Are you getting the picture here? Does it surprise you that there was an apparent lack of, say, *robins*, or *holly,* or *merry Santas* or even the odd *biblical crib scene including shepherds-complete-with-tea-towel-headdress* design? Bizarrely, it never occurred to us... it was just a wonder to see the tree lit up with these little lamps, which would occasionally and without warning flicker to the accompaniment of a noticeable and slightly menacing crackling sound coming from the bakelite plug. Such sparking eccentricities were made all the more dramatic by thus creating an enormous fart from the radio, should it be switched on to a seasonal carol service from Kings College, or *'Children's Favourites'* belting out a hearty rendition of *'Frosty the Snowman'*. In retrospect, I suppose that if Christmas tree lights *had* to have a nursery rhyme theme - though heaven alone knows why - then a more appropriate choice might have been *'Mary had a little lamb'* on the grounds that at least two of the characters central to the Christmas story would presumably have put in an appearance. But there you go... logic never got in the way of enjoying ourselves, and I have to say, Christmas in those days always seemed to be a very jolly occasion indeed. Although the wherewithal to indulge quite as freely as today was not available, it was still joyfully anticipated.

I guess this was in a large part due to the fact that, in the last decade before people started to become more socially mobile, extended families were still commonly to be found living within just a few miles of each other. Thus family get-togethers were much easier to organise, and seldom required the need to stay overnight. Because of their relatively short duration, this reduced the possibility for family feuds to take a real hold, and intemperate and ill-advised remarks about the quality and provenance of Auntie Eileen's mince pies could be more easily glossed over with the proffering of another small glass of sweet sherry before the fisticuffs could really take hold.

We also had loads of family party games. In an age when few people even had a TV set, home-spun entertainment played a much more significant part in our festive proceedings. And they didn't need to be very sophisticated either... for example, blindfolding Auntie Eileen and guiding her to sit on somebody's lap was seen as a fine entertainment. Not just the sitting there, you understand – for she had then to discover upon whose lap she perched by enquiring *'Ducky Ducky??'* If you still don't understand the complex and refined nature of this game, all will be revealed when I tell you that the unfortunate who was currently bearing Auntie E's not inconsiderable weight had to reply in a disguised voice *'Quack Quack!!'*

Laugh? Well, yes, we did. It was Christmas, after all, and it sure as hell beat the more sedate and academic game of *Charades*, especially when Uncle Stan's mime of *'a book, five words, fourth word three syllables'* turned out, after a mere hour and three quarters to be *'The South Portsmouth Telephone Directory'**. Also, of course, any game which involved blindfolding did allow those not similarly deprived to mouth messages to each other concerning the quality of the afore -mentioned mince pies and so on, so all in all, Ducky Ducky was a popular party choice.

'Sardines' was another well known game, which in retrospect might have earned its popularity by providing further opportunities for reasons other than innocent family fun. The essence of the game was that someone amongst the party revellers was secretly nominated by their selection of a specific piece of paper with an X on it. The lights throughout the house were then turned off, and the nominated person – the sardine - had to go off into some part of the house and hide, preferably in a location of small dimensions. Thus, broom cupboards were a popular venue, but it could just as easily be down beside – or even under - a bed. The rest of the party participants had then to also make their way through the house in total darkness in order to find the Sardine. They did this by whispering *'sardine? sardine?'* at any likely location. Once the sardine had been located in this manner, the person making the discovery had to squeeze in alongside the original sardine in the hiding place. Mind boggling yet? The theory was that other seekers stumbling around in the dark would eventually find the sardine, and add to his or her discomfort by making the squeeze that much tighter, or indeed intimate. The aim of this bizarre game was ***not*** to be the last person to come across the

* *It's a big book full of phone numbers. Everyone had one. You needed it to find out which number to dial. Honest*

- 232 -

darkened hiding place, which by now was beginning to bear a striking resemblance to the Black Hole of Calcutta. That the game could be somewhat protracted is an understatement, but it was generally agreed that if the sardine had not been discovered by Boxing Day morning, it might be just as well to call the whole thing off. Perhaps mercifully, most hiding places were fairly quickly revealed by muffled squeaks, groans, the occasional sound of a slap accompanied by the hoarse whisper *'I'll thank you to keep your hands to yourself Norman!'* or, more likely by a resounding crash as some essential part of the hiding place infrastructure gave way under the extreme pressure put upon it by merrymakers.

All this might seem a little weird – but at least *Sardines* rarely resorted to out-and-out physical violence. Another favourite, called *'Are You There Moriarty?'* certainly did. Although only played by two people at a time, it was in effect a spectator sport - and really not much more than a diluted form of the sort of things the Romans were fond of when they encouraged big blokes with pointy things to beat each other to death in the arena. Let me explain. Two *Moriarty* contenders were chosen by the assembled company. Each was invited to lie on the floor, where they were blind-folded and provided with a rolled up newspaper to be grasped firmly in one hand. They then held each other's free hand. So far, so good – although it has to be said, not tremendously exciting thus far. However, the first contestant was then invited to enquire of the second: **'Are you there, Moriarty?'** whereupon it was incumbent upon the second person to reply - thus giving the first player an indication as to the whereabouts of their opponent's head. With this directional information gained, the first player was then obliged to direct a blind-folded WHACK! with his newspaper, the aim being to hit the opponent on the head. Bit violent? Bit sacrificial? Well, yes – but the second player, rather than just sitting still was *allowed to move in any direction* in order to avoid the expected onslaught, provided their hands remained joined.

Moreover, should the first player miss, it would then be his turn to exact cranial revenge. And so the game went on until one or other received a smack round the ear-hole, or the contestants realise everything had gone a bit quiet owing to the fact that the onlookers had all sneaked off back to the buffet next door having become a tad bored with this writhing gladiatorial contest. Mind you, the first half hour or so really was most entertaining; I mean, watching two of your relations done up in their Christmas best thrashing about on the floor trying to beat each other to insensibility with folded up newspapers – got to be a winner, hasn't it? Of course it was an absolute hoot - and if the odd party-goer went home with a smudge of newsprint across his brow accompanied by a slight concussion, well, it was certainly worth it from the spectators' point of view. Such bizarre games were very amusing, and in the days before TV took over Christmas entertainment lock stock and barrel, you have to ask: who had the most fun?

'Ah – but what about Christmas pressies?' I hear you ask. Well, it would be wrong to suggest that we were any less acquisitive in the fifties and sixties than people are today; it was simply a matter of expectation and scale. I am certain that we looked forward to the big day with the same enthusiasm and eager anticipation, and all kids spent a great deal of time with their noses stuck up against the toy shop window positively slavering at the possibility of imminent ownership - often regardless of how realistic such a possibility might be. Bearing in mind the state of personal finances, disposable wealth was proportionately much smaller in those days, and the market place reflected that. Toys for example, were produced by a much wider variety of manufacturers, some of them very small by modern standards, and thus the choice available in any area could be unique to a locality. Yes, there were big manufacturers such as Hornby, Meccano, Tri-Ang, Subbuteo, Pedigree, Silver Cross and Mettoy. But there were also a myriad of smaller manufacturers producing a

huge range of pre mass-market merchandise, most of it quirky, some of it bizarre, and in a few cases some items that were downright dangerous... but the choice facing our limited resources was truly wide and much more individual than today.

The king and queen of presents were of course, the new bikes, and Christmas afternoon was the occasion when one either displayed one's good fortune by taking the first few wobbling turns up and down the street, or, more frequently, joining the much larger group of kids gazing critically from behind net curtains, each trying fairly unsuccessfully to repress the urge to wish the lucky kid on his or her new Raleigh Palm Beach Tourer the misfortune of hitting the kerb and sailing over the handlebars. And then, all of a sudden, just a few weeks following Christmas 1956, our lives changed a bit... well, quite a lot, actually. And why?

Believe it or not, the staid old BBC put on a TV show that was to revolutionise the world of popular entertainment, and as a result start to change the source from which *all* entertainment, Christmas included, was to be increasingly obtained. The programme was called "*The Six-Five Special*", and it was the first ever British modern pop music show on TV. It set the pattern for just about every one there has been ever since, including, of course, the much better known '*Top of the Pops*' which came along in the following decade. Looking back, its very inception was a huge surprise. As already mentioned, 'Auntie' BBC did not entirely approve of anything approaching modern beat music and so its adoption of such a revolutionary feature conveyed via what was then the totally new format of current bands playing their renditions to a live TV audience came as a complete surprise. Furthermore, that it was hosted by a lively and pop music savvy presenter was a production leap as huge for the Beeb as it was unexpected by the increasingly pop-starved population. Set in the context of the time, its very timing (at 6.05 pm, obviously) was equally astounding because right up until the end of

1956 BBC TV* had *shut down every day from 6pm until 7pm.*

'S*o why*', you are asking yourself, '*does a TV broadcaster who has a virtual monopoly of all broadcasting cease transmissions for an hour during peak viewing time?'*

Well, you may remember from Chapter 6, that the *establishment* culture of the post-war years was very paternal. The establishment (and by that I mean not only the national government, but the Local Authorities, the BBC, the Church and just about every other formal institution you could think of) KNEW BEST. The downside of the introduction of the welfare state, and the brilliant reforms it brought with it was that the authorities developed an entirely patriarchal role, deciding not only what services should be provided, but how, where and when they should be dispensed. Now this may seem a long way from an early TV pop show, but not so. The hour long TV closure from 6 – 7pm was perhaps the most extreme example of 'Auntie Knows Best', for it was called *'The Toddlers' Truce'*. The BBC was of the opinion that their shows were such a draw to the infant population (mesmerised as they were confidently expected to be by such delights as *'Andy Pandy'* and *'Muffin the Mule'*) that Mummies and Daddies throughout the land would be unable to get the little beggars to bed if they knew that the TV was still on. Hence the *Toddlers' Truce* – a time to get a hot cup of Horlicks down their necks and shove them off to bed with a threatening nursery rhyme or two before the early evening rave TV programmes such as *'What's My Line?'* could provide a massive juvenile distraction. And so it was that until the end of December 1956, parents across the land would be saying to their innocent offspring at exactly 6pm:

'There we are darling. Mr. TV is going to bed now, and so must you! He won't be on again until tomorrow comes, and Mummy and Daddy

---

* *The single BBC TV channel was all there was for most viewers. ITV was in its first year, and was not yet broadcast everywhere.*

will be sitting here in the dark until it's time for us to go to bed too! So night-night sweetheart, watch out for Wee Willie Winkie, the Bogey Man and any other weirdos lurking near your bedroom door, and don't even think about coming downstairs again before you hear the rattle of the Cornflake box in the morning'.

But with the threat of the challenge from ITV, whose penchant for broadcasting throughout the evening and apparently not giving a tinker's cuss about whether kids got to bed on time or not, it was clear even to the venerable Beeb that things had to change.

Given this background, it is therefore all the more surprising that the organisation should not only abandon the 'Toddlers' Truce', but that it should be done with a ground-breaking music programme whose foundation stone was the celebration of the new-fangled Rock and Roll. You'd have thought it more likely that a half way house solution might have been a programme on *'Pressing Flowers for Beginners',* or *'Interesting Church Interiors in East Anglia'*, but no... it was in at the deep end, and no one could have been more surprised than the up and coming teen generation. And so it was that in January 1957, the BBC broadcast a five minute news bulletin from 6pm, after which the new programme was launched – hence the title:

'Six-Five Special'.

Even the opening sequence was exciting, featuring film of a steam train thundering down the tracks accompanied by a lively Rock'n'Roll song sung by the show's resident group *'Don Lang and his Frantic Five'* to the words:

The Six-five Special's coming down the line,
The Six-Five Special's right on time
Coal in the boiler, burning up bright
A-Rocking and a-Rolling all through the night
And my heart's a-beating, 'cause I'll be meeting
The Six-five special at the station tonight

… and all this to the diddly-dum background chant of:

'Over the points, over the points, over the points, over the points'

Exciting or what?! The show's presenters were Josephine Douglas and Pete Murray, and if the words 'swinging' or 'hip' had been in use then, they would have been it – the very epicentre of being suddenly '*with it*'. Strange really, as these two and the musicians they introduced were usually dressed in a style that might have been described as 'everyday casual'... not at all glitzy, and light years away from the extravaganza of bizarre styles that were to become

OK – the graphics were not yet quite up to speed but for the young, the programme certainly was, with a catchy tune and lyrics which were easy to recall. Although some railway buffs might question why there should be 'COAL in the boiler burning up bright' rather than the more conventional WATER, it seemed a small price to pay... and we were in forgiving mood.

common currency just a decade later. In many respects, it was totally unselfconscious; the sets were minimal, the production pretty rudimentary and with virtually all the music being live, it was prone to the odd slip or two. But did we mind? You must be joking! Bearing in mind lots of us still had no direct access to a TV set, the programme was seen as totally unmissable... though of course, many did at least some of the time. And was it sophisticated? Well, no. A favourite rendition from Don Lang and his Frantic Five, for example, was a chirpy song called '*My Friend the Witch Doctor*' whose lyrics suggest that there was still a little way to go in terms of what later might later be called cultural sensibilities:

I told the witch doctor you didn't love me true
I told the witch doctor you didn't love me nice
And then the witch doctor he gave me this advice
… He … said … say
(Chorus) **Ooh, eeh, ooh, aah-aah, Ting, tang, walla-walla bing-bang**

Ooh, eeh, ooh aah-aah, Ting tang wall-walla bing-bang

Nevertheless, Don was a firm favourite, and some of the programme's artists did make big contributions to the emerging Rock and Roll era, which in turn started the fairly rapid replacement of skiffle group music. Famous among British talent were Tommy Steele with his song *'Singin' the Blues',* Marty Wilde with '*Endless Love'* and Wee Willy Harris, Britain's highly colourful response to America's Little Richard. And, of course, although they didn't appear on our screens at that time, the influence of American pop stars such as Elvis Presley and Gene Vincent was at the very heart of the Rock n' Roll revolution. Although the Six-Five Special only lasted until late 1958, it had done enough to set the pattern for just about every pop music type programme ever since, both here and abroad, and so it really was a trophy for the BBC to hang in its Hall of Fame

So, suddenly, we were Pre-Bop-A-Lula no more and the first few coins of the common currency that pop music was soon to become had been well and truly minted. By 1957, Gene Vincent's classic song was on everyone's lips, and you'd be lucky not to walk past the local shops without encountering a small group of teenage lads using the reflective qualities of Mr. Chandler's High Class Tobacconist and Confectioners shop window to further improve their Brylcreemed hair whilst giving Bebop-A-Lula a highly distinctive and locally accented rendition.

And then there was Radio Luxembourg. That this radio station broadcast beyond the reaches of the BBC gave it a romantic, an almost clandestine appeal. That it played Rock n'Roll, much of it American was marvellous, but it also had something else totally new – it had adverts. These had never been heard before by British radio audiences and Horace Batchelor's *'infra draw method'* of predicting football pools results from his office in Keynsham, Bristol *'spelt k..e..y..n..'*.etc etc became a much repeated logo. And don't forget those well nourished youngsters *'The Ovaltinies'*, clearly the world's *happiest boys and girls.* We were assured we could be similarly ecstatic if only we would knock back a cup or two of the famous drink before bed. Another less direct marketing strategy was for the station to employ announcers who had mid-Atlantic accents, and this together with the aforementioned properties made eager teenage listeners gather to their radio sets like moths to a flame. The only reason it didn't have a bigger effect on the burgeoning teen culture was that it was so damned hard to pick up on the cranky old radio sets we had at our disposal. The station's own much repeated advertising logo of: **'Radio Luxembourg, Your Station of the Stars on 208 metres on the medium wave band'** had many a kid searching the honey coloured dials of the family's venerable radiogram, vainly trying to find the elusive wavelength only to be rewarded with a mixture of static and the shipping forecast from Helsinki. Even so, Radio Luxembourg had an influence far greater than its size and broadcasting range would indicate: along with shows like the *Six-Five Special* it set the scene for the pop culture explosion soon to come, and was an integral part of the gathering energy and enthusiasm for all things new that characterised the age.

And that was the essence of the fifties, really. Forgive me if I mention it one last time, but it's sooooo important: History has a tendency to define the decade as one that was incomparably gloomy, with a worn-out people still recovering from a devastating war, tormented by continued rationing, and surrounded by a blitzed landscape. Not so. Whilst some of those things were true, they in no way diminished the sense of hopeful optimism that prevailed. It was an age noted for its sense of joyful security and eager anticipation. After the terrors of the war, we suddenly had the Welfare State, that would look after us *'from cradle to grave'* (or *'from sperm to worm'* as some less sensitive souls would put it). Whilst the main feature was, of course, our wonderful National Health Service, we also had much improved unemployment benefit and guaranteed paid holidays. There was virtually full employment, and factories were busy banging out all sorts of new products in all sorts of new materials... and, of course, we were now blessed with Sellotape. For the thousands of folk bombed out of their homes there was the short term benefit of prefabs, providing many with a standard of accommodation not known before, and underwritten by the promise and growing physical evidence of the new Council Housing estates. These were bringing permanence to a much higher quality of living for vast numbers of people who had previously been condemned to live in what was only a little removed from squalor. Hundreds upon hundreds of new schools were built in the fifties, the majority of them for Primary aged children. The fifties was vibrant, exploratory, colourful, energetic... and above all, ***optimistic***. Why it is that so many of the less well informed misinterpret the decade is that they confuse its energy and dynamism with its sparse material surroundings and lack of disposable income. And yes, of course, the decade did have its low points: the Korean War was ghastly for those involved, but the fact that it was so far away, made many of us feel - quite wrongly - that we weren't really that involved. There was also the embarrassment of the Suez Crisis, but can anything that was directly responsible for bringing us bubble cars really be *that* bad?!

Above all, there was the sense that the nation was on the brink of something monumentally exciting: we had everything to look forward to. There was huge optimism... and it was rightly placed. Although we didn't know it, perhaps the most electrifying decade ever was about to unfold. Clearly, this leap into the unknown required *stamina*, it needed *grit*, it demanded *determination*... which begs the question:

Were we well-hard Baby Boomers sufficiently well provisioned to sustain us for our biggest step ever?

Let's take a look.

9   Cupboard Love

There are lots of things in this day and age that we would find it hard to do without. These constitute the common elements of everyday life which we take entirely for granted and which provide such a sense of normality and total expectation that they disappear from our active consciousness. One such is the access we have to all manner of goods which, with the advantage of online shopping, are available for purchase twenty four hours a day, every day of the year. At the forefront of such total accessibility is the common or garden supermarket, which together with its poor relation, the open 'til late convenience store, provide a total wrap-around service for just about every day-to-day consumable you can imagine. Add to that the fast food outlets, the pizza deliveries and endless varieties of doorstep deliveries which now form an apparently indispensible part of our modern life, and you have 24/7 provision.

And yet these shopping habits, without which we would be left in something of a flat spin, are relatively recent. Nationwide online shopping has really only taken off since internet connections became widespread and reasonably dependable, and thus can only be said to form a normal part of life for the majority of folk since about 2015. Before that, the growth of hypermarkets and out-of-town shopping malls was a feature still new to some parts of the country around the time of the millennium. Clearly, our shopping habits over the course of even one generation have changed radically; go one step further to two generations, and you are in a different world altogether.

In the 1950's, there were *no supermarkets*. In case you think you must have misread the last sentence, let me reiterate: apart from rare experiments in London, there really were *no* supermarkets throughout most of the 1950's. There were also very few domestic fridges, no canned lager, no *sell by dates*, no *nutritional information* and absolutely no *health warnings* on anything. It's amazing we survived at all... and yet I can't recollect anyone wringing their hands in anguish and muttering *'Strewth! I hope someone invents supermarkets soon... I'm starving!'*

One of the unexpected outcomes of wartime rationing was that generally speaking, the population was in fact a good deal healthier in 1945 than it was before the war, and almost certainly trimmer than it is now. The term *obese* was virtually unknown, and because the nation had been forced to eat whatever was available, putting on a lot of unwanted weight was never a problem. It was not until 1953 – *eight years* after the end of the war – that sweets were off the ration book and as we have already seen, gave rise to the rapid development of the confectioners craft and the marketing man's artifice. But getting rid of rationing didn't change the fact that getting your everyday sustenance was, as it had been for centuries, a matter of daily visits to the local shops.

Picture if you will a traditional Christmas card scene: a snow covered street, a Christmas tree glowing with bright lanterns surrounded by a cherubic choir; a horse drawn stage coach makes its merry progress past the cosy candle lit cottages as the driver blows a cheery note on a brass horn of quite unnecessary length. Gathered in the background is a little group of angelic children, bright pennies clutched in their mittened hands and their noses pressed up against the tiny frost-encrusted window panes of the village shop, whose lantern lit display of goods includes all that is desirable in terms of things to eat and items to covet... and there you have it, a typical shop of the 1950's. Well no, not really. Typical in the sense that it was an individual property selling stuff of a particular type, yes, but in every other way a hugely overstated and much romanticised version of reality...but give us a break, *it's Christmas, OK?*

High streets in the post war years comprised a series of individual shops, the vast majority of which were independent businesses.

There were a few exceptions, the most notable being the *Co-op* and grocery stores such as *Home and Colonial* and *Liptons*. Nevertheless, the nation's needs were in the most part met by small traders who usually provided but one service each; if you were in the grocer's shop, and you also wanted bread, then you were directed to the baker's premises a few doors down. It was almost like an unwritten law... you didn't encroach upon the trade of another business, partly out

Slow and inefficient it might have been – but for many daily shopping was also a social opportunity.

of trade solidarity perhaps, but just as likely because others could no doubt do the same to you, and had such a competitive path been followed, you might well find yourself having to stock wet fish alongside your *petite fours* chocolate fudge cake display – not an entirely agreeable prospect.

What would be most notable today would be the fact that there was no self- service and each shop would be equipped with a long wooden counter behind which the goods would be displayed. Also behind the counter would be the shopkeeper and, depending on the size of the business, an assistant or two. Selection of goods was made simply by asking for, or pointing towards the display, and the staff would then go trotting off to retrieve whatever it was you wanted. Efficient? No... and it didn't always allow you to inspect what you wanted before purchase. On the other hand, it was certainly very much more personal, and many a customer/shopkeeper relationship was part of the daily social, as well as business round. Many premises provided the customer with a seat while the order was being collected and packaged, and this was as true of the local butcher as it was of the high street shoe shop or the greengrocer. That provision shopping was a daily chore comes into sharper focus when you realise that domestic fridges were a rarity in most homes in the fifties, and only became much more common by the mid sixties. As a result, perishable food was difficult to keep for even a day or two, and so most housewives had to build daily shopping into their regular routine. Whilst milk, and to a lesser extent bread would be delivered daily, every other perishable had to be purchased for more or less immediate use.

So, all of this might sound a bit primitive, but what might be harder to grasp is that, for some, it made shopping a pleasant social occasion. For ladies who otherwise spent much of the day doing those essential domestic chores (for which, as yet, there were very few labour-saving devices), going out to the shops was perhaps, a good opportunity to relieve the monotony - and of course, to catch up on the local gossip.

A typical 1950's shop with long counter and a customer's chair. The range of stock on display was relatively modest.

'*And what of the goods on offer?*' I hear you ask. Now, I have to admit to some personal insider information in this respect, as my dad was the owner of a grocer's shop into which I would casually drift from time to time. There's something rather nice about wandering around a food shop after it has shut – and opening and closing times were strictly adhered to in the fifties. Most shops closed at 5pm sharp, and many also had an hour off for lunch. If you got there at 5.01pm, well then, tough: unbelievable today, but just normal practice then. And by the way, apart from early morning papers, there was virtually **no** Sunday opening, and thanks to the Liberals' 1906 reforms, (which was one of the most improbable things that stuck in my mind when doing History O level... don't ask me why, but I suppose *something* had to stick eventually, didn't it?) shops closed for a half day each Wednesday afternoon. So there.

Now, back to my out of hours wander round my dad's shop. The range of goods available was, by current standards very small. Today's supermarkets stock a bewildering range of goods; not only is there stuff for sale the use of which I don't understand at all, (e.g. whether to eat it, polish the floor with it or apply to a small but irritating rash) there is always a whole range of different makes of this single product to choose from. In addition, there is so much to read: a list of contents, safety instructions, ingredients, who to complain to if it might unexpectedly kill you, which world-wide body is responsible for its overall quality... and all of this replicated in Spanish, Dutch, Cantonese and Polish too. Strewth. Not so in my dad's shop or countless thousands like it.

The majority of shelf space, right up to the ceiling – was taken up with the display of tins, jars and packets of every description. If the shopper couldn't see what she* wanted – which in a smallish shop was quite often - the assistants would have to go scurrying off round the back to the storeroom to retrieve the required item … efficient it

* *And yes, it nearly always was 'she' because working practices in the post war years were such that a housewife was just that...more often than not a married lady whose working life every single day was centred on the home while her husband was out at work being the breadwinner. In pre-war years, working married women were a rarity, and post-war before the 1970's were the exception rather than the rule. Women's lib was in its infancy then.*

was not, but it kept my dad & co pretty damn fit. Below the shelf display were the bins; not the type you tip your rubbish into I hasten to say, but really rather elegant storage units in which were put loose, large quantities of oats, barley, rice and other cereal type commodities, not all of which I could identify. The fronts of these built-in units were a shiny metallic green, and the bins were numbered in large gold numerals – making them look ever so much like a southern railway carriage. So, as a little boy let loose in an out of hours reverie, I would make the appropriate engine shunting noises as I went past each bin, inspecting the contents of each by lifting the heavy polished mahogany lids and running my fingers through the granular contents, which was a very pleasurable – if unhygienic – experience. All of these items were sold loose, and the shop would pack whatever amount the customer required into paper bags, and this included tea and sugar. The paper from which the bags were made was quite thick and coloured a matt blue; it was, of course, the original *sugar paper*, designed for use in the grocery trade, but used much more widely in primary schools throughout the country for making crappy Christmas decorations of the *chain link* or *Chinese lantern* variety mentioned in the last chapter.

Lots of other things were sold unpackaged in those days too; my dad took pride in boning and slicing huge sides of bacon, and hams and beetroot were cooked on the premises. Cheeses the size, shape and weight of a smallish pouffe would be delivered wrapped in thin muslin material – the original *cheesecloth-* and would await my dad's administration of the cheese wire to carve it up into pieces to display beneath a domed glass dish. I'm a little ashamed to say that after exhausting myself running my hands through the cereal products, I would pause for a well deserved rest and lower myself onto a cheese pouffe in order to catch my breath before deciding which hygienically unacceptable practice I would inflict upon the stock next. Licking the icicles formed on the inside of the fridge or testing the soft sweetness of the glacé cherries in order to witness my very precise finger prints left on their sticky surfaces were prime targets.

Naturally, my wanderings would eventually lead me to the areas where the chocolate biscuits were displayed. My abiding memory of these was that they were a lot bigger then than they are now. Take the famous and much loved *Penguin*, for example. Now my recollection is that in the 1950's, the Penguin was the size and weight of a small house brick – not the domino it is today. Weston's *Wagon Wheels* were so big you needed a friend to help you carry one home, and had to turn it on its side to get it through the front door. A bit of an exaggeration? Well, yes I suppose so, but I'm sure these products *were* bigger in the post war years. As I recall, P-p-p-picking up a P-p-p-Penguin in those days could very well leave you with p-p-p-pulled muscle at least, if not a h-h-h-hernia. Other biscuits were mainly produced by such baking stalwarts as Huntley and Palmer, Peak Frean, Jacobs, Crawfords and, of course, McVities (or McVitie and Price as they were once known). In an age before *Hobnobs* were even a gleam in Mr. M's eye, the population was pretty much sold on *Digestives*, even the ones unadorned by chocolate, and *Rich Tea, Lincoln* and *Garibaldi* were always popular additions to the daily sugar-rich assault on our teeth. And who could ever say no to a *Custard Cream?*... or a *Bourbon* – which half a century ago was covered with so much granulated sugar that it was quite likely to take off the roof of your mouth? It was only the tempting chocolaty

Not everyone used a cheese to sit on – but you can see the attraction, can't you?

cream-filled taste of the *Bourbon* that prevented many of us from using it as a small but handy sanding block for those hard-to-reach DIY areas. Nowadays, you can almost count the grains on the fingers of one hand … progress? Huh!

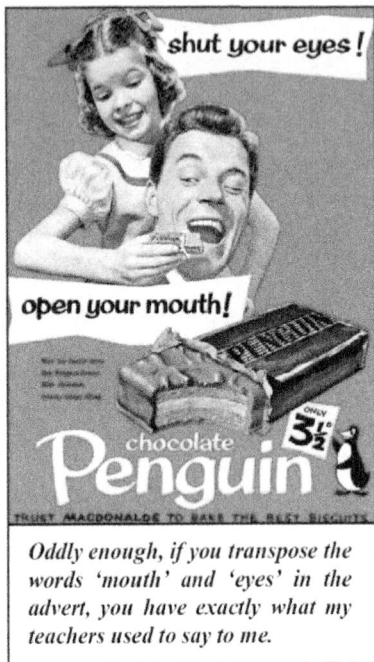

Oddly enough, if you transpose the words 'mouth' and 'eyes' in the advert, you have exactly what my teachers used to say to me.

As with so many products available in the local grocers, biscuits too were sold loose. Companies sent their products in large tins which were about one foot in each dimension. These would have a transparent cellophane lid to enable the customer to see and then select the bikkies within. Naturally, quite a few got broken in the process, and so most local shops put all the remaining bits in one box, and sold them as literally that – broken biscuits. And mighty popular they were as well, especially as you might get something chocolaty, or a wafer sandwich or two: the surprise was half the fun, and the cheapness made such bargain basement shopping keenly followed, especially by children.

The range of goods available in any one shop was tiny by today's supermarket standards, but nevertheless, the new mass marketing did lead to even the humblest establishment doing its best to meet local demand. As noted in Chapter 4, advertising in the fifties and sixties was pretty basic, and seemed more often than not to just involve adding an 'O' to the end of every product to make its use obvious, and to be immediately appealing to the housewife. Thus, in the domestic cleaning products area of our shop my dad stocked *Brasso, Brillo, Draino*, washing powders *Rinso* and *Omo* and nearby were cooking ingredients *Paxo* and *Oxo*. Sweets included *Toffo, Minto, Polo,* and *Rolo* - advertising for the latter sneakily making unreasonable demands upon a chap to question whether or not his affections for a young lady would entice him to part with the last sweet in the packet... '*Do you love someone enough to give them your last Rolo?*' Well no, not in the fifties, mate. You hung on to, and gobbled up every last one as fast as you could... don't forget, we were still duty bound to give our NHS dentist something to do, and anyway, post-war, *any* sweets were still regarded as items to be coveted and dieting had not been invented then, or so it seemed.

Tins used up a lot of shelf space, and I would sometimes spend an idle moment trying to count up how many of Heinz's '*57 Varieties*' my dad had actually stocked. Truth to tell, I never got very far, because as an easily distracted and quite feckless little git, my eyes would alight on some other desirable goody such as a *Marsh Mallow*, and thus my scientific marketing survey would grind to an abrupt halt. As you will recall, tea arrived in large wooden tea chests, later to be passed on to up-and-coming skiffle group hopefuls, and was bagged up according to customers' requirements. There were no tea bags around in those days, so a cuppa was made by adding the loose leaves to the pot. This meant, of course, that every household needed a tea strainer as part of its normal tea-drinking equipment; it was either that, or spending a few minutes picking out drowned tea-leaves from between your teeth subsequent to draining your cup. Although peculiarly satisfying, such a practice was not what you might call *sexy* – not on the first date, certainly.

Coffee, on the other hand, was not nearly so common, and our shop stocked only little tins (and I mean *very* little: 2oz to be precise) of the first instant powdered coffee made by Nestles. By the way, this company's name was always pronounced in exactly the same way as the word given to describe how a bird settles into its habitat for a comfy night in the treetops (a good position from which to watch many a cradle tumbling earthwards, no doubt). The modern pronunciation of '*Nest – lay*' was unknown.

The other contender on the coffee market was a bottled liquid called *Camp Coffee* which preceded the powdered version by a goodly number of decades. This instant beverage had been produced in the late nineteenth century by a Glasgow company which was responding to a request from the Gordon Highlanders. Evidently the soldiers were cheesed off because making coffee in the traditional way was slow and difficult when rushing about putting down uprisings in foreign parts. They wanted quick and easy coffee – and here it was, probably the world's first instant coffee. The inclusion of chicory gave the brew an individual flavour, which was evidently popular with the jocks because the famous adverts always showed a kilted officer knocking back a cup outside his tent. Lest you should be worried that such a pause for refreshment was an unnecessary distraction from military duties, just look at the flag's motto of '*Ready, Aye Ready*'. Whilst this might be seen as a reference to the coffee itself, it could also be taken as a description of military vigilance. Suffice it

This advert was amongst the most easily recognised in the 1950's

to say that the motto remains on the bottle to this very day – a longevity of almost a century and a half. Considerations regarding particular servant/master sensibilities didn't really have much of a priority in the first half of the century, and advertising, along with a good many other aspects of daily life in the post-war years was very unsophisticated compared with today.

Mind you, we do seem to have gone just a tad too far these days, haven't we? With products bearing names such as '*Persuasion*', '*Images*' and '*Impulse*', surely I can't be the only one who frequently reaches the end of a TV ad without the remotest idea of what was for sale, can I? At least the idea of just adding an O at the end left you fairly sure as to what was on offer; I have no doubt that had Viagra been available in the 1950's, it would almost certainly have been called '*Stiffo*'. Well, at least you would be left in little doubt as to what it was supposed to do.

The dietary range most people had in those days was also very limited. On Sundays there was the traditional roast, but this was nearly always roast beef, pork or lamb. Chicken, believe it or not, was a luxury item, and one we only had at Christmas (or turkey if you were particularly well-off), because all poultry was very expensive in comparison with red meat. Beef was considered to be

part of our everyday staple diet, and accompanied by roast potatoes, Yorkshire pudding and a sprout or two, it was the most common Sunday lunch menu – provided it was all afloat in a veritable lake of gravy. This latter accompaniment was often provided by yet another 'O' product – this time *Bisto*. For some reason, the advert featuring the *Bisto Kids* sniffing the meaty aroma of their favourite gravy really caught the public's imagination, and must have been one of the most successful promotions of the period.

Like most families, we always had a sweet to accompany the main course, and this was also the case with the majority of our meals in those days – although it was nearly always referred to as 'pudding'. On Sundays it might be something special like Spotted Dick or treacle tart, but for the remainder of the week would quite often be something cheaper, or a concoction of leftovers, such as bread and butter pudding. Regrettably, my mother, along with thousands of others, would all too frequently resort to things like blancmange, semolina or tapioca. I've often wondered about these items: everyone I knew hated them. Tapioca was often described as 'frogspawn' as its slimy but lumpy consistency bore a horrible similarity to its amphibian equivalent, and if anything, probably tasted slightly worse. I've no idea what semolina was or who decided that some whitish sloppy but sticky stuff bearing a remarkable similarity to wall paper paste might well be useful in providing a treacherous raft on which to float the obligatory blob of raspberry jam. Both it and tapioca seemed to hold heat for a long time, so all in all, the arrival of such delicacies on the table was not greeted with immediate joy; if you weren't put off by the texture and taste, you could still sustain a memorable scald to add to your misery. It almost made prunes and custard something to look forward to.

'*And what*', I may ask, '*is the point of blancmange?*' Needless to say, as a little lad I had no idea about French (apart from a rude song some of the big boys sang about the questionable exploits of some German officers which had a chorus of '*Inky – pinky parlay- vous*'). But in later, slightly more enlightened times, I learned that the literal translation was apparently '*eat white*'. I was not really surprised, because that's what it was like: eating a bowlful of '*white*'. Apart from being slightly sweet and generally doing a rather poor imitation of a jelly by wobbling about a bit, I could see no possible purpose for such a substance, other than to take up some space - and to be the centre of a philosophical debate as to its very existence.

So let's get back to custard. Mentioned all too briefly above in its association with prunes, this unsung hero of the pudding world could not be more different from blancmange or the horrors of tapioca. Indeed, I am of the firm opinion that along with string, sellotape and pickled onions, custard is one of those things which define our nation– a truly British, patriotic cornerstone of our very existence. A bit over the top? A shade overstated? Well, ask yourself, what other substance could combine so perfectly with sliced bananas and transform a long, thin, white-apart-from-the-many-bruised-bits tropical fruit into a pudding of such delight? What other colourful fluid is able to provide itself with a protective and entirely edible skin, the ownership of which led to many a childhood squabble? What other mealtime attraction could take it upon itself to turn into a solid if left to go cold? Case proven, I think.

The lack of labour-saving devices meant that jobs such as washing and drying clothes were hard work and time-consuming - and Monday was always the day devoted to this chore. Seems odd now, that virtually the whole post-war nation set about the same domestic task on a particular day in the week, but that's the way it was. Such womanly work also had an effect upon our diets, in that Mondays was always the day for leftovers from the weekend. Thus *Bubble and Squeak,* a fry-up of left over potatoes and cooked vegetables, was both common and popular. If any of Sunday's joint remained, that too would be added, usually accompanied by a blob or two of Branston pickle. The downside was that haste (and perhaps cost) dictated that this was the very sort of day when the dreaded tapioca might be scooped up from the garden pond and slithered into the pudding bowl, but sometimes there would be tinned fruit and evaporated milk: Hooray! Although relatively unfashionable these days, tinned peaches, apricots, pears and especially 'fruit salad' were very popular pudding partners with evaporated milk, which was normally supplied by two companies: *Ideal* and *Carnation.* Now, I challenge anyone to tell the difference between the milk tinned by these two manufacturers, but as is the way with people, there were those who swore by one, and wouldn't countenance the appearance of the other over the threshold: *Ideal milk?! Ideal milk?! Listen son, I'm a Carnation man, same as my father and his father before him! Ideal milk in this house?! Over my dead body!!'*

Yes, passions could run high over such fundamental issues, and I am certain for every *Carnation* fanatic, there was an equivalent *Ideal* man just down the road who would rather suffer a plague of frogs than apply ye olde tin opener to... 'a *tin of that... which in this house, shall remain nameless!'* Hey ho. Mind you, once the battle of the milks had reached an uneasy truce, there was the rest of the week's menu to consider. Red meat of one sort or another played a greater part in this than it does today, and mince was a frequent ingredient in many a lunchtime meal and played a fairly significant role. Equally popular was the (then) newly available tin of *Spam*. Introduced from the USA during the Second World War, the name of this startlingly pink meaty product was said to have been an acronym for 'Specially Processed American Meat' although this is but one of several equally plausible explanations. Regardless of its derivation, *Spam* was very popular, and would often be used as a main course with a salad and, at one time, an almost mandatory element in a sandwich.

If there was a temporary lull in the custard supply, we might have rice pudding to follow, and although quite a familiar presence in the pudding bowl, I didn't like it much because it had a skin. *'Aha!'* I hear you say. *'So too does custard. Are we talking double standards here? Is there an inconsistency in the narrative?'* Be still your beating heart... in our house custard was never around long enough to form a skin, or go cold and solid - so there!

From Tuesday onwards it was really just a matter of recycling the restricted menu we were used to: sausages one day, stew and dumplings another, a steak and kidney pudding perhaps, and of course, fish and chips. From a modern point of view, what was conspicuously absent was any sort of pasta, savoury rice, or indeed, any dish which had its origin abroad. The only sort of pasta I came across in the late fifties was spaghetti, and how it was presented was a world away from the long elegant bundles of pasta available now. We really only had tinned spaghetti hoops and these, like the much more common spoonful of baked beans, would often be served as a snack on toast. *Tagliateli? Lasagne? Linguini*? Never heard of them, mate! Neither did we have curries. Such food was considered quite exotic, and may have been available in sophisticated restaurants, but for the likes of ordinary working people, it was virtually unknown, as was Chinese food. International cuisine only really started making inroads into our dietary consciousness in the sixties, and even then it was of the *Vesta* instant meals type.

The advent of a new world – but early curries were often of the instant type

As regards breakfast, there was a veritable explosion of cereal choices from the mid fifties onwards. Up to that point, porridge had been the standard pre-curser to a slice of toast and marmalade, and as far as most of us were concerned, its only real competitors were *Shredded Wheat*, and a packaged product called *Grape Nuts* - the consistency of which was something akin to small pieces of road grit, and about as tasty as far as I was concerned. The only cereal flake product, dating from the

1940's was called *Force*. Although I never considered it one of my favourites, I was drawn to it because its packaging featured a character called *Sunny Jim* who seemed to be a confident and forthright sort of fellow, whose lively step would inevitably be bestowed upon all who partook of the boxed contents. That the flakes themselves were rather hard, and needed a good deal of milk submersion and generous sugar application to make them in any way appealing seemed not to matter that much.

That is, until *Kellogg's Cornflakes* suddenly became available, and as far as most of us were concerned, almost synonymous with the word 'cereal'. True, products such as *Puffed Wheat* were also on the market, but none had the meteoric success enjoyed by cornflakes: they were golden, they were crispy, you could float them for a minute or so in your bowl of milk before your mum told you to *'stop playing with your food – it's nearly time for school, and what's eight times seven..... OK, four times six then?'*

At that time, I don't think anyone I knew was aware of the fact that the co-inventor of the cornflake, Dr. John Kellogg, had been preoccupied with developing this new product not just for its own inherent benefits as a healthy food. Apparently, of greater importance to the good doctor was his belief that the ingestion of his product would *reduce the recipient's sexual urges*. As a Seventh Day Adventist, he had a particular abhorrence for the pleasures of the flesh, and was therefore particularly keen to stamp out masturbation. I kid you not. Evidently, in one of his books he stated:

'Neither plague, nor war, nor small-pox have produced results so disastrous to humanity as the pernicious habit of onanism. Such a victim dies literally by his own hand.'

Blimey. If any of the grownups I knew were aware of this by-product of our favourite breakfast cereal, they never let on... and I certainly wasn't aware of any increased monitoring of extra-curricular activity in the trouser department: cornflakes were just a nice nosh for breakfast, OK?

As time went on, and new cereal products hit the market, competition between manufacturers became that much more intense. Not only were the ingredients becoming ever more tempting with, for example the introduction of sugar coated cereals such as *Frosties* (which were ***Grrrrreat!!,*** according to Tony the Tiger), but the marketing became increasingly artful. Which brings me to the great – indeed, *gorgeous* - 1950's Vauxhall Velox.

During the course of one of my evening meanders through my dad's shop, my eye was caught by a colourful drawing of this gleaming and stylish vehicle on the front of a *Weetabix* packet. With curiosity aroused, my subsequent investigation revealed that, should my parents become the proud owners of the said packet of *Weetabix*, their son would have the opportunity to construct himself a shiny Vauxhall Velox whose coloured plans were printed on the reverse of the box: only a pair of scissors and some glue needed! Well, needless to say, my cereal affections and loyalties were re-directed straight away, and my mother was made immediately aware of my urgent need for a change in cereal to promote my physical well-being and happiness. OK. Giving up *Cornflakes* might make me more susceptible to some questionable personal habits as outlined by Dr. Kellogg, but wasn't the opportunity to be the proud possessor of a cardboard Vauxhall Velox worth the risk to my moral development? And it wasn't only cardboard cut-outs that became all the rage; soon cereal manufacturers were putting actual toys and puzzles inside the packet itself. Such a marketing ploy inevitably led to the near destruction of new boxes of cereal in the urgent search for the enclosed deep sea diver *'complete with helmet and breathing tube: to see him rise to the surface just add a pinch of baking powder'*.

And so it went on. To be honest, the dramatic pictures on the backs of the cereal boxes, be it aeroplane, plastic dinosaur or Vauxhall Velox set your expectations high, but reality seldom hit the mark. My diver, for example, stubbornly refused to rise to the surface. Even when I shook the bottle violently and tipped it over to a degree which threatened the integrity and water repellent capabilities of my mum's fablon-covered coffee table, the little swine just stayed sulking in a lather of frothy suds … the diver, I mean, not my mum. And the Vauxhall Velox? Well, I never seemed to have the right glue. Despite my natural inclination to resort to my old sellotape ally, on this occasion the vehicle itself turned out to be considerably smaller than the illustration would have led me to believe – in fact, even with the most delicate of application, a single piece of my sticky mate would have completely encompassed the whole front of the vehicle, giving it what would years later become a somewhat '*shrink-wrapped*' appearance – really no good at all.

The only thing that the cereal packets did do reasonably well was the face mask, and I can remember a certain '*Witch Haggy*' mask which *Weetabix* or some other company produced around the time when Halloween celebrations were at last dipping a tentative toe in the water. Thus we junior Weetabix munchers were encouraged to wolf down as much cereal as possible prior to becoming proud owners of the said mask. As I recall, it was really quite good, in a literally frightful way, and the artist who was responsible certainly gave it the warts and all treatment. Until then, I'd not been particularly aware of dermatological imperfections, but this poor soul had several, complete with a couple with realistic looking hairs per wart sprouting forth with what appeared to be unbounded enthusiasm. So, the whole ensemble complete with missing teeth and bloodshot eyes was really quite fearsome, and all you needed was a piece of black material to wear around your shoulders and a pointy hat to be fully kitted out to scare the crap out of innocent folk going about their business as dusk fell on 31st October. All OK so far? Well, as far as I was concerned, there was one slight flaw to this theatrical reign of terror. You see, the trouble with having a family grocery business is that you never seem to get the brand-spanking-new stuff off the shelves. What you do get, is the left-over stuff that no customer in their right mind would buy. Hence, we always got the funny shaped carrots, the cauliflower whose white heart had inexplicably covered itself in black and green speckled bits, and the toothpaste tube that seemed to have a bit of a split down the side. To be honest, I don't think we ever had a tin at home that didn't have a dent in it, or the label half missing. And remember, this was a long, long time before 'sell by' dates were even thought of. So what's this got to do with the revolting Witch Haggy? Well, as you might have guessed, come November, the dramatic allure of Halloween masks took a severe down-turn, and even with threepence off the price, selling such packets presented my dad with something of a challenge in the run up to Christmas. I suppose fair's fair: after all, looking at that awful face across the breakfast table when *'Jingle Bells'* is blasting out on the Light Programme is not a great combination. So, once we're in the New Year, the possibility of selling such graphically horrifying products was really a no-hoper… so they ended up in our cupboard. And I tell you, leaping out on people with a fearsome cackle and threats to turn anyone within a six foot radius into a toad… *in early April,* takes a lot of nerve. Believe me. I know.

In such circumstances, a little light relief was required… and so to the bakers. Again, these were usually independent local shops, the only real alternative being the Co-op, which in many towns did a daily delivery round in addition to the normal provision in its stores. Well, that was OK for your loaves of bread and buns of various types, but if you wanted cakes – especially fancy cakes, then a trip to the local independent bakers was a must. Although very much a luxury item, fancy cakes seemed to the likes of us to be the very pinnacle of ingestible excellence (not that I'm including sweets here, of course; sweets were sweets… cakes were *food* for heaven's sake). I don't know if the choice was greater in the fifties than it is now, but there certainly wasn't the packaging. Most shops displayed their sticky cream-smothered delights as naked as nature intended... which was great in the sense that what you saw was what you got, but perhaps not quite so good as regards keeping insect life at bay. But that didn't worry the likes of me: cream horns, meringues, Bakewell tarts complete with glacé cherry, sticky iced buns, even coconut cones ... that was living, wasn't it? Our dentist certainly thought so.

Prince among this cornucopia of delights was surely the *cream slice*. I'm not even sure they are made today, but if they are, chances are they will be entombed in a brilliantly illustrated cardboard box, or perhaps incarcerated under a transparent plastic dome, surrounded by lots of frilly paper only partly masked by a great big orange price tag that has the £ sign prominently displayed. I can't remember what the cost of a cream slice was in those days, but it was certainly a rare treat. It was also damn near impossible to eat. If you don't know what I'm talking about - and let's face it, this may not be the first time by any stretch of the imagination - then you need to know just how a cream slice was constructed.

Although not an expert in matters of fine confectionary, it seemed to me that the essence of the delight was a number of layers of very flaky pastry. So far, so good. Now, what you do next is insert between each of these strips a fairly lavish layer of cream. Some say it should be fresh cream, others that it should be something called 'confectioners' cream'. Did we care? Whether fresh or artificial, it made not a jot of difference, for the thickness of your cream slice has now increased significantly, and even at this stage has about it the look of a comestible that is becoming structurally unstable. But we're not finished yet. Unbelievably, a suggestion of raspberry jam is now inserted between cream and flaky pastry. I've no idea how this was done, but can only picture a baker sat up at the dead of night with a hypodermic syringe full of the necessary preserve, patiently injecting the stuff between layers… and probably up to his knees in discarded broken cream slices where a sudden jerk of the syringe has meant that more than a few of his products have met a messy and untimely end. By now, the successfully constructed slice is about two inches thick, and is awaiting the final administration of the icing. Now you may think that pastry, cream and jam is quite enough – but no! On the top layer was put a covering of the sort of icing that looks slightly transparent; it's nearly white in the same way as fog is white, but not completely so. It almost has a mother-of-pearl quality to it, making the completed sweetmeat all the more beguiling and enticing. So, all that remains is to persuade your mum that the difference in your young life between total happiness, absolute compliance with all maternal instructions from now on until the end of time, and by the way, that dress really suits you - and abject misery lies before her, and that it costs a mere 10½d. So, the deal done, the baker would scoop up the object of desire (again, I don't mean my mum) and deposit it upon a tiny cardboard tray, and commit the readies into the old cash till with just a hint of triumphant smirk.

Eating a cream slice was something else entirely. Looking back, I can only assume that the icing topping was there to hold the slice together. Once bitten into, the whole thing collapsed in a welter of flaky bits and a splurging jammy creamy mess. Some tried to attack it by trying to bite off the end – but the result was that as the end under attack compressed to a mere quarter of an inch, the other end opened up to about six inches, and all the jam and cream made a bid for freedom by shooting out all over the hearth rug. Some tried to restrain the opposite end by clamping it closed, but the only result was that the squidgy interior shot out both sides at the same time, so one way or the other, you lost. The only real way to eat a cream slice was to sit in the bath and hope for the best.

And whilst you were scraping the last of the destroyed slice off the taps, your eye may have been drawn to the range of bathroom products perched precariously on the curved side of the bath. Almost certain to be present would be a tin of *Vim,* or its rival, *Ajax.* What the cardboard tube contained was a granulated and really quite abrasive powder which you used to clean the bath and basin. That the grimy ring left around the high water mark of your bath may have spoken volumes about the infrequency of bath-taking in your household (and remember, hardly anyone possessed a shower even in the late fifties) attacking it with a gritty abrasive powder seems a bit OTT. I can well remember a noise not dissimilar from the application of fairly heavy duty sandpaper as the process commenced. So bathroom equipment may have been

reasonably clean, but it was seldom particularly shiny – indeed, some taps even had the chrome plating worn right off to reveal the underlying base metal. But *Vim* and *Ajax* were considered essential for the modern home. Indeed, when my sister set up her first flat in the early sixties, the fact that she had her own tin of *Vim* was a sign that she and her husband were now independent – they had made a home of their own – a sure sign of domestic responsibility. I well remember the wonderful Les Dawson doing one of his famous *Cissy and Ada* sketches with Roy Barraclough. As usual they sit side by side and are energetically engaged in running down another woman. Les, legs akimbo and arms folded beneath ample bosom, does the slight 'upward shuffle' of the arms that precedes many an announcement of great import, and out of the side of his mouth confides to Cissy: **'*Of course – she's a stranger to Ajax you know!*'**

Brilliant. And did I mention loo rolls? Well, yes I did actually, all too briefly in Chapter 2. If you ever wanted complete confirmation that Baby Boomers are well-hard, then all I need do is describe for you the situation concerning the two toilet rolls that were called *Izal* and *Bronco*. I'm certain that the following explanation will enable me to walk away with an insouciant *'Case proven, I think?!'* comment. You see, when it comes to toilet hygiene in those days, there were no cuddly little doggies running around the house draped in miles and miles of soft and strong, accurately perforated, delicately scented pink, sky-blue or dusky peach multi-pack rolls with which we fulfil one our most basic needs today. No. For the first twenty years of our lives there were really only these two almost identical brands of toilet paper. And just how did they differ from the modern version? Well, for a start, neither was soft, nor indeed, in any way absorbent. I'll just let that sink in for a moment – which was more than the loo paper would do, I can assure you. Now, having a non-absorbent quality was bad enough, but to have a shiny surface which was ever so slightly transparent as well, makes it – well, just about impossible, doesn't it? And remember, it was either that, or resorting to the outdated and even more unsophisticated solution of using newspaper cut to an appropriate size: not the sort of thing the modern family with a new *Vauxhall Velox* and a *Philco* electric shaver would sink to. So shiny hard loo paper it had to be. As far as I could see, its only saving grace was that it was cheap, and that it also worked pretty well as tracing paper if you happened to run short of the properly manufactured item and geography homework was due in the next morning.

So let's move away from such earthy considerations (the loo paper I mean, not the geography homework) and return to the relative safety of the bathroom shelf. You may recall that a few chapters ago we had reason to visit the dentist, and that such a venture was regarded with much trepidation by the likes of yours truly - and with good reason. You see, back in the fifties, the sort of hygienic practices we are accustomed to these days were more of a distant aspiration than a living reality, and none more so than in the realm of dental health. For a start, there was no added fluoride in drinking water, and so our teeth were therefore much more susceptible to the general lack of care little gits like me subjected them to.

Toothpaste was generally of the standard white stuff provided by Messrs. *SR* or *Colgate*, and some of us still had to make do with *Gibbs Tooth Powder*. As suggested previously, the best way this latter product could be described would be *Vim for teeth,* as it certainly seemed quite abrasive. It arrived in a tin about the same size as *Kiwi* boot polish, and as far as I was concerned was of about the same use. Once you had managed to prize off the lid, there was this pinkish powder stuff. So far, so good. Trouble was, to get the powder on to your toothbrush, you had to wet the bristles, and then apply them suitably dampened to the powder. This worked fine for the first go, but you may have spotted a slight flaw in the procedure: some of the wetness on your toothbrush inevitably escaped and happily settled itself amongst the hitherto dust-dry particles of unused tooth powder. And worse still, while you were busy beavering away at giving your gnashers a good going over with the old toothbrush, the rest of the powder in the tin was equally busy congealing itself into a hard concrete-like substance which had more in common with freshly constituted *Polyfilla* than it did with a useful dental product. So when *Pepsodent* came along, it was a big step in the right direction. *'Just a minute!'* I hear you say, *'What's the matter with Colgate... and what about SR? Wasn't that the first advert ever on ITV back in 1956? Didn't that fact alone make it an almost patriotic duty to purchase tubes by the dozen? Where's your product loyalty?'*

All very true, but *Pepsodent* had one of the greatest TV ads of all time, and its jingle remains with all true Baby Boomers to this very day. Sung to a chirpy little tune, the words echo down the decades and will, I am sure, enter the 'TV Ads Hall Of Fame'. Brace yourselves:

'You'll wonder where the yellow went
When you brush your teeth with Pepsodent!'

I mean, come on! It's got everything, hasn't it? Punchy, dynamic, scientifically specific and probably even reasonably hygienic too. Back in 1957, it really hit the spot for me, and I couldn't wait to examine the lack of yellowness after the first administration of the stuff. Suffice it to say that although the results were less instantaneous than I had hoped, I put it down more to the fact that I was still prone to resume my close encounter with a partially consumed gob-stopper well after lights out, and thus any remaining traces of yellowness were almost certainly down to my own sweet-toothed weakness. Anyway, *Pepsodent* remained the dental cream of choice… until *Signal* came along, that is. How on earth they managed to get the stuff to come out *in stripes* was beyond belief, and had about it the same measure of awe normally preserved for the lettering associated with seaside sticks of rock… or getting the jam into a cream slice.

Bathroom use was a lot less frequent in those days – mainly because there were far fewer of them; if you'd have mentioned the term *'en suite'* people would have thought you were from up north, and were referring to taking your ease on the family sofa. Also, there were not the products: roll-on deodorants, in fact deodorants of any type were virtually unknown, and talcum powder was just about the only product available to mitigate the malodorous effect of excess perspiration. Girls, of course, had loads of different bottles of spray perfume to enable them to waft about in a cloud of scented allure, but for blokes, it was a bit trickier. Shaving, for a start, was downright dangerous. Although the old open blade cut-throat razors had largely been consigned to the scrap heap by the fifties, their replacement, the so-called *safety* razor was sometimes anything but. For a start, it had to be equipped with a succession of quite lethal razor blades. This operation alone was, well, just that ... very similar to a real operation, given the amount of blood that all too often followed this apparently simple procedure. And as regards the decapitation of acne, whose proliferation with most teenage boys often reached a scale envied by Artex applicators, you can imagine the mess. Thank goodness for fag papers. For those of you who don't understand this last point, a lot of smokers rolled their own cigarettes, using very thin paper made by the *Rizla* company. Such was the thinness of this paper that even a tiny piece could be torn off and attached quite successfully to the bloody stump of what until a few seconds ago,

The bathroom surgery – tools of the trade.

had been a perfectly proportioned and snow-capped peak, the pride of your acne collection, now reduced to a minor foothill. So, seeing many a young bloke emerging from the bathroom festooned with bits of white paper, all of which had just a little tell-tale spot of red at the centre, was not at all uncommon. It was, in some ways, a mark of pride: it said *'Look! I'm old enough to shave, brave enough to lose blood and bristles in much the same proportion, and I have access to fag papers!'* And of course, it looked a lot better than sticking a bit of *Bronco* on your face.

But it was not all bad news for the blokes: we fellas also had *'Brylcreem... for men!'* Essentially, this was a scented white grease which came in a small pot, about the same size as a Marmite jar – and of about the same consistency. According to the TV advert, which showed a smart twenty-something getting ready for his date by rubbing the stuff into his hair with considerable vigour, he agreed completely with the accompanying jingle which went:

'Brylcreem - a little dab'll do yah,
Brylcreem puts life into dry hair!'

Oh yeah? Well, the bloke in the ad certainly looked good – his hair
was sleek and shiny, and the Brylcreem certainly seemed to have
done the trick, for did he not now have a beautiful young lady on his
arm who was clearly enraptured at the sight of his shining locks? In
point of fact, his hair was now so shiny that she could almost see
herself reflected in it; never would she suspect that just a half hour
before, his hair had been dull and lifeless. The trouble was, even the
slightest over-application of the cream left your hair slightly sticky,
so as well as putting life back into your dry hair, it also collected a
lot of other stuff that happened to be floating about in the
atmosphere: Ajax and fag papers for a start, and if you happened to
sneeze near a newly opened tin of Gibb's Tooth Powder, then in the
next few moments you were likely to have suddenly manufactured
your own crash helmet.

So let's get away from this alarming image, and return to the more
wholesome world of the shopping counter once more. By the mid
fifties, it was clear that supermarkets were going to be the future for
domestic shopping. As noted earlier, this was still pretty much a
daily routine, as few homes possessed fridges, and therefore keeping
food fresh was a real issue. The difference was that supermarkets
could not only offer most of the products currently provided by
individual businesses, they could also do it more cheaply because of
their bulk purchasing power. Suddenly it seemed that the days of the
small local shopkeeper (one of whom was my dad) were over. But
not so. For just in the nick of time, along came a knight in shining
armour bearing a Green Shield. Yes – small businesses were hitting
back with Green Shield Stamps - and from 1958, the battle of the
High Street was on!

Designed specifically for small independent businesses, it worked
like this: the shopkeeper purchased a large telephone directory-sized

book full of individually perforated Green Shield stamps. For each 6d spent in his shop, the customer would be given a Green Shield stamp to be stuck in his or her own little book. Once the book had been filled up, it could be exchanged for a whole range goods at the

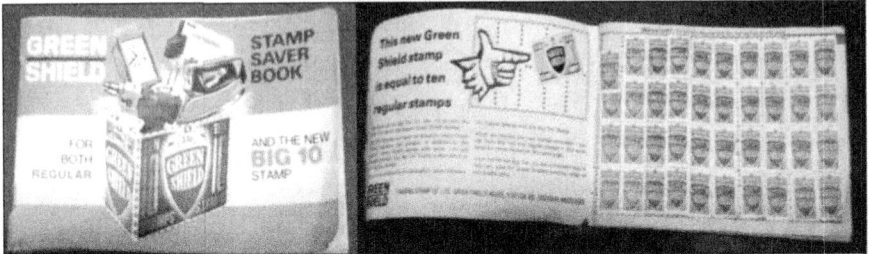

A collector's book outside and in. Promotion for the larger 'BIG 10' stamps is evident in both – perhaps an indication that inflation was becoming a factor in the economy.

local Green Shield Shop, which had opened in all towns participating in the scheme. And the redeemable goods were many and varied, ranging for example, from a dustpan and brush set at one end of the scale to a new TV the other. The only trouble was, you had to collect loads of stamps for each collector's book, and quite a lot of books to get anything really worthwhile. But it worked. Regardless of the fact that the independent traders' purchase of the stamps for distribution to their customers was quite costly, the retention – and even increase of subsequent trade - made it a viable proposition. For a while at least, those who could afford to buy into the scheme were able to counter the threat posed by the supermarkets, and thus preserved the traditional way of High Street shopping for a few more years.

And while all this was going on, most of the old door to door street traders were still adding to the daily routine of filling the kitchen shelf. There were the daily visits by the milkmen, some of whom were now offering a wider range of products, such as eggs and cream. The baker's boy was also a quite frequent visitor riding a strange conveyance that was half bike, half van. It was a bit like a pedal powered wheelie bin. Adding to the suburban street scene in the early 1960's, was the *Corona* delivery man, who was sophisticated enough to sell his bottles of the popular and multi-flavoured fizzy drinks from a rather snazzy and up-market van. At the other end of the scale was perhaps the oddest – and easily the most bizarre of all the domestic street traders - the French Onion Man.

Now I don't know if our Gallic chums have a particular affection for onions, or whether onions grown across the Channel possess some particular characteristic which places them head and shoulders above the more modest but equally eye-watering properties of the native species. Or it may just be that old French blokes liked cycling a lot. You see, the seasonal sale of French onions was brought to your very own front door on a bicycle which Pierre had ridden all the way from Paris. And they weren't stuffed in his pockets, or carried in a handy duffle bag – oh no! They were tied in a huge and unwieldy string which was tethered to the handlebars. Yes, really! Now I don't know if such a large number of onions swinging lazily about the handlebars in any way altered the road holding characteristics of the machine, but one can only assume this to be the case. And as regards travelling after dark, wouldn't the onions get in the way of the lights? And wouldn't it be a much better idea to put the damn things in a van in the first place, thus at a stroke eliminating cycling irregularities and providing a greater carrying capacity than just one crummy handlebar's worth? Obviously not. And so it was that once or twice a year, there would be a ring at the doorbell, and standing there with a Gitane dangling from his lips and an onion or two clutched in either hand would be Armand from Poitiers or Philippe from Rouen who would mutter something along the lines of '*Madame, sil vous plait, les onion?*'

Well, of course, being British, my mother took immediate pity on this poor French geezer. After all, had he not had a hell of a time wrestling with his wayward handlebars right across northern France, only then to be confronted with a windswept *La Manche?* And all of this just to bring a little extra flavour to the first course of Monday's *Cottage pie followed by bananas and custard* banquet.

So it was an easy sale, really - everyone was a winner. We got an eye-watering lunch, and were also happy that we had no doubt managed to reinforce the Entente Cordial, and perhaps had helped our visitor to forget that his nation was so utterly hopeless at wars in general, and Waterloo and Trafalgar in particular. As far as he was concerned, Pierre had got his 1/3d, and with a few more sales at that rate could probably afford to buy a complete new bike with even larger handle bars in a couple of months. It never really occurred to us that in fact Pierre may *not* have been a French bloke at all, or that his onions may *not* have been the fruitful produce of a foreign field that was forever England. Chances are, he might just as well have been a bloke called Dave who had a dodgy French accent gleaned from watching Maurice Chevalier films at the Gaumont, and had a shed full of old onions in a lock up garage in Southampton -*such* was the age of innocence.

And so to strawberries. Now, these were a very special treat because, unlike today, you only got them for a short period each summer... because that's when they were grown, OK? The possibility of getting fruit and veg from way across the world was unexplored in those days (- as indeed was quite a bit of the world itself, if I'm honest), and the prospect of getting perishable foods from places where they grew quite happily in out of season times was unheard of. I mean, discounting old Pierre and his onion-festooned handlebars, imported food was pretty limited, especially from faraway places with strange sounding names... except New Zealand, and you don't get much further away than that. Imports of frozen lamb from the other side of the world were quite common, and the vast amount of Anchor butter that found its way on to the upper surface of our Mother's Pride sliced white loaves just testified to the obvious lushness of the pastureland *downunder*. By and large though, perishable food was distinctly seasonal – and in a way this made it rather more appreciated.

My parents always looked forward to the first sprouts of the new season, and whereas their son didn't much slavver at the prospect of anything green and was much more interested in the first Bounty Bar of the year, I did get the point: anticipating the arrival of seasonal produce was all part of the yearly round, and gave a certain richness, diversity and appreciation which is perhaps missing today. OK, there is so much more to choose from these days, agreed – but the fact that it is so available – and in so many different languages, from so many parts of the world tends to make us all a little blasé, don't you think?

Back to my world of dented tins and packets of stuff that should have been sold last Christmas twelve month. Naturally, my family also got what was left over on the veg counter as well, and had I been more topped up with gorm and a bit more aware of the facts of life, I no doubt could have made much of the bum lookalike potatoes and phallic carrots that were our family's duty to consume without comment.

And all the time the supermarkets were growing in strength and popularity. Well before the days of the out of town hypermarket, these continued to be situated on the high street itself, and were often conversions of existing large buildings, such as old cinemas. Their very proximity to local independent traders thus made them even more of a threat, and by the mid sixties, many of the small individual businesses had gone to the wall. It was a bitter blow for many when the large supermarkets were suddenly included in the Green Shield Stamp merchandising promotion; thus, the single advantage given to independent traders was lost to the very people from whom protection was sought. And as for the customers – why not get all your shop under one roof *and* get your Green Shield Stamps at the same time? Can't blame them, can you?

At the same time, the purchase of items as diverse as milk, bread, cakes, sweets and cigarettes were increasingly diverted to the supermarkets with the inevitable effect upon not only the local confectioners, bakers and tobacconists, but on that seemingly essential part of our daily life, the morning delivery of milk bottles to each doorstep. Over the course of the succeeding decade, the clinking of the bottles and the electric hum of the milk float as it made its staccato early morning journey along the street became an increasing rarity. *'So what?'* you might say. Well, it was simply evidence that those things which society takes for granted – those elements which form the very *wallpaper* of the daily routine - were disappearing fast: they were seldom specifically registered, and only became noticeable when they ceased.

But life moves on with a shrug, and you search out the next bargain. And what a lot there were. By the early sixties, a lot of people were shelling out the loot – or using Hire-Purchase – to get themselves a fridge, and this made a very big difference to shopping habits. Now you could keep perishable stuff for more than a day or two, and what's more, you might even be able to keep ice cream and other chilly delights. True, I had tried several times to make ice lollies in my dad's fridge at his shop a decade before, but was always too impatient, and at best ended up with a stick that flopped about too much in a pool of cold orange slush. Not really a glowing success – but by the sixties many folk could get really good stuff like *Arctic Roll*, and keep it at home!

Fast drawing to a close were the days of paper bags filled with loose biscuits, or wedges of cheese cut with a wire and wrapped in grease-proof paper. Tea and sugar measured out and emptied into little blue bags made of sugar paper were fast becoming things of the past. Pre-packaged stuff all mass marketed in one supermarket was here to stay. So the only way to beat them was to join them. A decade later, counter service in many a small shop was redundant, and the only way to survive was to convert to the self-service open all hours corner shop. And for many it was successful, and continues to be so – but something was lost. The daily shopping routine was redundant, and with it went the opportunity to sit at the counter recycling the local gossip with the assistant. Perhaps a good job too? But don't forget, also lost was the possibility of buying broken biscuits at bargain prices, or of getting the assistant to find the cereal packet with the Vauxhall Velox on the back.

As for the likes of me, gone were the days of running my fingers through the bins of loose oats and rice before settling down to consume a brick sized Penguin sat comfortably on a conveniently placed cheese pouffe. Mind you, not having to worry about just exactly how the family business was going to shift that teetering pyramid of Bronco toilet rolls gathering dust on the top shelf now that Andrex had been invented was something, I suppose. Even if Miss Grant was still in post at Highland Road juniors, the chances of the school needing that much tracing paper seemed somewhat remote.

In the headlong rush towards supermarket modernity, I suspect that the range and diversity of products did suffer initially. Even though individual shops might not be able to stock anything like the variety of products available at the new *Fine-Fare*, they probably could do so *collectively*. In our street alone, there were at least two other quite sizeable grocery shops, and this was true also of confectioners, bakeries and butchers. So, if you were prepared to do a bit of walking, your choice was still pretty wide. Moreover, it was very individual – not only in terms of diversity of products but also in the *combinations* of merchandise available in each shop. Some of these were distinctly bizarre, and many could be described as quirky. Quite a few traders whose establishments bore the same *trade* title offered products that others didn't – and items that the early supermarkets would never even give a second thought to stocking on their shiny shelves.

For instance, close to my dad's business was Miss Eels' confectioners shop (itself only about six doors away from Mrs. Sutton's Sweetie Parlour) which sold a wide selection of traditional sweets including all our favourites, like pear drops, coconut mushrooms, liquorice pipes, sweet cigarettes, sherbet fountains and those ever popular four-a-penny favourites, Fruit Salads and Blackjacks. So far, so good. But she also sold a selection of model soldiers, some farm animals and little metal fences that linked together, and a cardboard slot-together barn. Oh, and pea shooters and wire pistols. As regards the latter, these didn't actually fire wire, you understand, they were just made of wire, and when loaded with the correct ammunition of a nice stretchy rubber band, could be used to terrorise the local spider community. Plus of course, Miss Eels always seemed to have at least a few superannuated fireworks available whatever the time of the year... and if the prevailing aroma in her delightful premises was anything to go by, she was also the purveyor of paraffin and boot polish as well.

So in her establishment alone, you could buy products that without the necessary application of *Gibbs Tooth Powder* would ensure an early visit to the dentist, enough explosives to further endanger your re-erected back wall and at the same time, set up your very own farm complete with livestock and outbuildings - and patrol it armed with the necessary ordnance to see off any possible rustlers with a well aimed rubber band.

OK, a bit bonkers it was, but it was also fun... and I bet you couldn't do the same at the newly opened supermarket.

At least, not in 1960 you couldn't.

10   **Class Wars**

You may recall that at the end of Chapter 6, life at Highland Road Juniors had come to an end for our year group – some of whom were surfing the wave of euphoria that went with the somewhat unexpected triumph of just scraping over the hurdle of the dreaded Eleven Plus. Actually, leaving the school site for the last time was pretty much a non-event. We simply said a fond farewell to Miss Grant and any other staff members we could find – all of whom gave us a pleasant smile in a '*Good luck and God help you*' sort of way. After that we simply zoomed out of the school gate as fast as our legs would carry us. No class parties, no discos, no proms and we wouldn't have known a stretched limo if one had come up and hit us… which, considering the state of our road safety awareness, was really quite likely.

If, however, any of us had given just one iota of thought to our current predicament, we might have noted that for the first time in our lives, we were about to go to *single sex* schools. This was standard post-war practice for the majority of eleven year olds, and we thought nothing of it. As an essential element of the burgeoning welfare state, our education was clearly in the hands of *those who knew best,* and seeing it was set within the context of a big construction programme ensuring many post-war children went into brand new school buildings, who were we to question - let alone complain?

On reflection, of course, the 'one size fits all' Eleven Plus system was deeply divisive, and girls in particular got the raw end of the deal. If my town was anything to go by, they had less choice than the boys, with only three selective schools as opposed to the five for their male counterparts. Also, the non-selective Secondary Modern system promoted courses that were designed to fill the requirements of the lower end of the employment market. Thus boys had many more practical, workshop based lessons, and the girls had subjects such as cookery and needlework as essential parts of their curriculum.

So, your performance in an intelligence test at eleven years old did, for many, dictate the future course of your life, for there was very little opportunity to move to a selective school once you were enrolled in a *Sec Mod*. True, there was the so called Thirteen Plus, but as mentioned in Chapter 6, the success rate via this route must have been minimal. For those few who did succeed to move into the third year of selective education however, I suspect that it must have been a monumental task to re-align and catch up.

It could be said, therefore, that social engineering was par for the course and the waste of talent and the in-built low level of expectation and aspiration for those who were unsuccessful in the exam was rarely, if ever challenged. As noted before, there were of course many children who enjoyed their Sec Mod experience, and some of these schools did sterling work in providing their youngsters with a good grounding prior to their entry in to the world of work... but I'm afraid it seems many did not. In similar vein, not everyone who passed the exam had a brilliant time either – far from it.

So, was the 1944 Education Act a failure in playing its part in the post-war revival? After all, if many children failed to reach their potential, and others were selected to attend a school for which they were clearly unsuited, was this not a balls-up on a grand scale? Well no, not really. You have to view it in the context of the time.

First and foremost – what did it replace? Pre-war education was something of a hotchpotch of make-do and mend. It varied considerably from one area to another, and had there been post codes in those days, success or otherwise could well have been determined by such a lottery. Also, the ability to pay for your education was still an important factor for many, and provision for the great mass of children was far more patchy and uncertain, especially for the post-elementary years. The 1944 Act was indeed a genuine effort to put all children on an equal footing, and this it succeeded in doing, so much so that education took its rightful place as a foundation stone of the post-war welfare state. What it failed to do was to take the rigidity out of the system, and recognise the huge reservoir of latent skills and talents that all too often were given no opportunity to flourish.

And where did all this leave me in the high summer of 1958? Well, basking in the brownie points that my surprise success in the exam had generated, of course - together with the hope that such merit might well be eked out for the blissful eternity that the summer holidays represented. So, it was with a light heart that my school pals and I embarked upon an extended period of self indulgence which included such highlights as the Summer Show on the pier, riding our bikes along the seafront, making a den or two, and of course, throwing stones: what more could anyone ask?

But, as time went on, the creeping realisation that BIG SCHOOL was getting ever closer made attempts to block it out ever more desperate; even going round to Auntie Una's house to see her new lino became a focus of immense interest - just so long as it kept the inevitable at bay for a bit longer. I was also becoming more than slightly aware of my lack of academic progress. Whilst I had got through the dreaded exam, I could tell from the relief (and surprise) so obvious in my parents' reaction to the news, that my success could only have been by the skin of my teeth. Until now, my attitude to learning had been that I did what I was asked to do with the bare minimum of effort because I had other, more important things to do: a cardboard Vauxhall Velox doesn't build itself you know! But now the storm clouds were gathering, and my sister's assertion that I made gormless kids look positively gifted was beginning to have an effect. Also, I had heard a new word – *feckless* - applied to my attitude. So I was gormless *and* feckless in the eyes of some eh? This didn't sound particularly complimentary so I suppose that in the same way that hopeless and careless people improve by becoming hope*ful* and care*ful,* it seemed logical that I should start to grapple with the rather uncomfortable ideas of working my way towards becoming *gormful* and *feckful*: clearly raised levels of both feck and gorm were definitely needed.

So, what of formal preparation for the new world of academia which was about to be revealed in all its glory? Well, there was precious little, I can assure you. These days, pre-school visits arranged between primary and secondary schools are just the normal – and quite proper – part of the transition process. Children may spend a number of days meeting their new teachers, sampling a lesson or two, going on tours of the building, having a go at some of the more practical and adventurous pieces of workshop and gym equipment and so on. Some schools arrange mentorship by older students to ensure the new youngsters feel at ease. In other words, there is a lot of pre-secondary school prep, and rightly so. I suspect that you will by now have a pretty good idea as to what my next sentence will be... so, in order not to disappoint you here it is: *It wasn't like that in the 1950's!*

The school to which I was sent was the Southern Grammar for Boys. In the pecking order, this was the second ranker, in that Portsmouth Grammar for Boys and Portsmouth High for Girls took the brightest and best, then there were the Southern and Northern Grammars comprising separate schools for either sex. This was where selective education for girls seemed to terminate, for all others were sent to their neighbourhood Secondary Modern. Not so the boys, for there was the Technical School, and still further down the list, a Building School. So, right from the start, girls were accorded less opportunity than boys. The social mores of the period were still very much influenced by the feeling that '*a woman's place is in the home*', and so the obvious discrimination was not really contested. What a waste!

As noted above, we were now well and truly segregated, and although some areas had co-ed schools, it was not common provision as far as I was aware. Mind you, I wasn't aware of much to be honest, and reflecting upon the uncomfortable fact that the most complicated words that I could spell with any degree of confidence were 'Vauxhall', and 'sellotape', I felt pretty damned vulnerable I can assure you. Nevertheless, even my own ostrich-like approach to life could no longer deny the fact that the inevitable was fast approaching, and apart from trying on my new uniform and watching my mum sewing in the name tapes, I had to admit that I was pretty much as unprepared as you can be.

That is, until I attended the *one* parents' meeting that my new school deigned to arrange for new entrants. I can't remember exactly when this was, but what I do recall is sitting near the back of this enormous hall, surrounded by other anxious and best-hat-wearing mums and dads with their tiny sons perched pale and goggle-eyed in between. The Headmaster gave some sort of oration, all of which went right over my head, as I was totally absorbed by the sheer size of the place. The hall could hold eight hundred boys: there was a full stage occupying one end, there was a cloistered pathway running the whole length of the hall beyond which was one of *several* football pitches, and the school had its own organ – a proper sit-up-multi-keyboard-loads-of-pipes-and-knobs jobby. And not a bean bag in sight. Blimey.

There were, however, a few problems. First, the school was almost brand new. '*So what,*' I hear you say, '*is wrong with that?*' Well, for a start it had been built in an area perfect for wide open spaces, and clear, fresh air. Great....except that it was therefore one hell of a long way away from where I and the other Highland Road intellectuals lived. The greatest irony was that the *old* Southern

Grammar for Boys building was ... guess where? Right next to Highland Road Juniors, that's where. Had I been just a little more aware as an eight year old, I could have *listened* to boys being caned just over the wall from where I was busy playing kiss chase with Susan Watts or having a sword fight with Kenny Hyde. The new, gleaming building was about three miles away, standing very exposed to easterly gales on the edge of some salt marshes, and served by only one bus route which came nowhere near where we lived. The journey also required a change at Portsmouth Prison. Ominous or what?

Back to the meeting. The second problem was that I didn't understand much of what the headmaster was droning on about. My eyes were drawn more towards what he and lots of other fierce looking blokes were dressed in i.e. some kind of long black cloaks and flat hats bedecked with a sinister black tassel, which seemed to me the sort of thing a judge might put on before condemning some unfortunate to death. As things turned out, this interpretation was pretty damn close to the truth. At the conclusion of the seemingly interminable lecture, parents were invited to talk to staff members... if you could find one. I rather regret that my mum did. The master concerned was the music teacher, and was known to my dad as one of his customers. *'Ahah!'* I thought, *'A chance for using the old family connection routine to ingratiate myself into this new academic world! I'd have rather he'd been the football teacher, but still, getting the first chance to have a bash on the school organ might give me a competitive start'.* But it was not to be. As I was to become painfully aware over the next few years, the masters – as they insisted on being called - were particularly proud of their sparkling brand new school, and it seemed to me that the last thing they wanted was a load of sweaty, ignorant and testosterone-laden louts cluttering up the place. So their main goal in life was to keep the juvenile riff-raff in its place. Thus, when my parents made a quite nervous enquiry of the music teacher regarding the extent and variety of provision their son and heir might expect, we were a bit taken aback when the incumbent stressed the need for *absolute obedience*, which if not forthcoming would immediately be dealt with by the generous application of *'the* slipper*!!'* I'm assuming, from the malevolent look he gave me that his threat was directed at me, but on reflection I'm not sure he wouldn't have set about my dad as well, just for the hell of it. Well, I suppose his view was that you might as well start as you intended to go on, so scaring the crap out of the new kids before term had even begun might delay by a nano-second or two the need to beat it out of them later. Hey ho.

With such experiences in mind, to say that many of us were all a tad apprehensive about our induction into the world of secondary education was an understatement, and encouragement from parents and friends along the lines of *'Oh, it probably won't be that bad'* or *'Well, your uncle Pete survived it, and he got a job as a milkman afterwards'* didn't do a great deal to alleviate the growing tension: there we were lambs to the slaughter, or so it seemed. To take my mind off the threat of being knocked about by big blokes wielding various forms of footwear, I decided to concentrate on acquiring all the equipment on the lists provided. And what a long list it was! Quite apart from having to shell out a lot for the formal uniform, complete with meaningful badges and a school cap, there was a PT kit, (not PE you'll notice... this was Physical Training – Education didn't come into it, like so many other aspects of secondary schooling, as it seemed to us then) football boots, shin pads and a workshop apron.

Also required was a whole heap of academic stuff, the most important being a fountain pen. Now you may recall junior school efforts with dip-in pens, crossed nibs, ink wells and the interesting splatter designs as outlined in chapter six, so moving into the realms of a pre-loaded fountain pen was something of a leap. There were a number of well known manufacturers, and a certain amount of prestige to be gained by having an up-market pen. *Parkers* were considered to be quite top-hole, and came complete with a pen top clip fashioned in the form of an arrow similar to the one adorning the front of the famous Golden Arrow steam train – though a little smaller, of course. Next came another classy make called *Conway Stuart*, which I remember having a rather distinguished blue livery augmented by a gold band or two. Clearly, gold bands and a double barrelled name spoke quality, but unfortunately did little in terms of excellent handwriting and impeccable spelling. Just as well really, as most of us went for the budget end of the market and bought a *Platignum* for about half a crown (two shillings and sixpence... remember? Thirty pence? A florin and a tanner? Half of something that did not exist?). Now, the purchase of a fountain pen was one thing, but of course, you had to load it, and this was before the days of those natty little cartridges you just pushed into your pen. Oh no. We had to buy a bottle of ink, and these were made by two companies, *Stephens* and *Quink*. They came in three colours: blue, blue/black and black. As with the great evaporated milk debate, there were devotees of each make, and some kids would swear blind that *Quink* was the only ink that actually improved your spelling, whilst others would make extravagant punctuation claims for the rival *Stephens* brand. Not that it mattered a jot of course, but doesn't equipping lots of little boys with small screw topped reservoirs of a highly indelible liquid to store inside their newly purchased leather satchel seem a little on the foolhardy side? Doesn't also providing them with a pen which could only be filled by inserting it in the said bottle and then operating a small and fairly inaccessible lever on the side of the pen seem a trifle optimistic? Well, yes... certainly a triumph of hope over experience at any rate, and mine was not the only satchel to be blessed with a complete internal redecoration from a light tan to a smudgy still-slightly-damp-after-three-weeks blue/black decor. Still, as I said to my mum, could have been worse... could have been blue.

Another way to waste ink was to draw lines with a fountain pen, using your ruler *the right way up*. You see the cross section of a ruler is often in the shape of a trapezium, thus: ⟨line drawing⟩

Clearly, it sits flat on the paper, and for the inexpert, or for those who have not succeeded in internalising the finer points of ink line drawing, you might rush headlong into committing fountain pen to ruler edge to fulfil your line-making wish. And initially, all might go well; the line will look straight and glistening in all its blue/black freshness. And you could be forgiven for basking in the reflected glory of a job successfully completed, and perhaps be considering awarding yourself a surreptitious *Opal Fruit* by way of reward for a job well done. But what you have failed to recognise is that rather than create a perfect line, what you have actually done is create a mini river of ink joining ruler to paper. So, half way through your *Opal Fruit*, when you eventually get around to removing your ruler from the paper - and regardless of how fast you complete this manoeuvre - your otherwise trusty straight edge, a piece of equipment which has hitherto contributed nothing but loyal and devoted service, will drag your micro-river of ink all across the page, turning what had once been a promising straight and pristine ink line into what can only be described as something for which the Tate Modern might, once again, express an interest. Even trying to get the ink rivulet to dry through frantic blowing had little effect and the only other prospect was to sit and wait for the ink to dry naturally, which could take a matter of days.

The answer to this line drawing debacle was, of course, to turn your ruler *upside down*. This means that the edge of the implement is no longer in contact with the paper, and thus putting it back in your satchel post a successful line drawing represented no significant challenge, and saved a considerable amount of ink. Although quite difficult to store in the average satchel, rulers were regarded as important personal items, for in addition to their line drawing capability, they also represented a handy weapon ready for use at a moment's notice... and they were also pretty good at measuring stuff, provided your mum got you the right one. Mine was purchased from a shop that clearly had a very long history in that its provenance must have dated back to King Eric the Length or one of his ancient mates. It was like the one below. Looks pretty normal? Look more closely. So why have we got **tenths** of an inch? No one used tenths – our measuring system worked in halves, quarters, eighths and sixteenths, even thirty-secondths ... sensible units drilled into us by Miss Grant. Tenths were for decimal people, and were far too abstract for us imperials

Similarly, the obverse of some rulers showed a veritable contempt for the natural order of things by introducing *twelfths*. If they were

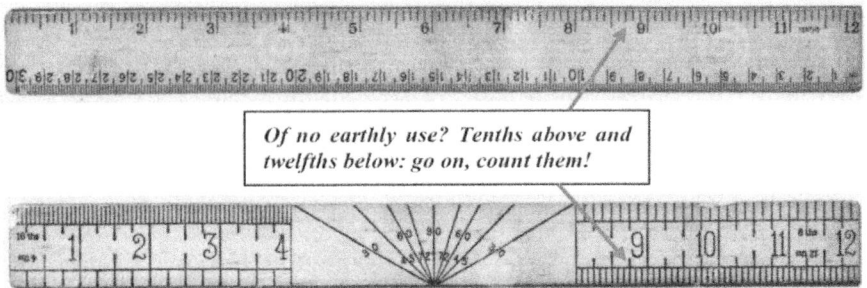

Of no earthly use? Tenths above and twelfths below: go on, count them!

hard to say, they were even more difficult to use, believe me; I cannot think of a single instance where you would need to measure something in twelfths. Perhaps the ruler makers just felt a bizarre unit would make their product so much more attractive to the schoolboy- about-town ...some young fellow on the lookout for something quirky and completely useless with which to equip his already bulging school satchel. And they say 'you can't put a foot wrong' – huh!

Another addition to the school satchel was the geometry set. Now these invariably came in a quite impressive-looking tin, and upon opening the hinged lid the aspiring junior Pythagoras was presented with a wide range of geometrical aids to delight the eye. First and foremost was the compass, complete with very spiky point at one end, and a small but easily breakable pencil at the other. This was held in place by a sort of ring, which when screwed down held the pencil firmly in place. That was the theory. In practice, the clamping ring often got cross-threaded and therefore ceased to exert such a manly grip on the pencil, allowing the latter to wobble about a fair bit. This had a knock-on effect in that in order to get the pencil to make contact with the paper all the way round the circle, you then had to lean the thing over. This would cause the spiky bit at the other end of the instrument to reach a dangerously acute angle. At the critical point it would give up on its prime function of remaining stationary and take upon itself to strike out for pastures new by tearing a small but ragged hole in the page. At this juncture any chance of securing a decently drawn circle might as well have been abandoned as it now resembled a rather unpleasant potato shape, and it was near to impossible to get the uncontrollable pencil to meet up with the point of origin. Also, your exercise book had suddenly acquired a sizeable hole in the centre of the potato ... good for looking through if you didn't want the bother of turning the page, but not particularly helpful in getting warm and fulsome praise from the Maths bloke.

Also in the geometry set were two little plastic set squares, one set at 45 degrees, the other at 30 and 60 degrees. To my certain knowledge, no one I knew ever used these for anything other than as a replacement if you had forgotten your ruler, and had a short line to draw somewhere. The only use the 30/60/90 one had was that, if held in the fist at the 60 degree point, it did look a little bit like a pistol, and when pointed at a fellow junior intellectual and accompanied with appropriate gunfight noises, could add a little moment of levity to an otherwise boring maths lesson. Now if the set squares were never used in the prescribed manner, at least we knew what they were. Not so another element of the geometry set - the dividers. This looked like a compass, but one where the bloke who puts the pencil and ring thing on has forgotten, and just stuck in another spiky bit instead. So this hinged implement had not one but *two* lethal looking metal spikes. All we knew about the dividers was its name. No one knew what it was for, but providing little boys and young adolescents with a double ended metal spike didn't seem like a great idea... and as no one had any idea what you used it for, a use was invented. As a result, this unsavoury mathematical weapon was used for the game of *stretch*. To play, you had a partner who was willing to stand perfectly still while the dividers were fully extended and thrown to stick into the ground as close as possible to the target's feet. If one of the spikes embedded itself in the ground, the target had to move one of his feet to the point of impact. The game ended when one or other person could stretch no further...or had been taken to casualty with an unexplained foot perforation injury.

Such a lethal implement made the final item within the tin seem something of a softy. The plastic protractor seemed almost benign: it couldn't be used as a makeshift firearm, or do a stint as a penetrative playing field game accoutrement. In fact the only thing it was pretty good at was measuring angles, and so should be awarded the '*most useful and least life-threatening member of the geometry set community*' certificate.

So, together with dinner money, bus fare, break time snack, tightly wrapped raincoat, picture of parents with '*Good luck son, stiff upper lip, try not to grizzle too much*' written on the back, we were ready for whatever grammar school could throw at us which, in fact, turned out to be quite a lot Remember my reference to blackboard rubbers in chapter 6? .

On the first day, having experienced the novelty of travelling to school by bus, (and so up-tight that I almost forgot at the bus stop to note how Mrs. Watts' season was progressing; perhaps I shouldn't have looked, for the 'Vacancies' sign was up... could it be an omen?) we little first years stood in uncertain groups in an enormous playground which rapidly filled with BIG KIDS. As the newcomers, we were subjected to all sorts of indignities, such as caps being pinched and flung around, sweets being demanded, satchels being swung on their straps and hurled sling like, with a range and speed to seriously challenge David's fine achievement against the giant Goliath – and so on. In the end, it was a relief when the whistle went and the teachers came out. During the next fifteen minutes the full extent of the lack of sophistication of the whole Eleven Plus system revealed itself. Being the result of a baby boom, there were a lot of us, and schools were therefore large. Ours had a five form entry, and once the bigger kids had been rounded up and herded into their classrooms, we were faced with four Masters each holding a list. Naturally, we looked at the assembled adults, and tried to pick out the friendliest face...and having failed to find any who met that description, in desperation invoked the alternative, i.e. the one which any human being would most like to avoid. As mentioned, there were five forms of entry, and the first lot to be rounded up was clearly the brightest and the best. I was neither so my name wasn't called ... nor was it for the second or third lot. When the teacher reading out the list for the fourth class got to the end, I must admit that anxiety overcame me and I let out a minor but embarrassing little squirt, and had to hold my satchel in the position normally associated with the sporran and hope that evaporation would do the rest. So, there we were, thirty plus anxious little boys, all eying each other, and I suspect I may not have been the only one thinking- *'Perhaps I haven't passed at all... perhaps it's a mistake... will my mum get the money back for the uniform? Well, not the trousers, obviously. At the very best, I'm now certain to be in the lowest class... the gorm form, the feck class.'* At that point, the fifth bloke came out to collect the rest of us. Unlike the other teachers who wore academic gowns, he was dressed in a tracksuit plus whistle. Oh dear. We were marched away to our classroom.

Over the next few days we were hurled into the unknown world of grammar school education. We had a Form Master, and a form room. We were told that the five forms of entry had the suffixes and went in descending order of intellectual prowess as follows: K, L, G, F and S and that these letters were the initials of the foreign language we would learn. L was for Latin, G was for German, F for French and S, for the dimmest boys, Spanish - *'because Spanish is easy to learn'.* I was in form 1S, the lowest of the low. Of course, it raised the question 'what the hell does K stand for?' I tried hard to think of a language starting with K - Korean? Unlikely, I would have thought. Knorwegian? – no, surely not. In the end the general opinion was that it must be Know-it-alls. Anyway, our class was left in little doubt that we were the absolute dregs, and as if to confirm it, our form room was down a long corridor opposite the workshops, and therefore had an aroma all its own – a combination of iron filings and oil, sawdust and urine...although, of course the latter might just have been due to my own slow evaporative efforts.

The change from junior school to secondary was really quite enormous, and could so easily have been eased by the thoughtful application of just one or two preliminary visits. As it was, we had to go from a small community of fairly scruffy kids who had just one teacher, no uniform, no homework, no corridors, no books to heave around from lesson to lesson, and no big blokes in gowns likely to give you a thump or two for the most minor infringement ... to the very opposite. Also, you were called by your surname - and almost unnoticed, we followed suit so that after a lifetime of greater familiarity, addressing each other in the same formal manner became the norm.

Thus it was that adjusting to life in secondary school became as much a matter of survival as it did of widening our academic horizons. We were the first years: there was no Year 7 then – we were first, second third fourth and fifth formers, with a Lower and Upper Sixth for any survivors. From our lowly perspective, the school yard was a blur of huge testosterone fired louts rushing about in a manner much enjoyed by starlings on a summer's evening, and about as predictable. The best thing was to keep out of the way, to melt into the background (or be ground into it) and wait for the bell to go so that at least there were a few adults around to restore some kind of order.

At least, that's how it seemed for the first weeks. I suppose it speaks volumes regarding human resilience in that we fairly quickly learned to cope with our new surroundings, and the regime of separate lessons conducted in various parts of the school started to have just a little appeal. For example moving between lessons was the perfect time for an illicit sweet or two, a chance to quickly crib any homework from a cooperative classmate, or an opportunity to thump someone who had dropped you in it during the previous lesson. Not that there was much of the latter; I have to say: we were starting to gel together into quite a tight-knit little self-preservation society.

Above all, the aspect of secondary schooling which affected us most, and with which we were least acquainted was the discipline imposed by the staff. Now I can't pretend that it was quite as despicable, inhumane or truly Dickensian as that described in Nicholas Nickleby's *'DotheBoys Hall'*, or went to some of the painful lengths recounted in *'Tom Brown's Schooldays'* – but pretty tough it definitely was. The threat and implementation of corporal punishment was the main method by which an orderly atmosphere conducive to a little occasional learning was achieved and maintained. Admittedly, there was detention or lines* for lesser transgressions, but the threat of physical violence was very much to the fore. What's more, this could be meted out by *any* teacher, *anywhere* and at *anytime.* And just as there seemed to be no rule about what may or may not constitute a misdemeanour worthy of physical revenge, there was certainly no restriction upon the weapon wielded by the black gowned individuals responsible for producing rational, reasonable and well-rounded citizens after half a dozen years of what sometimes seemed akin to legalised thumping.

Putting it too strongly? Well, yes, I suppose so. The ultimate form of physical punishment was supposed to be the cane – a thin whippy piece of bamboo produced in the pattern of a small walking stick. This was administered by the Headmaster or his Deputies, and seemed to be a fairly formal procedure for the most heinous schoolboy crimes.

Such administration was normally limited to 'six of the best' applied with some gusto to the derriere of the unfortunate victim who would endeavour to leave the Study without a murmur by gritting his teeth, scooting round the corner and then yelling *'Bugger! That really bloody hurt'* or something similar. In addition to these more formal beatings, other teachers had their own means of corporal punishment which would vary from strong slaps to perhaps the wielding of a ruler for non-mathematical purposes. It was of little use to try to forestall such a menacing approach by enquiring whether or not the instrument was marked in tenths or twelfths, or reminding the fast approaching big bloke that the ruler was still wet with ink

* *Lines: teachers might order you to write out a hundred or so times such restorative phrases as'* I must not be a complete twerp for the rest of my life'. *These had to be handed in the following day...or else! Detention just meant you had to stay behind after the end of lessons in the afternoon, usually for about half an hour. Certainly long enough to cause you to miss your usual bus home at any rate.*

after some forgetful non-inversion during line drawing, and therefore might leave a blue-black mark. You just had to take it, and hope you didn't let yourself down in front of your classmates. That is not to say that *all* teachers resorted to corporal punishment - some had little need to - but the deterrent was always there, and it was painfully apparent that even with the calmest teacher, there was a point where he might flip.

The most popular instrument of informal corporal punishment was undoubtedly the slipper. Not the fluffy footwear commonly used when sitting by the fire either: this was a large and rugged PE shoe which was held by the heel and swung with mighty force so that the large and deeply grooved sole would land with a ferocious *thwack* on the backside of the juvenile arch-criminal who had committed some trifling offence. Rumour had it that one teacher used spiked running shoes for the same purpose, but this was never verified and was, no doubt, spread by those who took pleasure in further terrifying the first years (i.e. everyone from the second year upwards). And I have to say, there were not many days which went by without witnessing some form of physical punishment being meted out by someone somewhere, whether in your own class or elsewhere; it was simply a fact of life. Boys could be slapped around the head, or even punched. I remember clearly attending a science lesson one early afternoon, when the teacher, normally a fairly restrained and quiet sort of bloke, said to us:

'You better not upset me this afternoon; I've just knocked a boy out!'

I kid you not. Naturally, we were all particularly well behaved that afternoon, and set about our studies of the common microscopic hydra with unaccustomed enthusiasm and devotion.

Now you may be thinking that the Southern Grammar was a real rough house, the sole educational establishment in the country populated by violent educationists – but not so: *all* boys' schools seemed to be like it, and comparing physical punishments with scholars from other establishments led to a certain pride in the fact that one set of teachers was more vicious and inventive than another. Also, physical punishment was the expected norm; boys had *always* been knocked about a bit, it was *'part of growing up'* we were told, and I suppose we just accepted it. What's more, we seldom mentioned such punishment when we got home, for the typical parental response at the time was to give you another thump on the grounds that *'Well, you must have done something wrong, so here's something else to remind you what you go to school for!'* Ouch. Now the vindication of being raised as well-hard babies became apparent; all that input of infantile terror was bearing fruit at last – the fear of the Trolls who lived under the bridge and were predisposed to eating you for their supper, suddenly made sense.

So you might think that because of all this totally random and unrestrained violence towards its pupils, we would hate our school. Bizarrely, the opposite was true; we actually liked it (the school I mean, not the beatings – what do you think I am? Kinky or something?) and became quite defensive in support of our teachers when their punishments were derided by kids from other schools. What's more, we were far from angels ourselves, and although chastisement was often excessive, it would be true to say that punishments *were* deserved on many an occasion. Boys will be boys, as they say, and disrupting lessons via all available means was a way of making the whole educational experience more entertaining. Chief amongst the weapons at our disposal was the common or garden fart, and one of our classmates earned himself huge popularity by developing the ability to generate, nurture and then *harbour* truly ambitious farts and then deliver them at exactly the right time. I mean, given such a talent, how could any schoolboy resist letting a particularly noisome example go during the breathless and dramatic pause when our history teacher had just asked us what did the relieving military force under General Roberts expect to find in the

Black Hole of Calcutta? We could not, of course, explode into laughter out loud, or burst into the applause that such a splendid and sublimely timed performance merited, but the number of scholars who became red faced and whose shoulders shook with barely controlled mirth was legion. And the great thing about farting was that our class perpetrator could always claim it was a natural function over which he had no control, and if any blame was to be accorded it might better be directed at the dinner lady who had dished up too many beans.

In retrospect, it is not that hard to work out why   people in general – and little boys in particular - find farting so funny. I suspect you could formulate a pretty convincing argument that farting was almost certainly humanity's *birth of mirth.* Don't believe me? Well, OK… picture if you will the very earliest stage of human development: a group of stone-age hunters have been sent out into the forest to capture tonight's meal which the missus has determined should be *'haunch of mammoth with a side salad of nettles and twigs'.* They wait in silence around the water hole, straining their ears for the approach of an overweight and hairy footfall. The tension builds… the nerves are at breaking point…. *'I'm sure I can hear something'* whispers the leader… *'Listen! Can you hear it too?'* Then some idiot cracks off a really big one, and they spend the next ten minutes peeing themselves with laughter.

So, having established its comedic origins, let us return to the classroom, where our little school community was having the greatest trouble in preventing the outbreak of spontaneous and appreciative applause for the latest effort from our resident aromatic artiste. The trouble with Mick, our expert class farter was that his growing – and quite literally - breathtaking talent drove him to greater and greater lengths. Whereas a more studied and circumspect approach might have been to at least mix the barrage with a few less obvious *'silent but deadlies'*, he ploughed on regardless, and thus started to reap the punishment for it which, ironically, also involved his rear end.

Some teachers were accorded a higher status because of their unique methods of applying physical remedies to any pupil misbehaviour or inattention. For example, a geography teacher we had came from Fleetwood. No one in our class had heard of the place, but he insisted that we should all be able to pinpoint its location on a map of the UK, for no other reason other than the fact that he was born there. Now I don't suppose the whereabouts of a fairly ordinary northern town featured centrally in the GCE O level geography exams for which we were supposed to be studying, but the failure of any boy to be able to accurately pinpoint his northern birthplace invoked this teacher's special punishment which was to pull victims up out of their seat by grasping the short hairs close to the ears and lifting. Not that it was *really* a punishment – it was just a bit of fun for the rest of the class, and a badge of honour for the recipient. I am certain that such bonkers behaviour was present in all boys' schools of the period, and suggest that you might find it illuminating to ask any old bloke of our generation to provide you with his memories of his secondary schooling in the fifties and sixties. I would be amazed if the memories did not include a misty-eyed account of '*old so-and-so who used to string us up by our thumbs for not knowing the opening line of Grey's Elegy ... he was such a laugh!*' or something very similar.

So it was against this background that we intellectuals of the bottom stream of the first year floundered our way through the first twelve months, and in doing so discovered the delights of homework, of school dinners run by the BIG BOYS, of prefects, of detentions, of cricket lessons (where it was rumoured that older boys had to wear a box when batting: why? what for? was it just to protect your willy? ... I told you we were naive) of cross country bloody running, of such facilities as laboratories, a gymnasium and a metalwork shop.

Many of us also discovered the dubious joys of riding our bikes to school – and with it the whereabouts of the bike shed which nationwide, always seemed to attract a school's low-life, and was the venue for many a juvenile punch-up. Equally, however, it was also a place to barter sweets and watch the big boys have an occasional crafty drag on a Woodbine before the start of the school day. So school life settled into something of a pattern and, like all others before us, we quickly learned to ride out the unpredictable moods of some of the staff. We also appreciated the odd occasion when the natural iron-clad frostiness of the teachers cracked a little to reveal an unexpected sense of humour. Still, we survived, and really enjoyed the long hot summer of 1959 when we were able to lounge about on the school field at lunchtime, and put our geometry set dividers to their only discernible use. So, for the up and coming lowlife that class 1S represented, gelling as a unit became a reality, and not only

Summer 1959: proof that we survived our first year. After sixty years the names of every classmate here comes readily to mind. Bearing in mind the fact that we had class roll-call several times a day for five years, such a recollection is not really that surprising.

because of the common cause of defending ourselves against the plentiful supply of adversity; we were from different parts of the city, from different backgrounds and with very different aspirations …
and more often than not, we got along pretty well.

There are two boys missing from the class photo on the previous page – me and a popular boy who went by the nickname of 'Bandy'. I missed the visit of the school photographer as I had convinced my mum that I needed a second week of convalescence to overcome my bout of Asian flu. So at the time the shot was taken, I was no doubt lounging about at home endeavouring to look convincingly *pale but interesting* whilst swigging back the old Lucozade. Clearly, my determination to work conscientiously towards topping up personal levels of feck and gorm was still somewhat patchy. As to the whereabouts of Bandy, I have only the suspicion that he may well have been in the school but have wandered off somewhere else, or got locked in the loo, or something. If ever proof was needed to demonstrate the inadequacies of the selective system, then Bandy would have been it. To be honest, he was very far from what one might politely term 'academically gifted', even by my standards. He was nonetheless, a surprisingly confident and belligerent little fellow, and although quite small in stature, seemed always ready to give someone a good pasting. Not that he was unpopular – far from it. In addition to the fact that he unconsciously provided us all with the warm glow that, however badly we were doing, we were probably doing *better than Bandy,* he impressed us all with the fact that he really didn't seem to care about anything, or anyone, teachers included. He had a fearless attitude, and despite being a couple of inches smaller than many, would square up to anyone, anytime, anywhere. He also wore the most decrepit pair of National Health spectacles ever. For a start, the wire frame was so bent that the two lenses were no longer parallel. Also, the glasses were far from being transparent in that they were permanently covered with what appeared to be a thin film of sticky thumbprints and other smeary deposits of questionable origin. In retrospect, I suppose he got away with a lot of his belligerent behaviour because when he felt affronted and squared up with his customary *'Who you lookin' at?!'* he was entirely unaware of the irony in that the recipients, looking at the asymmetric smear-covered qualities of his specs often, quite literally, had no idea who was looking at whom. Despite all of this he was a very popular boy, and the one who increased our level of literacy in the sense that his knowledge of *street talk* was extensive. It was him, for example, who introduced the class to the term 'bum bandit'. I certainly had no idea what the term meant, although of course, laughed and nodded along with the rest of the boys in a vain attempt to make it look as if the expression was in constant family use, and the social circles within which my nearest and dearest revolved were thick with bum bandits. I have no doubt that my unfamiliarity with such expressions was common; we were all busily engaged in the process of coming to terms with the adult world, and if Bandy could help to illuminate the murkier depths of our naiveté, so much the better. So in some respects, the least academic boy in the class probably added more to our level of 'whole world' literacy than did any teacher.

As mentioned earlier, a really big change in our circumstances was the opportunity to travel to school by bike. Although this may not seem too revolutionary an idea, the actual travelling part for many of us really was a big deal, as the school's catchment area was large, and thus a lot of time and effort went into travelling to and from. My case was pretty typical, and a world away from the convenience of the Junior School just around the corner. First of all, it meant that I would have to ride about three miles due north, the route incorporating a very busy main road which in winter especially, was very exposed to easterly gales sweeping in off the sea. Bearing in mind the need to transport a pretty heavy book-laden satchel, games kit and the necessary weatherproof bits and pieces, meant also that the old bike was pretty heavily laden, and therefore demanded the attachment of a sizeable and unwieldy saddle bag. Worst of all, my bike was highly unfashionable, being **a)** small - it only had an eighteen inch frame, and **b)** being hand painted in brilliant red, it looked absolute crap. Neither of these features did my street cred any favours, and so I was delighted when my dad agreed to loan me a sub to my pocket money just sufficient to enable me to fork out £17 for a second hand Raleigh *Jack of Clubs*. This came complete with trendy drop handlebars, five speed derailleur gears, a hub dynamo to power the lights, and a fair amount of rust. Nevertheless, I was made up, and with the swift application of white handlebar tape to obscure the worst of the rust, the days of having the piss taken out of my 'kiddies' bike' were over...my place in the school bike shed – if not behind it - was secure, and I could wave farewell to the protracted bus journey with the interchange at the grim prison. And the change of bike came just in time, for suddenly, the need to carry loads of stuff increased almost exponentially as a result of my decision to join the school Combined Cadet Force, the CCF. Let me explain.

In the 1950's, most grammar schools tried to maintain vestiges of the Public School system, presumably to increase their status, and to at least keep up with those semi-public schools which offered many places to boys who had won scholarships. Thus the Southern Grammar had school houses, house masters, inter-house sports, Speech Days, an impressive and elaborate Achievement Scroll upon which the names of alumni were inscribed and a prefect system which accorded significant rites to those selected. We also had the CCF. The connection between education and the Armed Services goes back a very long way. In the fifties, an inspirational example of where such an association might lead would be organisations such as the University Air Squadrons and those of the Army and Navy which did such tremendous service in the Second World War. Thus, the incorporation of some aspect of the military was seen as a prime example of the maintenance of the establishment, the very fibre of our nation. Well, that might have been the intention; as far as we were concerned, you got to wear a snazzy uniform, do a lot of stamping up and down the playground, and best of all, have a shot or two on the rifle range. *'A rifle range?'* I hear you ask. *'In a school? With proper bullets?!'* 'Yes' is the answer to all. The phrase 'behind the bike sheds' has all sorts of connotations, most of them rightly dubious. Ours was a little different in that, not only did it provide a small area for initiation into the illicit world of smoking, but even more spectacularly, it housed our purpose built full-sized .22 rifle range and armoury, with proper rifles and bullets and targets and everything. Blimey. Looking back, putting a load of teenage hooligans within easy reach of doing themselves and others a whole lot of harm does seem a tad reckless, to say the least. But to us, it was all part of the scene, and the opportunity to make lots of bullet holes in something seemed too good an opportunity to miss – plus the fact that on one day a week, you

Tuesday was CCF day. With military cycle clips shone to perfection, I was off to do battle. Mind you, every day was something of a battle at the old SGS. Why a small ghost should choose to join me remains a mystery.

didn't have to wear your school uniform. OK, you had to wear a very scratchy and ill-fitting service uniform instead, but you also had big boots with hob nails in them which made an even more impressive noise on the playground than ye olde footy boots had done in junior school, and there was always the chance that you might meet some girls on the way to school ... and what female heart would not be set a-flutter in the proximity of such good-looking military might? Well quite a few unfortunately, but we lived in hope.

Of course, getting a go on the rifle range was dangled as bait. Before we got our eager little hands on any ordnance and started blasting away, there was a certain amount of training to do, and we all had to enter the Basic Section (army) for a year before deciding which of the three services would be graced by our presence after a year's instruction in the absolute essentials of the military life. The prime component of this was learning to march, and considering that most of us aspiring combatants could already walk, taking a year to learn how to march – a process which after all, is little more than simply *walking together* - seemed excessive. Not so. Marching, we were told, is a skill, and has its own set of impenetrable rules and regulations, and requires in its initial stages at least, a good deal of stamping accompanied by much shouting of the well known military mantra: **'One, Two-Three, One!!'**

To those of us who pictured ourselves as the protectors of our nation, armed to the teeth with hand grenades, flame-throwers and a sub-machine gun in each hand, this stamping about shouting out a series of numbers seemed to lack the manly and heroic actions we were all anticipating. And why did this mantra never go beyond three? Wouldn't 'One, Two-three, *Four*' make a lot more sense? Did the military suspect that counting beyond three represented too great a mental challenge for the standard Tommy? Who knows? Anyway, this was what you had to shout out when you were undertaking some kind of marching move, such as coming to a halt, and its purpose was to ensure you all kept in time. Thus, on the order to halt, the corporal in charge would bellow out *'Squaaaaaad...... HALT!!!'* Now the theory was that on hearing this, our little group of tiny soldiers on taking their next step would shout **'ONE'**, then, to the chorus of **'Two-three** raise the accompanying knee so that the military thigh was now parallel to the ground - before finally crashing the hovering boot to the ground as the final **'One!!'** rang around the playground ... sorry, the *parade* ground. As I say, that was the theory. The practice was somewhat different. Quite often, kids didn't bother to stop at all, and the concertina effect of someone in the fourth row cannoning into the warrior in front sent off a chain reaction right to the leading rank. Another common problem was that despite shouting the final **'One!!'** together, the final crash of boots onto the concrete was seldom the required single sound. It was much more like the staccato rattle of the machine gun we were all hoping to use on the drill instructor, especially as our little squad had within its ranks the most uncoordinated, un-military recruit I'd ever met.

Cadet Penny was a really nice classmate. He always – and I mean *always* – had a smile on his face, but when the Almighty was handing out coordination skills, young Penny had presumably been in the celestial loo, and had been missed out. For a start, not only couldn't he stop, he couldn't march either. As already mentioned, if you consider marching to be no more than organised walking, you would have expected most youngsters to have at least achieved a level of locomotion consistent with moving along together. An essential element of this united motion is that your arms must swing in the approved military manner, so that as your left foot goes forward, your right arm swings up to a position parallel with the parade ground. On taking the next step, the opposite arm does the business, and further ambulation establishes a pattern of the arms and legs taking complementary but necessarily *opposite* actions. Not so cadet Penny. When he marched with left foot forward, *left arm went forward as well.* The next step continued this ungainly and utterly disastrous motion with the right arm and leg proceeding at the same time. The result was what one can only describe as an exaggerated swagger, and left the cadet officer bloke in charge either open-mouthed, head in hands, or bursting into tears. And that was not all. Despite his best efforts, dear old Penny was about the most unmilitary person you could imagine. Whereas most of us occasionally looked reasonably smart, he most certainly did not; to be honest, however new and clean his uniform was, he had the skill to make it look like he had just spent a torrid night in it, haunted by appalling nightmares, and the whole effect was somewhat *corrugated.* Added to that, his crowning glory was the military beret, with which we were all issued. Most aspirant soldiers managed to polish up the badge, and all of us wore it perched on the head with the right hand side pulled rakishly over the accompanying ear. Cadet P never achieved this level of sophistication. Despite being told a thousand times, he insisted on pulling the beret down around his head to ear level, which meant that - **a)** there was no slack left to pull the rim down to the ear in the approved manner, and **b)** he looked like Benny Hill. Alright, a *smiling* Benny Hill, admittedly, but not the sort of appearance to put the fear of god into the enemy.

And that was not the only comedy which made our square-bashing rather more entertaining than the military powers intended. Marching instructions were full of opportunities for juvenile insubordination: for example, an instruction to get a row of soldiers into a perfectly straight line requires the command:

Riiiiiight dress!

Each warrior would then clap their right arm on the left shoulder of the next bloke, and do a little shuffle to ensure he was in line. That we all did it together was an instant recipe for chaos, and so it proved – but more especially as most of us were already in stitches because one wag, on hearing *'Riiiiiiiight Dress!'* had muttered *'Wroooooong Trousers!'*

Another example of mutilated parade ground orders furtively exchanged was on the instruction: *'Eyes ..... right!'* to mutter *'No you's not!'*

Clearly, such mirthful insubordination had to end somewhere, but schoolboy humour being what it was, it was hard to know when to stop – and the orders were soooo vulnerable: I mean, who could resist naming other body parts on the instruction:

'Shoulder.... Arms!'

That the odd juvenile was prone to add *'Bollocks…. Knees!'* is hardly surprising, is it?

After a year of all this banging about each and every Tuesday evening, we were asked to choose which of the three services we would like to go in, and being a kid from a naval town, and knowing lots of grownups who were in the navy, and being surrounded by uniformed sailors whenever we went out anywhere, I of course, joined the RAF section. Why? Well, the uniform looked nice, I liked planes, and I was a rotten swimmer. So, an informed and logical choice, obviously. In consequence each Tuesday I became a *Cadet Aircraftsman*, and was allowed at last to have a go in the rifle range. Bearing in mind the rifles we handled were the real thing, the rules and regulations as to how they were handled were strictly enforced, and rightly so. There is a certain aroma that you get in any military location – it's not unpleasant, but is a curious combination of moth balls overladen by a frisson of what I can only describe as tarry saltiness – and no more so than in the dimly lit interior of the school rifle range. Compared with the hurly burly of playground thuggery being played out just a few yards away, the lunchtime gathering in the rifle range was strangely quiet and well ordered. Except for the occasional crack as the rifles fired, it was ironically just about the most quiet and peaceful place in the school.

Another advantage of being in the CCF was that you occasionally got trips out of school. Nowadays, off-site educational visits are a common and often important part of the curriculum. In the sixties they were an absolute rarity – in fact I can only recall one school visit we made in the whole five years of my tenure at the Southern Grammar, and that was only down to the local dockyard to see a visiting Spanish ship (remember, we thickies were learning Spanish, *'because its easy!'*) But membership of the CCF opened up another opportunity for off-site visits, and – for all the wrong reasons - I well remember one I took with the RAF section to Old Sarum aerodrome near Salisbury.

On this occasion we were told that we would be going up in a small RAF passenger aircraft called an Avro Anson. With great excitement we all scrambled aboard, got ourselves seated and belted and listened to the two engines being started up. And then listened to them being turned off. And then listened to an officer who told us that the aeroplane was poorly, and that we wouldn't be going anywhere in it today. *'Shit!'* We all thought. And then the good fairy appeared, in the form of our woodwork teacher, who doubled up one day a week as our RAF officer. *'Who has never flown before?'* he asked. I was the only one. *'Right, Burden* 'he said, *'They've got a Chipmunk ready to take just one cadet up for a quick spin, and you're it – so off you go'*.

Blimey. So with the imaginary daggers of all my mates in my back I made my way across the tarmac to where this aeroplane was spluttering away at the end of the runway. Now the Chipmunk is a very small two seater training aircraft, and I was invited to sit in the rear seat behind the driver chappy. The only problem was, there were no seats – just a sort of metal tray. To overcome the apparent in-flight discomfort this might suggest, it was traditional – if not absolutely obligatory – to wear a parachute and you sat on that. I was informed of this unexpected addition to my person by the aircraftsman in charge, who made me stand with my legs and arms akimbo while he strapped this unwieldy piece of equipment on.

Now you may recall that to date, I had not been the most alert of students, and although by now I had had at least a couple of years in secondary school, my levels of gorm were still alarmingly low. So there I stood, having a parachute strapped on me, whilst at the same time trying to pay attention to what the bloke was saying, which went thus:

'You puts these straps over yer shoulders like this, and clip them into this 'ere big buckle in the front. Now you brings the other two straps between yer legs, and clips them into the same buckle like this'
So far, so good. Parachute firmly in place. Then came his final, and to my mind, the most important part of the instructions:
Nah then, to release the parachute all you 'as to do is turn the front of the buckle by forty-five degrees, and then smack the front of it hard with yer 'and. Easy!'

With that I waddled off towards the Chipmunk. I say waddled because, as the parachute is also your seat cushion, it was strapped on in such a way as to curve around your bum. Thus walking normally was impossible, and I looked more like Quasimodo ascending the bell tower at Notre Dame as I shambled across to the plane – not quite the heroic mad dash to the cockpit that I had seen in so many war films, you understand. When I got there, I was supposed to swing my leg up to the height of the step by the wing and pull myself over the cockpit rim. No chance. After a couple of futile attempts, I managed to get my foot on the wing, but I could swing it no higher. Luckily the parachute bloke came up and lifted me on to the wing; I was sure Douglas Bader never had this trouble, and he had tin legs!

The flight itself was wonderful, and a complete revelation to me. The little aeroplane had a huge Perspex canopy which came right down to knee level, and so the impression was more of sitting on top of the aeroplane, rather than being inside it – quite extraordinary.

On returning to the ground, I had slightly less difficulty in extracting myself from the cockpit, and waddled back to the parachute shed, where I stood waiting uncertainly. *'Go on then!'* said a voice. *'Release the bloody parachute, like I told yer.'* I was about to say *'But we're not in the air...'* when the awful truth struck me. When he had told me how to release the parachute, I thought he had meant *that's the way to make it work in an emergency – to open the silken canopy and drift serenely to the ground'* but now I realised, it was the way *to take the damned thing off!*

So, picture the scene. The Chipmunk's engine splutters and dies at 5000 feet. *'Sorry old boy, but we'll have to bail out'* says the skipper. *'You know the drill, don't you'.*

So, here I go... stand on the wing and jump.... now, what was it he said? Oh yes, *'to release the parachute, turn the front of the buckle forty-five degrees and smack the front of it hard with your hand'.* Well, here goes!......

What a ghastly picture.... me going one way, my parachute the other. It never occurred to me to look more closely at the parachute harness itself. Perhaps had I done so, I might have noticed the big red handle on the front had **RIP CORD** written on it. I told you I was gormless. And so back to earth.

At the end of the summer term 1960, the little chaps of our form found out to their surprise that there would be some big changes curriculum-wise as from next term, the start of our third year. Instead of doing Art and English Literature, we would be doing 'Workshop Practices and Processes', and 'Engineering Drawing'. *'And furthermore, to make way for these changes, you won't be doing Music either'.* Now the latter was quite pleasing for many of us – music to our ears, you might say – as we were very wary of the erratic slipper-wielding bloke who took us for the subject... oh and not many of us were that keen on Rachmaninoff's Prelude in C sharp minor either, if truth be told. Nevertheless, there was a degree of consternation.

'And just what', may we ask, *'are Workshop Practices and Processes, when they are at home?'* Well, on closer examination, it turned out that they were... well, Woodwork and Metalwork really, but in keeping with the increasingly trendy times the new decade brought us, the name had been changed, and therefore everything was *MUCH BETTER*. Oh really? And *Engineering Drawing* ...

what's that for Pete's sake? Well, we were told, it was something to do with engineering, and involved a certain amount of drawing...so it was a bit like Art really, in that the word 'drawing' cropped up in both subjects. It was just that the free expression bit, the copying of the Great Masters, the detailed sculpting of superb life-forms and the creation of the occasional masterpiece well, yes, those would all be missing... but in its place you get your own T square, and a drawing board full of pin holes!

So why am I banging on about this curricular change? Well, for a start it was unannounced, and neither the little chaps wallowing about in the bottom stream of the second year, nor our parents had the slightest knowledge of the forthcoming change. Consultation? Never heard of it, mate. Clearly, the message was: *'You lot are at the bottom of the school, therefore you'll never aspire to anything greater than being a craftsman, a stout-hearted artisan type who has no need of the refinements of art and literature – and as regards music, as long as you can hum along to 'Music While You Work', that's all you'll ever need. Now get down the workshops and do some bloody filing'.*

We touched on social engineering in Chapter 6, and here was another prime example of the establishment knowing best. Yes, we did languish in the lower streams, but to deny a large group of youngsters the opportunity to benefit from further exposure to the fine arts was heavy handed at best, and could easily be interpreted as downright life-limiting. All right, we did muck about a bit, and the insertion of a finely timed fart still caused huge merriment, but that's no reason to decapitate any latent artistic ambition.

And yet, that was just so typical of the age. Boys of higher ability will be taught an academic curriculum including those things which will enable them to benefit from, and later contribute towards the higher aspirations of mankind; those at the bottom will be happy to be the technical or commercial class, and won't need to be exposed to subjects beyond their predetermined destiny - a case of a self-fulfilling prophecy if ever there was one.

So, did we protest? Did we create slogans and daub paint on gaudily coloured banners (thereby confirming the artistic promise so cruelly terminated) and descend upon the Headmaster's study proclaiming our disquiet at such high-handed treatment which was depriving us of our artistic and cultural heritage? Well of course we didn't. I don't suppose it even occurred to us. Mind you, we would all miss our Art lessons... a lot.

Of all the zany, bizarre and downright odd individuals that populated our school staff, Wilf stood head and shoulders above them all for *bonkersness*. He was without doubt the king of the eccentrics, whose erratic and inconsistent teaching methods left one bewildered, frequently threatened, occasionally attacked... and incredibly well entertained. Although I'm not sure he ever really understood it, he was very popular in the school: he was our Art teacher and we loved him.

The art room was a far-flung location at the end of a long corridor, and immediately preceding Studio A, the engineering drawing room, and the craft workshops. As the lowest of the low, we were accorded the sumptuous surroundings of the metalwork shop as our form room, and had the pleasure each day of perching on the edges of grimy workbenches while the register was called. The upside of all of this was that we didn't have desks, but were provided with lockers which were right on the corridor, just a few yards from the Art room. As a result, we always had a grandstand view of the comings and goings of our much admired neighbouring odd-ball.

Now schoolboys are noted for their pranks, and flicking ink pellets at each other or putting copious amounts of pepper in someone's desk was all pretty much par for the course. What may not be quite so well known is the habit and quite exquisite skill of goading and baiting teachers. Even though retribution could be swift and often quite brutal, I am pleased to say that during our earlier years at the school, when the level of feck was still pretty minimal in most of us, making a teacher's life as awkward as possible was a flourishing pastime, and certainly enlivened many a lesson.

Such behaviour during the first two years when we were actually taught art by dear old Wilf was a prime example. He was a small, quite old, greyish sort of bloke with receding hair, gimlet eyes and thin lips ready to part in a snarl at any moment. He also had not the faintest idea how to motivate boys, and I'm sure he saw each day as a constant battle against the forces of anarchy and destruction... or schoolboys, as they are known. He was the school's only art teacher, and when he could be tempted to put aside his constant quest for the source of class disruption and turn his hand to a bit of drawing or painting, it was clear that he was an exceptional, talented and quite fondly admired artist.

Unfortunately, however, he never used his great skill to inspire us to do well in the subject, and I am a little sad to say that during our two years with him we actually learned very little in terms of artistic interpretation and practice. Lessons would usually consist of us filing into the art room in the centre of which was placed an item to draw, such as a lawn mower. Wilf would tell us to sit and draw it. So far so good. If there was ever any talking he would point to the criminal responsible and shout *'Look, shut up YOU!!'* To my certain knowledge, he never remembered the names of any of the kids in the class – we were always just the target of his pointed finger and called YOU!! What teaching there was consisted of us shuffling up to the desk to present our finished masterpieces, and his response to proffered work would always be one of two outcomes: if all was OK he would say:

'Ooooh, lovely stuff, Excellent A old man, Excellent A!' and then proceed to scrawl the mark in the corner of the drawing. The much more frequent response however, always went like this: he would

look closely at the drawing, and you would see his lips tighten across his teeth; his eyes would bulge and he would yell:

'There's nothing there! Take it away!! Take it away you damned lout and SHADE IT UP!!'

By this time he was getting really wound up, and it would only take a few muffled titters from the assembled host for him to launch into a full-on tirade, often comprising such rants as *'Shut up each and every one of you; cut out the fertivity, or I'll knock you down!!'* At this point he was a little ball of almost uncontrolled rage and any chance for the lesson – if you can call it that – to progress to anything like an educative experience had been well and truly lost. Never mind. We all enjoyed it immensely.

So now, at the beginning of the new decade we were condemned to a utilitarian future, with no art or literature to nourish the cultural desert within us. *'Serve you right, if all you could do was take the piss out of the poor art bloke'* I hear you say. Not so. The fact is that Wilf was like that with all of the boys right across the school. OK, there were a handful of very creative and gifted kids who did produce many *'Excellent A's'* but the vast majority benefited more from the notoriety he created than the merest smidge of cultural accomplishment. That this state of affairs was allowed to persist seems unreasonable by today's standards, but that was the fifties for you: teachers could do more or less as they liked in their fiefdom, provided the school got the GCE* results at the end of the course. Our art teacher was extraordinary, of course, but he was not alone in his bizarre behaviour. There were plenty more who would do and say all sorts of odd things, but it was accepted as just part of schoolboy life – indeed, we actually enjoyed most of it, and were surprisingly

* *General Certificate of Education. There were two levels – Ordinary Level, taken by all students on the completion of their fifth year, (now year 11) and Advanced Level for those who completed a further two years in the sixth form. At that time, most youngsters left school at sixteen, many to undertake apprenticeships or further educational courses at local colleges. A relatively small proportion stayed on to study for A levels.*

protective of the bizarre behaviour of those in charge, and surprisingly jealous of our school's reputation. I suppose that in the grand scheme of things, the result of the on-going confrontation between staff and students was about equal: both sides gave the other hell, but the equality which this implied meant that each felt relatively secure.

Seems crazy? Well yes, I suppose it was in a way, but the proof of the pudding was that it seemed to work. As an educational objective, the combination of co-existence and armed truce does not feature very highly in pedagogic texts, but that was what we had. a sort of happy war, and I dare say that had one or the other side gone beyond what was anticipated or expected, there would have been collective outrage. From the juvenile perspective, being openly cheeky or letting rip a whole barrage of perfectly timed farts in just one lesson would be pushing your luck. Like most kids, we were keen to identify personal idiosyncrasies or mannerisms in our teachers, and then use them to take the piss. As far as Wilf was concerned, he hated to be called names. One of these was '*Buller*'. Not very aggressive, not even rude, and to be fair, it was pretty accurate in describing one who was apt to tell extremely tall tales. On the odd occasion when he was not yelling that he was about to '*knock each and every one of us down*' for some petty infringement (he never did) we could sometimes persuade him to launch into a long and elaborate account of his personal experiences. Chief amongst these was to get him to talk about wartime recollections. Wilf was useless at this, but thought he was quite good. Some of his stories were clearly fabricated, but the most outrageous tale I recall was when he claimed to have been '*the rear gunner in a Spitfire, old man...*' Now to try to convince anyone of a fictitious military skill, the last thing you should do is to choose a subject where most of your audience know a damned sight more about it than you do. Thus telling a lot of aeroplane-loving little boys that he was a rear gunner in a *single seat fighter* was a story too far ...and contributed to earning him the school-wide title of '*Buller*'.   However, unlike most teachers, who seemed to more or less accept their titles, Wilf became utterly enraged with his.

Now you may think that road rage is a recent phenomena. Not so. On one cloudy afternoon in 1960, many boys were on their way home. At a nearby stop, a number were waiting with a few members of the general public for the arrival of their bus. So far so good. But coming up behind this small collection of passengers was Wilf on his very unfashionable little motor scooter. Just why a teacher was puttering off home so close to school closure time is not really the focus for this particular account, but nevertheless, there he was, dressed in beige raincoat and trilby hat which, on any other person might have been described as 'jaunty'. Not so Wilf. His teeth were exposed in customary tight lipped scowl, as he proceeded at a stately twenty mph, and he cast no glance at the schoolboy group as he approached. In fact there was no visible sign that he was aware of anything at all, until one brave bus stop lad yelled out 'Buller!' just as he drew level. Immediately, and without the slightest reference to the '*I am intending to slow down and stop*' hand signal procedures so clearly outlined in the Highway Code, Wilf put on the brakes, and brought the scooter to a halt about twenty yards beyond. He then pulled the machine up on to its stand and stalked back to the bus stop. Once there he cuffed the boy firmly about the ear, and then calmly returned to his scooter which he kick-started back into life and drove off. And all of this without a word, and under the gaze of the bus-travelling general public, whose interest was absolutely minimal. A schoolboy getting knocked about in public? '*So what?*'... '*He probably deserved it anyway!*'

Despite being denied curricular access to the finer things in life, our scientific studies were allowed to proceed relatively unmolested. I guess the thinking was, '*Well, these kids are destined to become the technical / tradesman type, so we might as well give them the skills to wire up a house, or set off an explosion or two'.* The labs were at one end of the school, and always had a strange chemically-cum-armpit type smell to them; not surprising, I suppose, when they were all equipped with gas taps and Bunsen burners, and stoppered glass bottles containing some pretty damn corrosive acids and preservative solutions. Taking a deep breath in such an environment was therefore to risk a sudden onset of giddiness ... mind you, considering we were always accompanied by our resident 'farts on request' colleague, our class may have been rather more immune to the effects of such inhalation than many. Nevertheless, a visit to the laboratories was always fraught with some degree of risk; naked flames, bottles of acid and many colourful liquids and powders do not necessarily constitute a safe and ordered environment for a mob of adventurous little gits, all of whom were thinking ' *I wonder what would happen if I were to just chuck a bit of this blue stuff in with the old hydrochloric....?*' etc. etc. And don't forget, these were the days before we had health and safety: there were no safety glasses, no latex gloves, no labels all over the place with lots of exclamation marks all over them. It's quite amazing that some of us didn't vanish in a sheet of flame from time to time. Mind you, the constant threats of physical retribution played a part in keeping the more adventurous amongst our throng from embarking upon their own lines of enquiry.

As well as a complete lack of safety equipment, there was also a glaring absence of one part of the science curriculum – namely sex education. Nowadays, even children in the primary phase of their education are given a pretty good idea of what goes where, whose bits are whose, what to expect when you get older, and not to worry if your 'thingy' gets stiff. Not so in the fifties and sixties: we had no formal sex education of any type that I can recall, and even bearing in mind that I was not the most alert of students, I'm damn sure any reference to the difference between boys and girls, and why some of the latter had bumpy bits when we didn't, would have alerted my attention. Suffice it to say, the only sex ed to date was courtesy of our schoolmate's memorable discovery of a discarded copy of '*Health and Efficiency*' during the final year at Highland Road Juniors.

So bear in mind that, as boys approaching the start of their third year at Grammar school, our attendant increase in testosterone was far outstripping the equally necessary input of gorm, and thus many of us were in an even more confused state than ever. Why, for example, was it that our voices were experiencing a sudden change of gear, making the rendition of '*Onward Christian Soldiers*' at morning assembly sound more like a yodelling competition? Why was it that the thought of girls made you feel suddenly hot all over, and that the sight of the headmaster's secretary had a magnetic attraction for eight hundred pairs of eyes when she walked into the hall? Don't ask me. Like the vast majority of my mates, we had no idea how sex worked... zilch, nada... and the school did next to nothing to fill in this rather glaring gap in our education. I say '*next to*' because, evidently, the process by which human reproduction is accomplished was covered very briefly and in a very oblique way one Thursday in the biology lab. According to my mate Ken, with whom I battled against a strong east wind on our bike ride home shortly after, sex ed had indeed been covered that very afternoon. '*Really?*' I said. '*I thought he was talking about rabbits and burrows and stuff*'. Surely I couldn't have dozed off long enough to miss anything really interesting... could I? '*Yeah, it was about rabbits*' said Ken, '*but there was the bit when he said the buck rabbit puts his thing in the doe and that's it!*' Not wishing to appear any more dim than my reputation already prescribed, I simply replied '*Oh yeah*' and was deft enough to quickly change the subject by asking if he had any of his Mars bar left.

Mind you, a little surreptitious enquiry the following day left me in no doubt that I was far from alone in my total lack of grasping the importance of the feeble attempt by the biology bloke to provide his charges with some information regarding the facts of life. As a result, it was all left to hearsay, gossip, a mass of misinformation from mates, and general stumbling about in the dark until early adulthood. I guarantee that few of us had any idea that girls had a menstrual cycle that made them a bit tetchy from time to time, and such things as birth control were way off the radar. OK, we knew that there were French letters, and a popular joke was to ask a fellow pupil whose name happened to be John... *'Can I borrow your rubber, Johnnie?!'* a phrase rich in innuendo, but lean on fact. Now this missing link in our developmental education didn't mean to say that we weren't interested in sex – of course we were. Being at a boys only school meant that meeting with girls of similar age was pretty hard at the best of times, and as a result, out of school organisations such as youth clubs were very popular in the sixties. Like many, I was brought up to go to church each Sunday, and in the early years this took the form of attending Sunday School. As a result, meeting girls of similar age in their best frocks etc. was quite common for me, and no doubt, like many other kids, my enthusiasm for Sunday School attendance was not wholly the result of religious zeal. The fact that the lovely Vivienne - whose slender waistline and warm smile challenged even the comely Cinderella in the recent Walt Disney cartoon - was going to be there, made my attendance that much more urgent.

These early associations then developed in the teen years into membership of the church youth club, and bearing in mind we are talking about the very epicentre of the whole sixties thing, it played an important part in our lives. More of that in the next book, but now, back to school.

If sex ed was virtually absent from our formal education and the vacuum thus created filled with a load of utter tosh, make-believe and scare stories (*'you only got to touch some girls and you get the crabs!'*) other parts of our unofficial education were better provided for. A prime example of this was our introduction to cigarettes. Now you have to understand that smoking was far more common in the decades just after the war than it is today. There were no health warnings, cigarettes were advertised everywhere, and amongst adults, you were far less likely to find a non-smoker than someone who lit up first thing with their breakfast fry-up. People walked the streets smoking, went about their daily business smoking, even served in shops smoking... it was just part of adult life. To us boys, it was a role model waiting to be followed. Many, if not most of our teachers smoked, and if you were asked to take a message to the staffroom at lunchtime, you had virtually to cut your way through the smog created by the loads of fags on the go all lunchtime, every lunchtime. That some teachers stank like an old ashtray was common-place. For teenage boys, having heavily nicotined fingers was seen as a badge of achievement, a token of being grown up in a man's world. The adverts on bill boards all around the town, and now to an increasing degree on commercial TV, only added to the allure of the habit – plus the fact that fags were pretty cheap, *and* as far as impressionable young teenagers were

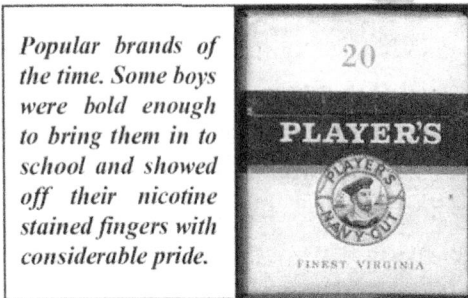

Popular brands of the time. Some boys were bold enough to bring them in to school and showed off their nicotine stained fingers with considerable pride.

concerned, when you got good at it, *you could blow the smoke out of your nose!* How good was that? How sophisticated! So it's hardly surprising that ciggies made a pretty early appearance in the uniform pockets of a number of classmates. The more daring would even put a packet in their breast pocket, thus advertising their street cred – until the teachers appeared on the scene, when they were discreetly removed to a less obvious location, to await the lunchtime break. Now you've heard me mention the 'back of the bike sheds' before, and I don't suppose there was a school in the land whose identical facilities didn't provide the nation's youth with much of its extra-curricular education. True, some of this could be described as *'finding out about sex from those least qualified to give an opinion'*, but that was minimal compared with the first spluttering steps in the art of smoking. There can hardly be a schoolboy alive who was not at least *aware* of the daily gathering of a certain clientele at the hallowed location. As a result, a number of boys increased their personal status greatly by developing really splendid coatings of nicotine on their smoking hand. Somewhat inevitably, it was Mick who achieved this much admired height of pubescent respectability in our class. Thus, as we became a little older and more sophisticated, even his famous – nay legendary – 'silent but deadlies' were surpassed by the rich aroma of nicotine and fag ash from the finest Virginia tobacco that a half-used *Player's Weight* could provide. The boy was moving on.

And so were we all. The third year saw the start of something more sinister... preparation for the dreaded O Levels and even to the most ostrich-like little soul of Class 3S, it was obvious that there was a real need to sit up and pay just a tad more attention. Also, there was a discernible change in the attitude of the teachers who seemed a lot more conscientious in really getting us to *understand* stuff. Perhaps they had suddenly become aware that this rabble of unruly little gits would shortly be responsible for the school's reputation as a centre of academic excellence…. or not.

Blimey. Things are getting serious. Seems like it's time to extricate the head from the sand, and to pay a lot more attention. But with that thought in mind, there's also a need for some light relief.

What time's Youth Club tonight?

Post Script

So, here we are, dabbling our toes in the 1960's. The Second World War seems a long time ago and threats of further damage to our back wall seems a lot less likely after a good number of years notable for their total lack of land mines, or any other variety of destructive ordnance. Indeed, the only *shake rattle and roll* we've endured in the interim has come from dear old Bill Haley in 1955, and even that early rock and roll comes across as a bit old-fashioned at the dawn of the new decade. It seems skiffle is on its way out too, and even the great Lonnie Donegan appears to have had a change of style with his new release *'My Old Man's A Dustman'*... quite funny, but hardly an earthy derivative of rhythm and blues.

Although getting to hear the latest records on the radio is still very difficult, the range of music on the new vinyl discs increases every month. We've now got Elvis belting out *'It's Now Or Never'*, the Everly Brothers worrying about *'Cathy's Clown'* and The Shadows doing their tricky little two-step routine whilst banging out their terrific instrumental *'Apache'*. Now in our early teens, the Baby Boomers are fast becoming soooooo sophisticated. With newly acquired BO protection, luminous socks (carefully concealed at school) and voices that continually break into what might resemble a yodelling competition, the world is our oyster…. isn't it?

Mind you, most of us have still got no complete or well-rounded understanding of sex. At best, there's a highly questionable mish-mash of lustful speculation, overheard comments from adults and smutty innuendos from older kids. The latest of these has been egged on by the recent publication of D.H. Lawrence's *'Lady Chatterley's Lover'*. Evidently, a particular few pages of this book have become seriously tattered after being passed around many a sixth form common room: not the whole book, mind you, just a few pages. The resulting rumours as to specific details of this steamy passage have then Chinese whispered down to those of us in the lowlier forms... and added yet another layer of cloudy misinformation.

Still, not to worry eh? We're in the 1960's for heaven's sake, and there's a pretty good chance that by 1970 we might all have just about got it sorted out. Otherwise, things are changing fast. All around the city, bomb sites are disappearing along with the remnants of the old 'two up two down' slum buildings from the nineteenth century. And in their place? Why, the shiny, new and imposing high-rise blocks of flats, that's what. These new 'villages in the sky' we're told, are the modern way to live, each apartment having internal loos, built-in kitchens and a fine view down to the concrete playground far below. Why, each block even has its own express lifts to every floor – so what's not to like?

Shopping too is changing: a lot of towns now have a supermarket or two – places where you can get a whole load of stuff without the inconvenience of having to trail around to the little local shops with a pocketful of heavy copper coins giving your trousers a curiously lop-sided look. Even so, buying things for a farthing won't be possible in the future, because the littlest of our coins ceases to be legal tender at the end of the year – so no more buying a single Fruit Salad or Blackjack, and it may well be that the old bicycle association will be the only way in which the little coin with its tiny wren imprinted on the obverse will be remembered in the future. Shame really.

Although events on the national and international scene have not played much of a part in our lives so far, I suppose we are aware of the fact that, as a nation, we're struggling a bit to keep up with the Yanks. Although the new Vauxhall Cresta has wrap-around windscreens front and back, and sports very snazzy tail fins and white wall tyres, it's still not as glamorous as the equivalent Cadillac. Also the US ships visiting the dockyard are so much bigger than ours – and so are their sailors who whistle at the girls on the seafront. On the other hand, Mr. Macmillan tells us we've *'never had it so good'* and despite a number of boys muttering *'most of us have never had it at all'*, I suppose he could be right. At the social and domestic level there's a lot of optimism in the air, and many homes now have access to a television set with two whole channels to choose from. This new window on the world has been a revelation, and has perhaps made even the dopiest amongst us a lot more aware of what's going on both at home and overseas.

Mind you, not all of this is comforting: it seems that the Yanks and the Russians aren't hitting it off too well, and there's been a fair bit of sabre-rattling of late. In addition, there's now a space race between the two countries, with the Ruskies getting off to a good start with their little bleeping *Sputnik* satellite in 1957. In response, the Yanks tried to follow up with their own orbiter later in the year, and we found it hard not to snigger when this televised attempt was a monumental failure. The rocket exploded just a moment or two after launch, causing the newspaper headlines to christen the failed attempt *'Flopnik' 'Stayputnik'* or *'Kaputnik'*.

You might notice that the good old UK is not really involved in this race – mainly because we can't afford it. But worry ye not: we have spent a lot of time building our very own Lovell Telescope, so even if we can't join in the race, at least we can watch what the others are up to. And what's more, we've now got HMS Dreadnought, our own nuclear submarine – full to the brim, we're told, with nuclear missiles.

It's just a good job that we boy warriors in the school's CCF understand these military matters so well, otherwise we might be getting just a little jumpy. When it comes to polishing up the mighty army boots to a glossy finish or daubing blanco all over our gaiters we are second to none. Those of us in the RAF section are vying with eachother to see who can grow the most elaborate air force type moustache first, but as we are all only in the 'bum fluff' stage of facial decoration (and acne doesn't really count) it seems we'll have a while to wait yet.

Question is: do we spend time catching up on how to do logarithms, revising just a little bit more about the 1906 Liberals... or even on reading the papers to find out how the economy is doing? Or shall we just tune in to the first show of a brand new ITV series called "*Coronation Street*"?

You know ... I think we'll do that.

Looking Back, Looking Forward

I hope you've enjoyed this canter through the decade and a half that followed the end of the Second World War. For those of you who are members of the Baby Boomer clan, I suspect that some memories will have been revived. I would also like to think that younger readers are now in a better position to understand the very *differentness* of the 1950's experience to that of today.

As mentioned in the Foreword, I've been mindful of the tendency to look at the past through rose-tinted glasses, but I believe that my account is an honest, appreciative and accurate appraisal. More to the point, I sincerely hope that I have demonstrated that the fifties, far from being the bleak, austere and careworn decade that is often its modern day representation, was in fact a time of huge optimism, of great innovation and excited – almost tingling anticipation. Now we are in to the next decade, and teenagers throughout the land are agog as to what's in that long and intriguing pipeline.

And speaking of the sixties, I hope you might like to join me again on what amounts to a gallop through that tumultuous decade, arriving breathless and gasping amongst the debris of the seventies. The second book in the '*All in Good Time*' series is entitled:

… And About Time Two

Come with me on a journey which hits the highs of Carnaby Street and the Summer of Love - and the lows of the cold war, the threat of nuclear annihilation… and the horrors of home-brewed booze and shell suits.   Overleaf you'll find a brief chapter synopsis, but first, let me ask you something:

Question: When is a battleship not a battleship?

Answer: When it's aground!

Quite why HMS Vanguard, the Royal Navy's last battleship ended up scaring the socks off the customers of the 'Still and West Country House Tavern' by grinding to a halt just a few feet from the Public Bar is a mystery to be unravelled in the next exciting volume of the *All In Good Time* series entitled:

'… And About Time Two'

And just to give you a flavour of what to expect, here's a little look at the sort of thing we'll be delving into chapter by chapter…

Chapter 1 Two Tin Cans and a Piece of String.

The tranny's arrived! Why is there never a pirate around when you need one? Wrestling with photography, tape recorders and cine films, plus printing problems and getting all doolally in the Banda cupboard.

Chapter 2 A Dedicated Follower of Fission.

A time to be afraid – when the Cold War nearly went hot. Kruschev's visit and the unfortunate Buster Crabbe. A reluctant battleship. Watch out! It's the Cuba Crisis! Y Fronts, fall-out; and James Bond.

Chapter 3 Sky Hooks and Elbow Grease.

The big wide world – job opportunities and adolescent options; Technical College and an unexpected trip to Bletchley Park. Initiation: sky hooks, and elbow grease; wages and motor bikes plus a highly illuminated Lambretta.

Chapter 4 Two Thirds of Sex, Drugs and Rock'n'Roll.

The essence of the Baby Boomer years. The glorious Summer of Love and why most of us missed it. The explosion of exuberant style, music and culture that was the heartbeat of the Swinging Sixties. The wild drugs scene… so *'far out man'* it was invisible. Missed that too.

Chapter 5   Vertical Hold.

Tuning in: if you think losing the TV remote is a nuisance, it's a doddle compared with balancing on the dining table and waving an aerial about to get a half-decent picture. The telly takeover, and the big screen fight back. Getting spaced out with Apollo 11.

Chapter 6   Shell Suits, Vertical Artex and Other Mistakes.

Losing the plot? A lament for the Seventies plus the woes of decimalisation. DIY in Technicolor, but why so much brown? Woodchip, polystyrene and artex regrets. Home-Brew: falling down and throwing up. A shock in the mirror: shell suits and snorkels.

Chapter 7   Acid Drops.

Some very uncomfortable issues; acknowledgement of failures but also a defence when seen in the context of the time. The realities of life in the fifties and sixties and the risks associated with challenging the orthodoxy of a bygone age.

Chapter 8.   So Far So Good.

Not so much 'abandoning ship' as watching its progress from a comfy lifeboat. Mouthy competition from the next generation; travelling and Napoleon; muddling along: a British skill. Environmental awakening;   startling revelations about J Cloths and pentagonal crisp bags.

Chapter 9   Hindsight's a Wonderful Thing

So, what have we learnt? Indeed, who understands *anything* any more? Keeping a sense of generational perspective. Who was it who said *'The older you get, the wiser you get'*? I need a word in his ear.

Anticipated publication date: Christmas 2021

Acknowledgements

Without a doubt, the biggest single influence on my commentary has been the collection of reminiscences and reflections residing in the mental archives of my contemporaries, the Baby Boomers themselves. One of the benefits of writing a book over a protracted period is that you get to meet a lot more people, and I had the added advantage of chatting to hundreds more when for several years, I was invited to give talks about my earlier (railway) books. Get a load of oldies together, and it's a sure bet that once the essential comparison of recent ailments and matching treatment has been dispensed with, someone will pipe up with a '*Do you remember when*' type comment, and that is enough to start the memory avalanche. So to all of them I say a very big thank you, and hope that I've done you proud. But of course, there were many others who gave me more specific help and advice, and to whom I am indebted for their patience and generosity.

As you will have noted, Meccano features quite strongly in my tale, and I am most grateful for the friendly advice provided by Paul Voaden and Alan Esplen – both of whom pointed me in the direction of Jim Gamble, a man who probably knows more about Meccano than anyone else alive, and to whom I am indebted. I would also like to thank Spin Master, the current owners of the brand. The only puzzle remaining is the origin of the imaginative French advertisement.

I am very grateful to my sister Daphne Rex, who gave freely of her time trawling through the draft manuscript where she discovered an unsettling number of blemishes.

Paul Bunce was particularly obliging with publishing information, and my old SGS friend Paul Knox provided helpful and much appreciated observations and advice.

Dave Vickers offered many snippets of information in addition to a whole lot of well-timed encouragement.

People of my generation don't always take the world of modern IT in their stride, and so I am particularly grateful to my daughter Kathryn for her support and advice concerning IT applications, and to Paul Langton for his excellent technical solutions.

Tracking down some of the transport photos in Chapter 5 proved quite tricky but contacts in Portsmouth came up trumps. In particular I'd like to thank my old friend Howard Jones, and Melanie Bushell, the Development Director at Portsmouth Grammar School who helped me source the rare trolley bus photos.

In similar vein, I'm grateful to Dave Couch of the Japanese Motorcycle Club who enlisted the support of Jim Pike and Roger Leversuch, the kind providers of the motorcycle combination set photos.

David Higginson of the Vintage Wireless Society provided images and a wealth of information concerning valve radios and radiograms, and I am equally indebted to Brian Robins of the Veteran Cycle Club for putting me in touch with Ian Hall, whose photo of his lovely penny-farthing bicycle appears in Chapter 6.

Chris Walker of the 'Railroad Bill' skiffle group was very helpful (he is the tea-chest bass player in the photo), and put me on to Andrew Jeffery, the photographer. My thanks to them both.

I received a lot of assistance and information from the owners of several well-known domestic brands, notable amongst whom were Premier Foods for Bisto and Vesta and R.H. Amar Ltd., the current owner of the Camp Coffee brand. Amber Viner at The Advertising Archives also provided a lot of useful information.

Picture credits

I have an admission to make. On the preceding page I mentioned the benefit of writing a book over a lengthy period. Trouble is, if you're as wayward as me, there's also a downside. You see, back in the early days when publication was only a vague aspiration, I would add to my own photograph collection by trawling through the internet seeking suitable images to illustrate a point, and I'd get these from here there and everywhere. And did I bother to take note of where each came from? I suspect you already know the answer. So I've spent a lot of time recently trying to re-locate images, and I've been pretty successful...but not completely so. A very small number remain hidden in the depths of the internet, and I can't find them. In addition, I've written several times to some photographers, but have received no response. So, if you are the owner of one of the illustrations not mentioned below, can I please offer my apologies? I could spend yet more time scouring the internet, but *tempus fugit* and all that jazz - plus there's a pandemic on and I'm not getting any younger! Nevertheless, rest assured that any omissions or mistakes brought to my attention will be corrected in future editions.

Most contributors have been extremely generous, often providing their illustrations free of charge. To them I offer my sincere thanks.

Introduction.

Invalid carriage: *Imperial War Museum.*
Invacar: *Elvis Payne at www.3-wheelers.com*

The Well-hard Babies.

General Jumbo: *Courtesy of DC Thomson, archivist David Powell*
Pedal car: *Courtesy Frank Loft Moreton Hampstead Motor Museum.*

The Lino Years.

Triumph estate: *Classic Car Catalogue.*
Meccano: *Courtesy Spin Master, owners of the Meccano brand.*

Let There Be Sellotape.
Prefab: *Courtesy of Robin Wiltshire, Sheffield Local Studies Library.*
Street scene: *Evening Standard.*
Milk float & delivery bike: *Courtesy of Mike Smith at IGG.*
Horse-drawn float: *Courtesy of Alan Henderson, Brentham Society Archive.*
Three wheelers: *3-wheelers.com*
Messerschmitt and Isetta: *Moreton Hampstead Motor Museum.*

A Dog's Dinner.
Lord Snooty: *Courtesy of DC Thomson, archivist David Powell.*

Ode Tetnyaah!
Semaphore: *Malcoma at Wikimedia.*
Trolley buses: *Courtesy of Tim Runnacles.*
Leyland Seafront Service bus: *Courtesy of Roger Cox.*

The Three R's: Reading, Writing and Rubbing Out.
Penny–farthing: *Courtesy of Ian Hall.*
Football and boots: *Courtesy of the National Football Museum, Manchester.*

In Sickness and in…Bed
Dentist drill: *Wikimedia.*
Dr. Finlay: *BBC Archives Photo Library.*

Pre Bop-A-Lula.
Radiograms: *Courtesy of David Higginson.*
Skiffle group: *Courtesy of Andrew Jeffery.*
Football fan's rattle: *Courtesy of the National Football Museum, Manchester.*
Pompey sailor cartoons: *Courtesy of The News, Portsmouth.*
Penny slot machine: *Courtesy of Paul Coppin, 'The Penny Arcade'*
Firework photos: *Courtesy S. Johnson, Firework Heritage Museum*

Cupboard Love.
Shop counters: *Courtesy of Saltash Heritage Museum, Cornwall*
Domestic products: *The Advertising Archives*
Looking Back, Looking Forward.
HMS Vanguard in Portsmouth: *Courtesy of The News, Portsmouth*
Book cover.
My thanks go to Leah Jeffery at Cornerstone Vision, Plymouth.
And last but not least:
For the countless chats we've had about our shared Baby Boomer history and her willingness to keep me focussed on the task in hand (not to mention her self-restraint in not asking *'finished yet?'* too many times), I owe much to Lynda, my ever patient, unnervingly wise and resourceful wife.

****

The piece at the end of chapter five concerning the *diddly-dum, diddly-dum* sound made by railway carriages – and their interpretation by the great Reginald Gardiner – is an extract from a book I wrote in 2013, and published by Wessex Books. It concerns the extraordinary life of one of the oldest railway carriages in existence, which is now restored to its former Victorian glory and maintained at the Bodmin and Wenford heritage railway in Cornwall.

This generously illustrated book is still available via the station bookshop.

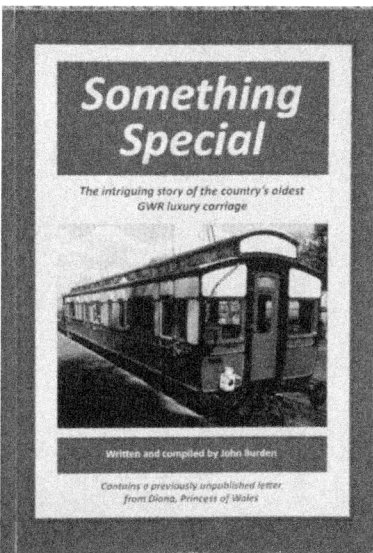

Don't know about you, but I'm worn out. Fancy a drop of oil?

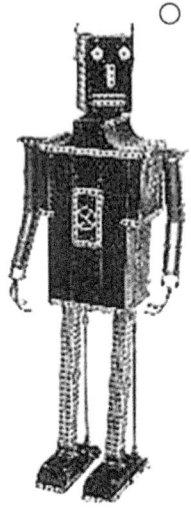

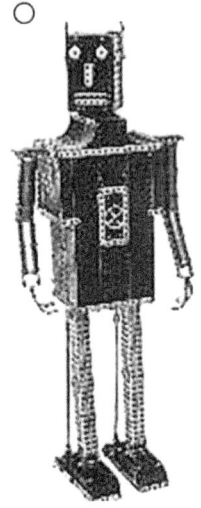

****

jb.allingoodtime@gmail.com

Printed in Great Britain
by Amazon

41632214R00188